The Art of Driving

According to the Guidelines of
Benno von Achenbach

Max Pape

Foreword by
H.R.H. The Prince Philip, Duke of Edinburgh, K.G., K.T.

Translated from the German by Frank Haydon
and Anne Weber
and illustrated by Gisela Holstein

J. A. ALLEN
London

British Library Cataloguing in Publication Data

Pape, Max
  The art of driving.
  1. Driving of horse-drawn vehicles
  I. Title   II. Die Kunst des Fahrens. *English*
  798'.6   SF305

  ISBN 0-85131-339-6

First English edition published 1982

Reprinted 1988

Published in Great Britain by
J. A. Allen & Company Limited,
1, Lower Grosvenor Place, Buckingham Palace Road,
London, SW1W 0EL

The original edition in German was published by
Franckh'sche Verlagshandlung Kosmos-Verlag, Stutt-
gart, under the title Pape, *Die Kunst des Fahrens* (The
Art of Driving) ISBN 3.440.04056.9
© Franckh'sche Verlagshandlung, W. Keller & Co.,
Stuttgart 1966, 1976

Printed in Great Britain by
St Edmundsbury Press Limited, Bury St Edmunds,
Suffolk

Dedicated to
Benno von Achenbach
founder of
the art of driving in
Germany

Contents

Foreword

by H.R.H. The Prince Philip, Duke of Edinburgh, K.G., K.T.

When I decided to take up driving I thought it would be a good idea to read as much as I could of the available material on the subject. I discovered that most of the modern books in English were about breaking and training harness horses and ponies and about the basic techniques of driving singles, pairs and teams. Anything more advanced, particularly on the subject of driving a four-in-hand, dated from the 19th Century. Edwin Howlett, who taught four-in-hand driving in Paris and whom Achenbach acknowledged as his teacher, wrote his book *Driving Lessons* in 1894. Fairman Rogers published his book *Manual of Coaching* in 1901. These books are most valuable, but they are basically about coaching and are really more concerned with traditional harness, coaches and driving techniques than with a practical analysis of the whole art of driving horses.

In 1972 I attended the first World Driving Championships at Münster in Germany and there I met Max Pape. He was a small, elderly man, neat and wiry with an infectious enthusiasm for driving, and he was kind enough to give me a copy of his book.

It so happens that I spent many holidays and a year at school in Germany, but the war years and subsequent lack of practice have considerably reduced my fluency and comprehension. However, enough remained for me to appreciate that this book *Der Kunst des Fahren*, now translated into *The Art of Driving*, was just what I was looking for. I read it, rather laboriously, from cover to cover, and I still use it quite frequently as a reference book.

I am sure Anne Weber and Frank Haydon would have thought of translating this book anyway, but I do remember discussing its merits with them and when I heard that they had started on the translation I tried to encourage them to get on with it because I was convinced that it would be immensely valuable to the growing number of people in the English-speaking world who are showing an interest in driving.

Now at last it has been published and the translators and publishers deserve the thanks and congratulations of a very large section of the world's driving fraternity.

Benno von Achenbach
His Work and Life

Benno von Achenbach was born on 24th July 1861 in Dusseldorf and died on 15th October 1936 in Berlin. He was the founder of the German method of driving and his name will forever be connected with his insistence on the highest artistic impression in driving.

His practical experiences go back far into his childhood. He was the son of the famous landscape painter Oswald Achenbach from whom he inherited his talent as an artist. This enabled him to illustrate his book *Anspannen und Fahren* (Putting to and Driving) with very clear and comprehensive drawings. He also painted in oils, his main subjects being riding or driving.

From early childhood Achenbach travelled extensively with his parents, and his passion for driving began at a very early age. Even as an eight year old he always asked to sit next to the coachman and be allowed to hold the reins, if only at a walk.

During travels with his parents to Italy he developed such a disgust for the cruel treatment of horses and other animals that already he began to devise means of easing the hard work of horses.

When a student of driving in Dusseldorf at the age of twelve he was allowed to drive the tandem belonging to Freiherr von Eppinghoven. He never missed an opportunity to drive whether it was a single, a pair or a four-in-hand. He bought every available German piece of literature on driving and finally managed to get hold of a British publication, *The Book of the Horse*. From this he adopted, to a very large extent, the English method of handling four-in-hand reins.

In the 1880s he frequently went on 'driving' visits where he used to drive a four-in-hand every day. During the years when coaching and tandem driving flourished in the Rhineland, particularly in Cologne, his name was always prominent. Many of his coaching and riding pictures were created during that period. In 1882 he was awarded the first gold medal for stylish driving when he drove a coach belonging to Graf Bismarck at Baden-Baden. In the 1890s he went three times to Paris to visit Edwin Howlett whom he considered his tutor.

Achenbach drove a marathon through the Swiss Alps and Italy, and later he drove Geheimrat Vorster of Cologne, who owned horses of excellent quality, with his coach from Munich via Innsbruck to Bad Gastein. He also drove for years all the coaching routes in Britain. He watched the driving élite of the world, particularly the Americans, at British horse shows, and drove with them, too. With this background, and with his enthusiasm, his thirst for knowledge and his excellent powers of observation, it is understandable that his life's work had to be something that was thought out to the minutest detail.

His reputation as the great expert, particularly in the field of producing horses in harness, caused Wilhelm II in 1906 to call him to the Royal Stables. There he was put in charge of the driving section, but he also modernized carriages and harness using both his expert knowledge and his artistic eye. During his years of service in the Royal Stables he was sent to attend the British Horse Show at Olympia on three occasions.

His booklet *Stil-Anspannungs Grundsaetze* (Principles on the Style of Turnouts) was produced in 1899 originally for the Deutscher Sportverein but was also recognized by the Kartell fuer Reit- und Fahrsport as 'Hints on Driving'; it was later considered by the Reichsverband as the Manual for the Horse-Show Rule Book (Turnierverordnung).

Achenbach became the great German Driving Apostle. It is easy to imagine that, because of his high standards, he was at times severely criticized. However, he defended his opinion with unyielding logic in the magazine *St. Georg*. He often told me: 'Only very few take the trouble to think and re-think; they make statements based on theory but have never tried them out in practice.'

His knowledge in the equestrian field was unlimited – and not only in driving. His great artistic gift and his thorough knowledge of 'High School' riding undoubtedly would have qualified him to judge Olympic dressage competitions. I was frequently present when he and Ludwig Koch, author of *Die Reitkunst im Bilde* (*The Art of Riding in Pictures*), discussed the finer points of the '*haute école*' or the mechanics of the movement of the horse.

Achenbach transferred the high standards expected of a dressage horse – in responsiveness, obedience, fluency of movement, exercise, training and collection – to his artistic demands of the harness horse. In a short period of time he was able to transform four horses into one team by quietly adjusting reins and bits or changing horses over. It was fascinating to watch him handle a four- or six-in-hand in a driving test, or observe him working horses to achieve beautiful positioning and elevated stepping. Whilst he was my tutor I had to drive him every day with a four- or six-in-hand through Berlin's busiest streets. At first I was grateful when he took over the reins and helped in difficult situations. However, under his guidance I gained confidence to drive safely. Benno von Achenbach was always available to help anybody. He never forced advice, but gladly gave it when asked.

During the Aachen Horse Show in 1931 he was honoured in a public ovation. This was initiated by Oberlandstallmeister Gustav Rau who recognized Achenbach's work in a toast.

On 15th October 1936 Benno von Achenbach died in Berlin at the age of 75. He had lived to see his system adopted by the German Army, included in the rules for showing harness horses, and taught at every school for driving in Germany as well as being recognized in Switzerland, Sweden and Turkey.

As long as there is the sport of driving, his directives will remain valid everywhere.

2

General Views on Driving Techniques

With this book I wish to present something for everyone interested in modern driving, not only for those who wish to turn out and exhibit in style. Achenbach, whose principles on turnout are authoritative for the adjudication of harness competitions under the L.P.O. (German National Rules), has amalgamated the best from the driving methods of various countries. He was greatly influenced by the English style of driving and particularly that of his tutor, Edwin Howlett. Britain was the origin of the sport, and unequalled, especially in the field of turnout and coach-building.

For decades the English had retained only that which was recognized as practical. However, Achenbach checked out every point, and only recommends that which is practical for the intended purpose and which results in a picture of perfect harmony. Harness must fit the horses and horses must be suitable for the carriage. Therefore, when judging a turnout in competition, there is a mark for 'General Impression'. I will refer to this again in later chapters.

The uninitiated will give a correct judgement on 'General Impression', particularly from the viewpoint of harmony, without being able to say how this judgement was achieved. He likes horses and carriage well matched, a settled and fluent performance and an elegance of movement which comes only as a result of careful training of the horses. What love, care and diligence is produced by the Vienna School to achieve the artistic accuracy of their high school horses! Years of groundwork are required to create such living works of art. It has taken cen-

turies for the art of riding to develop to such heights. I am convinced that the road to perfection in the art of driving is hard, but our standard of training is becoming more and more impressive. Drivers try to do justice to the dressage requirements and the standard improves continually.

Firstly I would like to enlarge upon the purpose of the modern turnout and the driving doctrine. The aim is to ease the work for the horses by whatever means, while still observing the greatest possible safety for driver, passengers and public in modern traffic, and to achieve this by the method of harnessing, bitting and driving. Both are in causative connection; one is a supposition of the other.

Any car driver must pass a test before he is allowed to drive alone; he must prove not only that he has mastered the technique of driving but also that he knows the highway code and understands his car. The driver of a horsedrawn carriage, however, is not required to prove either that he possesses sufficient knowledge of driving or of the treatment of horses. Horses are not machines but creatures full of life which are entitled to decent and correct treatment. It is incomprehensible that no government has as yet demanded proof of proper training, but leaves it to private initiative to gain expertise.

It is interesting to note that people are often of the opinion that driving is no art and that anybody can do it. The opinion is particularly widespread amongst riders. What a big mistake! A rider is only concerned with himself and his horse. He can use his legs, his weight and the reins. But a driver, for instance when driving a pair, has only two reins and a whip. If he wants to do his job safely and correctly he must have a comprehensive knowledge of driving including the effect of bitting his horses, fitting the harness, as well as the design of the carriage.

A driver has considerably greater responsibility too. He is solely responsible for the safety of his passengers and/or the load he carries, as well as for the safety of the public in road traffic. Before setting off on a journey he has to ensure personally that reins and harness are in order and sound, that the carriage is safe and the brakes work; that the turntable is properly greased, the load is placed correctly and securely and that all possible safety precautions are taken.

Another difference between rider and driver is that the rider can 'feel' (one talks of riding sense – feeling). To the driver this only applies in a figurative way. Certainly, he can feel in his hands whether or not his horses are pulling, but he has to find out why they pull, and which one is the culprit of the two or four horses he is driving. The driver must see, think, think again and only then act. The kindness of the hand is in the head!

The demand for 'thinking and observing' goes like a thread through the Achenbach doctrine. 'Giving' aids, not pulling at the reins which only unsettles the horses and does not make work easier for them.

Some drivers, because of a special gift, excel at the art – but cannot explain their skill. If a system is to benefit everybody, however, it cannot be explained in vague terms of 'feeling'. It must be based on firm rules.

Such a system, which builds up logically from a single harness horse to a multiple-in-hand, has been given to us by Benno von Achenbach.

Benno von Achenbach, centre, with General Adam, right, and the author. Photographed at an international show in Aachen in 1933

A rousing ovation for von Achenbach on his 70th birthday. The author is in the foreground

American roadster to a runabout. Typical yoke attachment at the pole

A jucker four-in-hand on the marathon

Pair of Hackney ponies to a viceroy wagon

The vehicle depicted is too low. The reins drop on the horses' quarters

A Russian troika

A four-in-hand used on the farm. Useful training for young horses

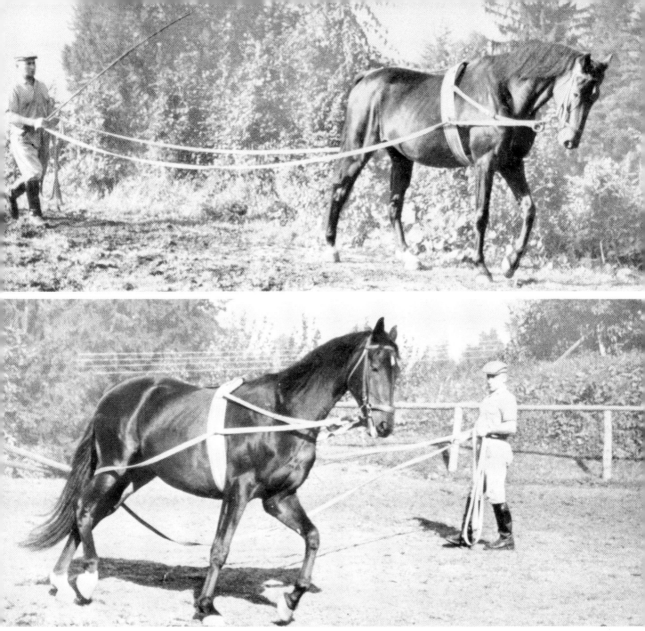

Long reining on the circle, above, and pupils, below, at the driving apparatus

The Kladrupi team
exhibited by
Czechoslovakia at the
European
Championships held
Sopot, Poland in 1975

Imre Abonyie from
Hungary, former
European and World
Champion

The Polish competitor
Symoniak with his
Trakehner team

3

The Reins

Before discussing the Achenbach reins, which are derived from the English reins, I would like to discuss certain types which are still in use and, even today, are made by harness-makers. German harness-makers are craftsmen, not drivers, and therefore a large number of drivers still prefer to use reins that were made years ago rather than new ones.

First and foremost, reins and harness must be practical. That means they must be accurate in all measurements. Parts which have to take strain, such as reins, pole straps, collars and traces, must be wide and strong; pads, belly-bands and back-bands may be comparatively light. The beauty of the harness should be of secondary consideration.

For instance, it is no use having attractively decorated reins if the measurements are wrong and splices in the leather are rough. Rein splices that get stuck in the terrets when driving a four-in-hand can cause very bad accidents.

Reins of incorrect measurements are very uncomfortable for the driver. He can get the splices of the lead reins in his hands when loop-ing, or the buckles of the wheel reins can be in the way because they are too close together, or too far forward, and out of reach for adjustments.

By describing unsuitable reins I want to create an understanding for correct reins. 'Bad' reins are rounded, stitched reins (these incidentally are also incorrect for Hungarian harness) and double-stitched reins. The reason for their unsuitability is that they can only be made from thinned leather which has been flattened at the edges. As long as these reins are new the stitching may make up for the weakness, but with use the stitching will rot and eventually burst. Such reins are also difficult to adjust at the coupling.

There are two types of reins quite frequently used in Germany which are as different as they are impractical.

Firstly: cross-reins with detachable hand-parts – the so-called 'Handstutzen'. They are sometimes made of hemp, even in multiple colours. The couplings are so short that they cannot be adjusted from the box seat. They have three round holes instead of oval holes and, therefore, the tongue of the buckle stands up rather than lies flat. The doubled leather and the short roller buckles also make them difficult to adjust. Whenever one comes across such reins one often finds that they are still buckled in the same holes as when they left the harness-maker. Some drivers, because they want to couple one horse shorter and thus distribute the work more evenly, make a few more holes in the billets. This not only makes the reins look ugly and untidy, but makes any adjustment from the box seat impossible. Altering reins at the bit is insufficient for any major adjustment.

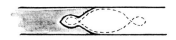

Rein splices – two methods of stitching

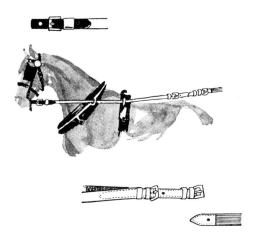

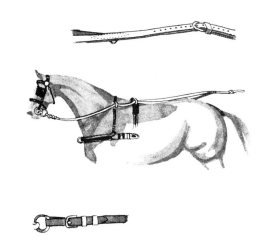

German coupling reins and billet

Vienna reins

Secondly: the worst form of reins are those with couplings so long that the buckles are beyond the driver's hand. These, however, are preferred by quite a number of drivers. They say: 'I can drive my horse with four reins and it is much easier to cope with sudden difficulties because I have each horse under direct control.' This may be so for the expert, but for the average driver, it has nothing but disadvantages. The right hand is permanently engaged; the keen horse, which should be held back to stop it

from doing all the work, will pull the reins out of the driver's hands, whereas the lazy horse, which should have the longer reins, is being dragged along on short reins, thus hanging back even more. The necessary continual adjusting of the reins unsettles the horses because it creates a sawing movement of the bit in their mouths.

I would rather recommend 'Vienna Reins' with the horses bitted with a snaffle. They are in principle Hungarian reins (Szecheni reins), consisting of two continuous reins. The outside rein has a metal ring sewn to it through which the inside rein is threaded. Adjustments are made by means of a movable coupling buckle, the so-called 'Frosch' (frog), not by a coupling buckle sewn on to the inside rein. Each rein has up to 20 holes (i.e. a total of up to 80 holes).

By adjustments it is thus possible to move this 'Frosch' as far in front of the driver's hand as is wanted. At a sharp pace it is even possible, when the horses are well bridled, for the 'Frosch' to be held in the driver's hand. However, this style of driving, with arms stretched out, is neither beautiful nor particularly gentle.

Buttons – whether leather, wood or ivory – or cross-pieces on reins should be avoided, certainly on four-in-hand reins, as they impede any subtle looping.

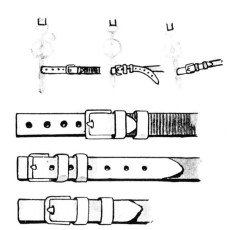

Rein billets

Black billets are incorrect. Repaired billets should be sponged off with a soda-and-water solution until the new leather matches the old in colour. They should then be left to dry, and when dry should be oiled.

Leather-covered buckles, although popular, are very dangerous. The buckles rust without being noticed and, eventually, the tongue of the buckle will only just reach the leather. It then only requires one good pull and the tongue slips through the buckle.

Achenbach Reins

Now to the advantages of the Achenbach reins which were developed from the English reins. Achenbach reins consist of outside and inside reins, the inside reins being buckled to those on the outside. Both are made from best natural back-hide (not spongy belly leather). Several pieces of leather are spliced together so that they appear to be one long piece. The splices should be without decorative stitching and the points should be stitched flush together for a distance of about 10 cm.

The reins should be 25 mm. wide. (This is also a suitable width for small hands.) Even better are 27 mm. wide reins which taper down to 25 mm. Narrower reins are impractical. The advantage of the wider reins is that they can be held with a hand only half closed. With narrow reins the hand must be kept firmly closed to prevent the reins from slipping. The firmer the hand is closed, the more the blood circulation is impeded, and thus the hand gets very cold and stiff in winter.

The measurements of the outside and the inside reins are such that the couplings are about 30–40 cm. in front of the driver's hand. This makes it possible to adjust the reins without having to halt. It is very unpleasant to have the coupling buckles too close to your hand, particularly when making a sharp point, or at bends, or when going down a steep hill – and even more so when your hands are cold.

One of Achenbach's main improvements is the adjustability of the reins which makes it possible to cope with any requirement. The

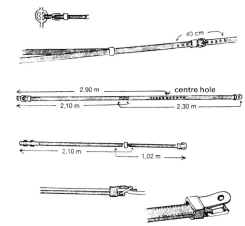

Measurements for Achenbach reins

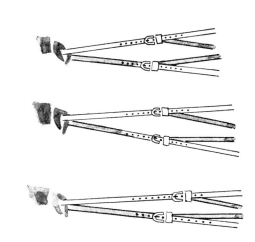

Rein adjustment. Reading from top: Incorrectly adjusted reins; Correctly adjusted reins; Reins correctly adjusted for a keen horse on the left side, and a lazy horse on the right

holes – 11 in all, and oval – stretch over a distance of 40 cm. and are 4 cm. apart. (Reins that have not been adjusted for some time show a dark imprint above the hole that has been used. This imprint is made by the metal buckle-tongue and cannot be removed.) It is possible to protect the reins by stitching a thin piece of leather with a large oval hole to the keeper. If the tongue is pushed through this piece of

7

leather and the leather then tucked away under the buckle, it is hardly noticeable.

The billet has only one oval hole and a long buckle that is easy to use. The point is tucked away through either one or two keepers.

Approximately 40 cm. from the coupling buckle, a keeper is sewn on to the coupling rein to keep the two reins together.

The coupling buckle is slightly curved and easy to operate.

The coupling reins (inside reins), when buckled into the sixth hole (standard hole), should be 12 cm. longer than the outside reins because they cross over and cover a longer distance. Changing them over makes correct driving impossible as it pulls together the horses' heads. The horses should go parallel to the pole, their heads pointing forward with a slight tendency towards the outside.

One rein has a small buckle at the end, and the other has a point. The rein with the buckle should always be attached to the horse on the left (near side) and the rein with the point to the horse on the right (off side).

I have already mentioned that it is possible to adjust pair reins whilst on the move, from the box seat. This is of great importance when driving highly-spirited and restless horses, particularly when not accompanied by a groom (though, in fact, one should *always* be accompanied by a groom). To be able to adjust the

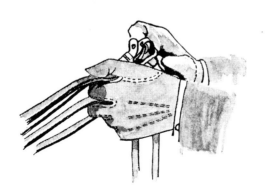

reins without stopping is invaluable and, after some practice, it can be done without even changing pace. If a groom walks alongside the team it can also be done with a four-in-hand.

The technique is as follows: shorten the reins so that the left middle finger is just in front of the left coupling buckle. (The Hungarians drive in this fashion when they place their hands in front of the 'Frosch'.) Place the right-hand rein, very much shortened, underneath the left thumb so that the horses walk straight. Then take the coupling buckle with your right index finger and push your finger between the buckle and the tongue. Using thumb and middle finger, push the right-hand rein up. This lifts the tongue and releases the rein. Pull the rein off the tongue with thumb and index finger. To lengthen the right-hand rein, push it forward under the left thumb until the required hole is level with the tongue. Then push the tongue through the hole. It is, of course, important to remember how the reins were buckled originally. After the right-hand rein has been adjusted, push it on to the middle finger and then proceed with the left hand to adjust the left-hand rein as above.

As the box seat is on the right-hand side, the right-hand coupling rein is closer to the driver. Therefore, if the left-hand rein is to be adjusted it is necessary to take the right-hand buckle quite far up behind the driver's left hand in order to keep the horses straight.

With enthusiasm and practice these alterations can be made without disturbing the horses or changing pace.

Now, back to the explanations of the Achenbach reins and coupling them. The coupling reins should be buckled in the sixth hole of the outside rein, i.e. the centre hole of the eleven holes which are evenly distributed over a distance of 40 cm. This makes the coupling rein 12 cm. longer than the outside rein, and will suit horses of average size (1.68 m.) [16.2 h.h.] in full collar harness – provided of course they have the same length of front. The horses will move straight, with the correct distance between them and their heads pointing ahead. If the total number of holes this side of the coupling buckle (the driver's side) is more than ten, the coupling reins will be too long for average-sized horses, and too far apart. However, this would fit large or broad horses. For small, and very small horses the total number of holes this side of the coupling buckle should be eight, very rarely only six.

When fitting the reins it is important to make sure that the coupling reins are not too short, otherwise they will pull the horses' heads together, and the horses cannot go straight. As a result they will hang away from the pole. It is better to have their heads pointing slightly to the outside. This will stop them from hanging away from the pole and leaning into the bend.

When attaching the coupling reins to the bit it is important to remember that the rein of the horse with the higher head carriage crosses over the other. The same applies for a horse that has a tendency to throw up its head. By observing this small point the other horse will not be disturbed in the mouth. It is important to remember this if the horses are bitted with a curb. The head of a sensitive horse cannot be pulled down! Therefore, coupling rings which hold the coupling reins together should not be used, certainly not with curb bits.

When coupling the reins, different conformation of the horses and different lengths of front must be taken into consideration. A horse which bridles more should have a shorter rein. However, if he is put back one hole, his mate must be let out one, so that the total number of holes this side of the buckle again adds up to ten.

When adjusting for different temperaments the keen horse should have the shorter rein. This stops it from doing all the work. His lazy mate, put on the longer rein, will have to take its share of the load.

There should be no difference in the length of the traces. Any adjustment is made by the length of rein.

Keen horses on the shorter rein should be bitted mildly, the lazy horses may be bitted more severely. It is also important to use the whip correctly.

I have taken the technique and the basis for fitting harness, as well as some other information on measurements, from Achenbach's book *Anspannen und Fahren*.

In the extract quoted below I have omitted some points already mentioned.

'In an establishment which has both large and small horses, it is advisable to have two standard measurements, because the coupling buckles must be close enough to the driver's hand so that he can easily adjust them from the box seat. If the pole, measured from the splinter bar to the pole end (without the crab) is 280 cm. long, a coupling rein of 290 cm. from the bit to the centre pole is suitable for average-size horses. The horses should be put to not longer than 162–163 cm. i.e. the length of the traces, measured from the splinter bar to the centre hole of the traces. If this distance is longer, the coupling buckle can only just be reached from the box seat which is neither comfortable nor practical. The best measurement for correct harnessing – not too short – for the outside reins, measured from the bit to the end of the rein, is 430 cm. and

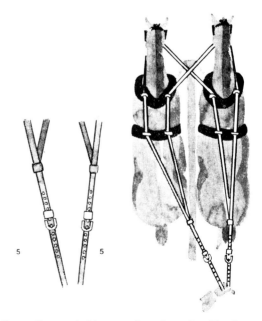

Correctly-coupled horses of medium size. (The figures refer to the number of holes in the reins appearing before the buckle)

9

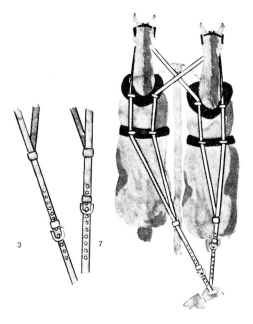

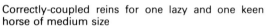

Correctly-coupled reins for one lazy and one keen horse of medium size

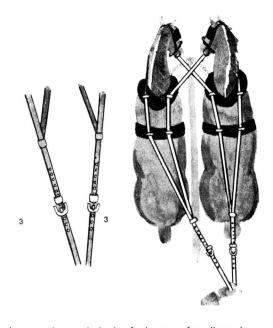

Incorrectly coupled reins for horses of medium size

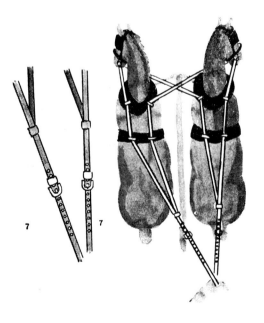

Incorrectly coupled reins for horses of medium size

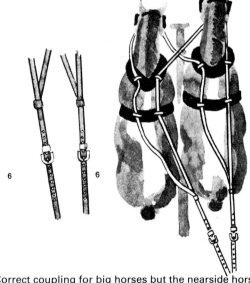

Correct coupling for big horses but the nearside horse is not working and should have a reminder with the whip

10

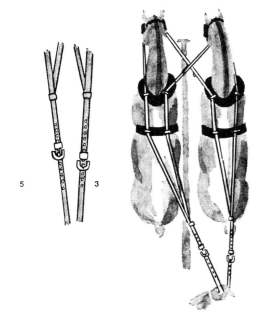

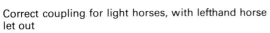

Correct coupling for light horses, with lefthand horse let out

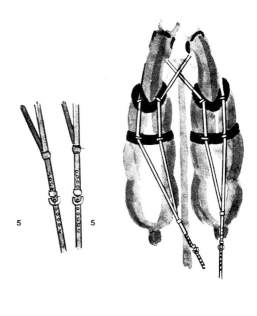

Incorrect. Inside reins are on the outside and vice versa

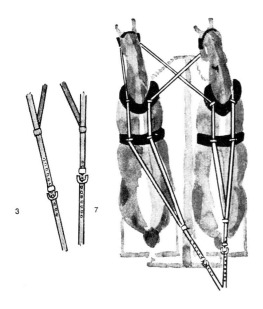

Horses badly coupled

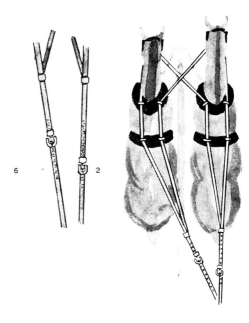

Standard coupling for light horses

11

from the bit to the centre hole, 290 cm. The coupling rein, when buckled in the outside hole, should be 12 cm. longer than the outside rein; this should fit average-sized horses of 1.68 m [16.2 h.h.] in full collar harness. On some carriages the box seat is so far forward that, by using the above measurements, the buckles get into the driver's hands. In this case all four parts of the reins should be shortened at the splices by the distances required.

'The inside billet is fitted in reverse. This has given cause for a number of wrong explanations. It is thought that, spliced in this way, the buckle would not turn over and thus not show the rough side of the reins.

'The coupling reins should be arranged so that the smooth side faces the other horse (by looking at the billets it becomes obvious which is the coupling rein).

'When using new reins for the first time the driver must take care that the coupling reins are in the right position. This is best done by catching hold of the billet before moving off and turning it like a corkscrew (left rein clockwise, right rein anti-clockwise). Should the coupling rein turn over during the journey, it is usually possible to turn it back by twisting the coupling buckle to the inside until the coupling rein turns back in the terret.

'The neck strap of a breast collar should be without terrets. They are of no use as they do not give any support if a horse is sharply in work. The coupling rein goes straight from the pad to the bit. If English cross-reins are used with breast-collar harness the coupling reins should be only about 8 cm. longer than the outside rein, i.e. the coupling buckle should be closer to the driver's hand. This still leaves sufficient holes for adjustment to suit different temperaments. The most suitable width for new reins is 27 mm. which, with use, will shrink to 25 mm. The four reins from the coupling buckles to the bit carry the same load as the two handparts and, therefore, need not be as strong. It is thus recommended to have the whole of the coupling rein 25 mm. wide and the outside rein 27 mm., tapering to 25 mm. from the first hole down-

wards. Some harness-makers disagree with this as they feel it is bad craftsmanship. This is nonsense. It may be new and strange, but it is sensible. After short use the handpart shrinks, and it is only the part with the eleven holes that retains the original width of approximately 27 mm.

'The reins have a buckle at one end of the handpart and a point at the other. This makes it easy to distinguish between the left-hand rein and the right-hand rein. In a properly run stable the rein with the buckle is always used on the left-hand horse. With Vienna reins, however, both parts are identical. Therefore, if the reins are taken off immediately after driving – which is correct – and are unbuckled for cleaning, the right-hand and the left-hand rein can easily be confused. If both horses are of the same temperament, have the same mouths and lengths of front, and the driver sits right in the centre, this would be of no consequence. However, such a perfect set of circumstances is unlikely.

'Cross-reins have only one hole in each billet and, when buckled to the bit, look perfectly even. Any adjustment is done at the coupling. This, in a large stable, makes life much easier, because a book can be kept recording how the various pairs of horses work best. When using Vienna reins it is impossible to keep a record, and with English reins, because of the number of holes in the billets, it is very difficult. For the reins recommended here, only one figure need be recorded for each pair, at the most two. I have already mentioned that each rein has 11 oval holes which are evenly distributed over a distance of 40 cm. English reins occasionally have 11 holes, but mostly 13 or 15. This does not achieve any more than the 11 holes in our reins because, whatever the number of holes, they are still distributed over a distance of 40 cm.

'Now we come to the crux of the matter. With 11 holes the sixth hole is the centre or standard hole. When the coupling reins are buckled into this centre hole each coupling rein should be 12 cm. longer than the corresponding outside rein. The total distance by which the coupling reins are longer than the outside reins is therefore 24 cm., which is the distance between the heads of the horses from bit to bit. The holes this side of the coupling buckle (towards the driver) add up to 10, i.e. 5 either side. Therefore, with a total number of 10 holes above the buckle we have a total extra length to the bits of 24 cm. as each coupling rein is 12 cm. longer than the corresponding outside rein. This also gives the distances between the horses from bit to bit. If both couplings are moved by one hole towards the driver, the number of holes adds up to 8. This reduces the distance between the bits to $24 - 4 - 4 = 16$ cm. The heads of the horses are now closer together. If, for instance, the left-hand coupling rein is lengthened by one hole and the right-hand rein shortened by one, the horse on the right-hand side has been let out on both sides, whereas the horse on the left-hand side has been brought back. However, because the total number of holes above the buckles is still 10, namely 6 plus 4 (standard), the total distance between the bits remains at the standard 24 cm. (Left-hand rein 16 cm., right-hand rein 8 cm. = 24 cm.)

'To use the above reins – which are suitable for horses of about 1.68–1.72 m. [16–17 h.h.] (coupling reins 12 cm. longer) – for small, narrow horses we take each coupling buckle one hole up. The total number of holes above the buckle then adds up to 8, i.e. 4 + 4; or, if the horses are of different temperaments, adjust to 3 + 5 or 2 + 6 or 1 + 7 or even 0 + 8. The reverse applies if the same reins are to be used for a pair of big horses. This means letting out each coupling buckle by one hole, thus making the total number of holes above the buckles 12 (6 + 6), which gives a distance between the bits of 16 cm. + 16 cm. = 32 cm. If the distance between the horses is correct at 6 + 6 holes (32 cm.), any adjustment for different temperaments or distribution of work must be kept to this total number of 12 holes above the buckle – 6 + 6 or 5 + 7 or 4 + 8 etc. With the total number of 12 holes, the distance of 32 cm. between the horses is automatically retained (10 holes = 24 cm. for average-size horses, 8 holes = 16 cm. for small horses). If for any reason the driver wants to bring the horses' heads together, or further apart, or couple one horse shorter than the other, this can be done after some practice without stopping. It is important to experiment, as only then can it be determined whether the measurements are suitable for the horses. The tests should, however, only last a few moments; and one should never fumble, a common sight with Vienna reins.

'Horses are different in conformation, in degree of submission, mouth and temperament. Ideally, for a four-in-hand, all four horses should be bitted so that they are equally light on the bit. To achieve this, bits of varying severity are required and, of course, the driver has to assess correctly the temperaments of his horses. For instance, with one keen horse and one lazy horse a fast pace will only excite the keen one while making the lazy horse even lazier. A sensitive driver will easily find the pace that suits both. This is where the "art" of driving begins. With English cross-reins, a good driver will balance out his team by giving each a suitable bit, adjusting the reins according to the temperament of each horse and finding the correct pace at which to drive them. One may ask: "But what if I am in a hurry and have to drive fast?" The same end can be achieved with a good average speed, if necessary without a walk. The sensible driver will arrive – with dry horses – before the fast driver who, in the end, has to walk his horses because any excitable ones are covered in lather.

'A wise driver will also apply this "average" speed when driving a four-in-hand uphill and downhill. On good roads, with a very light vehicle, this is of little importance; with heavy vehicles, however, like a coach or char-à-banc, it is of utmost importance. They have to be driven fastest when going slightly downhill; excitable horses will then keep calm, and none of the horses will have to work hard. The time thus saved can be used when going uphill.

'Here are some hints for driving enthusiasts on how to bit horses. For a horse that is inclined to over-bridle: broken mouthpiece, bit high up in the mouth, do not drop the curb but put it rather steep (although not severe) or on a loose curb chain with the reins buckled single cheek. For a horse that pokes its head: slightly lower curb. If the horse is very sensitive in the mouth use a leather-covered mouthpiece, roller curb, small or large port, Segundo mouthpiece; experiment with the length of the curb chain. With a puller, leave the curb chain twisted and tie it up higher with a strap to the throatlash.

'Driving a pair in English reins puts emphasis on the acceptance and observation of the re-actions achieved by the correct use of the whip. The hand should be held high and, although gentle, should hold on firmly until the horses accept the bit. Halt, walk on again, halt, rein back. An excitable horse is usually sensitive to any disturbance. It will become restless if the lazy horse next to him is touched with the whip. Why? Because, as a reaction to the whip, the lazy horse will suddenly accelerate, pulling the driver's hand forward before dropping back again. However, the excitable horse, proceed-ing nicely as the driver's hand goes forward will run against the hand (bit) as soon as the driver's hand goes back. Therefore, the lazy horse should have a sufficiently severe bit on a long rein so that it runs against the collar rather than pulls forward the driver's hand. To bend the right-hand horse to the right, drive closer than usual to the right-hand kerb. Then use the whip quietly, and without dragging the lash along the horse's body. To bend the left-hand horse to the left, touch it with the whip on the left. Of course, the horses must have been taught beforehand in long reins how to react to the whip, just as a riding horse reacts to leg aids.

'The strict accuracy of the English or Achen-bach (cross) reins is invaluable in getting a horse to accept the bit by using the whip. To start off, it will lie on the bit. If four individual reins were used the horse would pull its own reins forward, while the reins of the other horse remained short. In order to correct the reins, it is neces-sary to stop in the middle of the exercise and start all over again. With cross-reins this does not happen. If a horse pulls its reins through the driver's hands it will also pull forward the reins of the other horse. Therefore, the balance be-tween the horses is always maintained. When training with the whip, hold the reins very short. This way the attentive hand can counteract firmly but gently. Firm hand and supple elbow joint! The right hand should always be free to use the whip. If the right hand is holding the reins as well as the whip it only results in "fum-bling" and jerking the horses in the mouths. Fumbling whip aids result in a driver relying on his strength and the weight of the whip, irre-spective of success. Laying on the lash (without any noise) is carried out at intervals and the skilful driver will yield as soon as the horse obeys, both with hand and whip.

'Few drivers recognize the importance of ad-justing the coupling reins correctly. For instance, if the left-hand horse is positioned correctly but the right-hand horse turns its head a shade too much to the outside, what must you do? There are several ways of putting this right. Firstly, establish whether the left-hand horse is on the bit or whether it is hanging back. If it is a lazy horse, the chances are that it is behind the bit and the whip is required. The rein adjustment was correct. Why? As soon as the whip is effec-tive the head of the right-hand horse will be positioned correctly and the head of the left-hand horse will point slightly to the outside. The following has happened: as soon as the left-hand horse accelerates, the splinter bar pulls the forecarriage forward and the pole moves over to the right. At this moment every driver, in-tentionally or not, puts less pressure on the right-hand rein in order to keep straight. This overcomes the positioning to the right. If he then continues to push the left-hand horse by using the whip, both horses' heads will soon (in approximately one minute) be positioned to the left because the left rein has exercised an increase in pressure in order to keep straight, thus achieving the left positioning. If, however, the left-hand horse was on the bit, the outside positioning of the right-hand horse was caused by the fact that the left-hand rein was too short (right-hand rein too long). The driver then has to give the left-hand horse more freedom by taking the coupling buckle up by one hole and letting the right-hand coupling out by one hole. Because the horse was on the bit, this will move the forecarriage, and thus the pole, more to the right. The driver, therefore, does not pull at the right rein as he did before and, as a result, the horses' heads will not point to the right-hand side either.

'If both horses look to the right, or the left-hand horse hangs away from the pole because the pole is uncomfortable at its front leg, the vehicle will always pull to the left – much to the annoyance of the driver. Novices usually try to correct this by wrongly shortening the coupling rein of the left-hand horse – thus holding the horse back, instead of letting it out so that it can turn the forecarriage and pole to the right. As a result, the carriage will pull even more to the left. The right-hand horse that has done all the work gets jerked in the mouth because it seemed not to follow to the right, and becomes frightened and excited. If the driver then, with the best of intentions but little knowledge, changes the horses over, he will think he has found the answer because it works! The over-excited right-hand horse finds the left-hand, short rein suitable for its energy. However, this is unlikely to work for any length of time; as soon as the horse has calmed down because its mate is helping, the vehicle will again pull to one side.

'In order to learn all the effects of rein-adjustment, the novice driver must investigate every possibility with the use of correct cross-reins, but he should do this without working with the whip. For instance, if the horse on the right-hand side keeps poking its nose to the left – the inside – an experienced driver should soon find out why. Obviously the horse does not want to bend to the right. Perhaps the horse is hanging on to the left rein or leaning against the right-hand rein. The cause for both is the same but the horse is using different means of defence. If you have a horse with bruised bars it may even do both. Coming straight out of the stable the horse will not take the bit on the side with the bruised bar; it may do so after a little while, or perhaps not until the return journey. It will be a little unsettled at first but will then take hold of the bit with force. The novice may try to cure this by bitting the horse more severely on the right-hand side. This will lose him the battle completely because the severer bitting will squeeze off the nerve and the horse will use force to avoid having to bend to the right. A sympathetic hand may be able to achieve something by severe bitting on a sound mouth but only if it tries to achieve the positioning to the right without forcing the horse to bridle at the same time. The cure is always the same provided one knows the cause of the problem. If one meets the trouble described above, put the reins on single cheek both sides, loosen the curb chain, drop the bit away from the bruised bar, let out the reins one or two holes on both sides, and walk the horses on a loose rein so that they can stretch their necks. The horses will straighten out immediately. Why? The answer is simple. It was less painful for the horse to lean against the right-hand rein than it was to bend its head in a bridled position at the lower jaw and have the parotid glands pinched. This cannot be corrected so easily with any other reins except the Achenbach reins.'

4

Harness and Harnessing Up

When buying harness it is important to ensure that it is suitable for the required purpose. Generally speaking, harness should be such that it guarantees full use of the 'draught power'. Together with the draught arrangement on the carriage it should ensure complete safety in traffic. The horse must not be impeded by the position of the harness.

Therefore, harness used with a light carriage for pleasure purposes must be different from harness used for heavy transport. Certain points, however, are valid for every type of harness. These are explained in the following paragraphs.

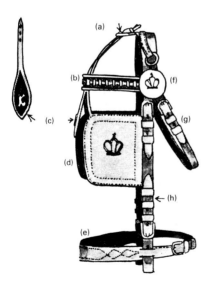

The harness: (a) stay strap; (b) winker; (c) facepiece; (d) winker; (e) noseband; (f) rosette; (g) throatlash; (h) cheek piece

The Bridle

A badly fitting bridle can cause pain. This is very often the reason for upset horses which, in their agitation, can endanger the safety of both horse and man.

For that reason the bridle requires some explanation. The first condition is that it must have sufficient margin for adjustment to fit the shape of the head. The browband should rest just below the ears and fit smoothly around the forehead. It should be neither too narrow nor too wide. If the browband of a set of double harness is too narrow, temporary relief can be achieved by putting only the cheek piece through the loop of the browband, where there should be no bosses, not the throatlash.

The Winkers

A separate chapter will deal with the purpose of the winkers. Most drivers believe that the centre of the winker should be immediately opposite the eye of the horse. Wrong! To achieve this they have the winkers cut out at the buckle. As a result the top rim of the winkers on both sides rests on the temple bone, pressing and rubbing badly.

Correct winkers are not cut out. The eye rests behind the upper third of the winker and the top rim rests in the cavity of the temple bone; the cheek piece fits closely along the whole of the cheek thus avoiding any pressure. The winkers are kept in place by correctly-made winker-stays. They are forked and made in one piece. The winker-stays are buckled to the poll piece. This point should be easily adjustable, and the winkers should stand away from the eye at an equal distance either side so that the eyelashes cannot press on to the eye, which happens with incorrect winkers. Unsuitable winker-stays are those which finish in a loop. The loop can move along the connecting strap between the two winkers and the winkers can apply one-sided pressure. Winkers are only used for blood horses. A working team, particularly of heavy horses, does not really need them.

The Throatlash

It is a peculiar fact that very often the throatlash is buckled too tight.

The reason for this is the intention to have the throatlash buckle level with the buckle of the cheek piece, although the throatlash was too short in the first place. Levelling up of the two buckles only needs to be done on the outside. It should be mentioned here that it is very wrong to adjust the cheek piece to match up with the throatlash buckle. This would push the winkers up too high. A correctly-fashioned throatlash should leave sufficient room for a hand to fit comfortably between the jaw and the throatlash.

The Noseband

Very few nosebands are correct! The cheek piece should go through the noseband, not the other way round as is often produced by harness-makers. It should be able to move on the cheek piece. The noseband should have slits through which the cheek piece is threaded so that it can be moved up and down. This will ensure that it is always placed correctly, neither too high nor too low. The noseband should have three slits on the inside which allow adjustments to suit the size of the head. It should not be placed too high, and should be buckled tight enough so that although the horse can still chew, it cannot open its mouth. With incorrect nosebands, which cannot be adjusted, the distance to the winkers cannot be changed whether the head of the horse is large or small. They are as useless as trouser-braces which cannot be adjusted. A further reason for the noseband is to keep the cheek pieces, and thus the winkers, in place.

I do not, as yet, want to go into detail as to whether full-collar or breast-collar harness is more suitable. I only wish to explain the general requirements of suitable harness and its correct fitting. Wherever heavy draught is required, for instance in mountanous areas or for heavy vehicles, full-collar harness is used. On the flat, and for light work, breast-collar harness is preferred. Once again the Achenbach principle

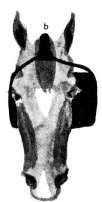

Winker stays: (a) correct; (b) incorrect finishing in a loop; (c) Incorrect noseband as it pulls the cheek piece backwards and therefore the bit forwards, and leaves the curb chain dangling; (d) Winkers incorrectly shaped as they press on the temple, and the throatlash is too tight

applies: 'Make work as easy as possible for your horses by correct harnessing.'

Full-collar harness spreads the draught because the collar rests with its entire length against the shoulder of the horse. It therefore distributes the draught over a much larger area, which makes work easier – provided, of course, the collar is of the right size and is positioned correctly. A good collar should be anatomically correct; that is, it should not be egg-shaped but more pear-shaped. It should have sufficient room for a hand to fit comfortably between the windpipe of the horse and the bottom end of the collar. The draught arms must not be too close to the elbow joint. A correctly made collar avoids rubbing of the tugs. For working harness, soft under-collars are recommended. Hame ter-rets should be movable, not rigid. This avoids jerking in the mouths, particularly if you have horses with a lot of action.

The collar must be fitted in such a way that when the horse is in draught the collar neither lifts away from the shoulder nor from the chest. Hame strap and kidney-link can help to make a collar fit better. Therefore, a well-run stable should always have a number of various sized kidney-links in stock. For working harness, adjustable collars are obtainable.

Some horses have such large heads that the correct-fitting collar cannot be pushed over their heads. In this case a larger collar with an under-collar should be used. Under-collars are flat 'bolsters' made from ticking and filled with horsehair. They are open at the throat and can be put on after the collar is in place. They are buckled to the collar with leather straps so that they cannot move but form one unit.

Breast-collar Harness

This has the advantage that it can be adjusted to fit horses of various heights and sizes. It has, however, one great disadvantage. In heavy draught it can never lie correctly. It either hinders the freedom of the shoulder in the forward movement or presses on the windpipe. There-fore, as already mentioned, full-collar harness is more suitable for heavy work. Breast-collar

harness is ideal for light horses in light carriages provided that movable bars are attached to the rigid splinter bar. If this is not done, the rigid splinter bar with its roller bolts will result in sore shoulders.

Because of the loose neck-coupling strap, stopping is very difficult. With a heavy load, going downhill, horses can fall quite easily because the coupling strap has slipped forward up to their ears. It is therefore essential that the neck-coupling strap is put through the loop at the top of the neck strap and, below, through the ring on the breast collar.

To facilitate any sudden halts a breeching is advisable. In hilly country it is a necessity. The breeching is fitted by adjusting the hip strap so that it rests flat about one hand below the ichium bone. When the horses are in draught the breeching body should have sufficient room for one hand to fit comfortably between it and the body of the horse. The whole breeching must never impede the horse. If fitted correctly, the front edge of the hip strap should rest one hand behind the highest point of the croup.

The Harness Pad

Saddle marks at the withers indicate a badly fitting pad. Like a riding saddle a pad must be fitted, taking into consideration whether the withers are long or short, or even hardly visible, and whether the back is flat or pointed. Pads made for narrow horses with very long, tapering withers cannot be used for a big horse. They will rub and pinch at the sides. Pads for big horses used on small horses will cause sores at the top of the withers.

The frame of the pad is made from iron and must, therefore, be fitted by a blacksmith. The padding is done by a saddler. Felt underlays may be used as a makeshift until the job can be done properly, but they must not become a permanent arrangement. When the girth has been fastened, the pad must fit closely and evenly to the body and must leave adequate room at the withers.

The firm location of the pad is secured by a correctly fitted crupper strap. This must neither be too short, as it will only irritate the horse, nor too long, because it would serve no purpose. The crupper strap, particularly if the crupper itself is heavily padded, is also a very good remedy for 'rein-catchers'. It makes it impossible for a horse to lock the reins under its tail.

Farm horses very often show saddle marks on their backs. These are caused either by badly fitting pads or by 'broken draught' i.e. the backband was too short, thus breaking the draught and putting pressure on the back of the horse.

Whether the horse has been put to correctly and whether the harness fits properly must be checked at the halt as well as in work. If this rule is obeyed a 'broken draught' will not be overlooked. Unfortunately, very few coachmen take the trouble to check even when they have changed the harness on to another horse.

Requirements of the Carriage

Let us now turn to the load to be pulled, the carriage. Even with the best fitting harness, work can be made difficult for the horses. The weight of the carriage should be as low as possible. However, because of the purpose for which it is used there are limitations. It must be borne in mind that the weight of the horses should be in proportion to the weight of the carriage.

It is also possible to improve the movement of a carriage by keeping wheels and lock always well greased. Furthermore, front and rear wheels must keep track, otherwise the rear wheels have to break new tracks which increases the ground friction and thus creates heavier draught.

The shorter the carriage and the wider the wheels the better. The height of the wheels has certain limits but the higher the wheels the easier a carriage will run. The application of the draught depends upon the height of the wheels. This can be easily observed when watching a working team or a pair of horses on a farm. Because the tractive power should be connected with a reduction in the leverage, the draught angle should be 10°–20°. The main bar of a pair in work on a farm, for instance, must therefore be fitted either above or below the pole.

The point of the pole should be level with the shoulder joint. The pole should not be carried by the horses' necks because this would place too heavy a load on their front legs.

The manoeuvrability of a carriage depends on the connection between the fore and the rear carriage. This connection should be as far forward as possible. For farm vehicles, in order to have a good lock, it is advisable either to have vehicles with high wheels and a narrower body or, with a wide body, the lower wheels underneath.

Every vehicle must have a brake. Where it is fitted depends on the purpose for which the vehicle is used, but normally it is in the front of the vehicle.

Good manoeuvrability is particularly important for agricultural vehicles. This can only be achieved by a certain independence between the fore and rear carriage which, in turn, can be safeguarded by the friction pin. The pole should not follow every unevenness in the ground but should move easily up and down.

The pole must rest firmly in the turntable and should have very little vertical play so that the vehicle can be held back even without a brake. It is painful for the horses if the pole rides up and down and the bars hit their hind legs. If in addition the loose neck coupling strap is used it will produce another one of these pitiful sights we see too often on downhill roads.

To put only one horse to the pole makes it difficult to keep the vehicle straight because the pole will continually pull to the other side. It also puts a one-sided load on the forelegs. On uneven roads the pole will always hit the horse and, if the pole chain is too short, the pole will rub the shoulder-joint. In addition, the horse is never straight.

5

Long-Reining and Breaking Horses to Harness

Long-reining

Long-reining prepares young horses for their work in harness, saving a lot of sweat and toil and preventing damage to horses or carriage.

Before starting on the actual long-reining I would like to describe the tack. Anyone who has much to do with breaking horses to harness will have his own long-reining tack. If this is not available, one half of a set of full-collar double harness can be used, without the traces but with the crupper. The correct tack for long-reining has the advantage that it can be used on any horse, whereas a properly fitting collar is not always readily available. Long-reining tack is best made of a breast-plate with a neck strap, two reins and a roller made of either leather or very strong canvas. It is advisable to fit a crupper to stop the roller from slipping forward, which would cause sore withers. The crupper also has the advantage of getting the horse accustomed to feeling the rein under its tail. The reins should be 17 m. long with billets either end which buckle to the rings of the snaffle. The front part of each half of the rein should, if possible, be made of rounded stitched leather (for a length of about 2 m.), as this moves more easily in the guide rings on the neck strap and the large rings on the roller. It is also recommended to have the centre part of the reins made of canvas rather than leather as it makes them much lighter. From the roller the reins should be sufficiently low to stop the outside reins from getting across the horse's back.

The long-reining tack is put on in the stable. However, be gentle; talk to the horse, give it a pat and feed it a carrot. Talking to the horse gives it confidence. Do not tighten the roller immediately and take care when putting on the crupper. It is practical to use a crupper with a buckle on the left-hand side.

After the bandages have been put on the front legs (knots on the outside), and the brushing boots on the hind legs (lifting the front leg on the appropriate side), lead the horse into the indoor school or the exercise paddock. With a difficult horse (or if it is the first time, with any horse) fit on a cavesson or a strong halter with an ordinary lunge-rein which is held by a groom. This prevents the trainer from being pulled over should the horse start plunging. The lunge-rein is essential if a horse is long-reined for the first time in an indoor school where, at the same time, other horses are being worked. Whether it will be necessary to repeat this precaution will be obvious at the end of the first lesson.

As already mentioned, if special long-reining tack is not available one half of a set of full-collar double harness may be used. If this is not available, a breast collar with rings either side of the neck strap will suffice. The rings are required to simulate the directions of the reins in driving. Pad and crupper should fit, but not too tightly. The back-band is buckled in the first hole. The belly-band must hold two large rings, at least as large and as strong as the ring on the kidney link of a full collar. If the belly-band is too long, it can be shortened by making a knot in it. The rings must be put in low, to prevent the outer rein getting over the horse's back. An ordinary riding snaffle may be used as a bit.

Achenbach says: 'The reins for long-reining can be made very easily by joining a strong single harness rein and an ordinary lungeing rein. For this purpose cut approximately 15 cm. off the ends of the single harness rein, fix a strong buckle to one end and a strong point to the other. Accordingly, the lunge-rein should have a buckle instead of the usual hand loop. An ordinary lunge-rein is approximately 8 m. long and the two parts of a single harness rein together about 9 m. This gives you a rein suitable for long-reining of 17 m.'

If an additional cavesson or halter is used, the lunge-rein should be attached in the stable on the left-hand side. The rein for long-reining is only attached in the indoor school or in the exercise paddock. The horse is asked to stand. Then move behind the horse as far as the reins will go; lift both hands, holding them quite far apart, and move the reins gently up and down the outside of the horse's legs. Be patient and careful so as not to frighten the horse. If the horse remains quiet, walk over to the left until the right-hand part of the rein gently touches the horse's thigh. Then try the other side until the horse is absolutely relaxed. If the horse

kicks, resists or tries to run away, allow it to let off steam, initially in a large circle with the aid of the groom who is holding on to the lunge-rein. If the outside rein does get under the horse's tail leave it, but do not pull. Give rein and keep on the circle. When the horse knows what to do but resists, then it should be restrained. Assuming the most difficult case, the horse will buck and kick around the circle. However, this is only short-lived. No horse can keep it up for longer than a quarter of an hour. It also has the advantage that the horse gets rid of its freshness. It will realize that its efforts are futile – and neither horse, nor man, nor carriage have suffered any damage. The only possibility is that the horse might have lost a shoe. Therefore, check its shoes afterwards, particularly the hind ones.

Once the horse is settled on the left rein, practise the walk and the halt until the horse is fully relaxed. At the halt, hold on to the rings of the snaffle and pull the reins forward so that the horse can stretch its neck. Now tell the groom to attach the lunge-rein on to the right-hand side and then start to work the horse on the other

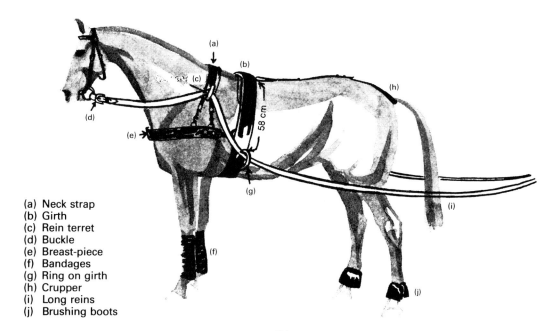

(a) Neck strap
(b) Girth
(c) Rein terret
(d) Buckle
(e) Breast-piece
(f) Bandages
(g) Ring on girth
(h) Crupper
(i) Long reins
(j) Brushing boots

rein. The changed position of the rein can result in renewed kicking. However, this will soon stop. Make the horse walk until it has settled down to work and only remembers the period when it obeyed. (Only if you have a ruined horse, or a mare that appears to be permanently in season must you expect more trouble the next day.) The trainer should take up the reins immediately and walk back to make the circle as large as possible. Take care that the reins do not dangle down as they could trip up the groom who is holding the lunge-rein. Once the horse is working quietly and without problems, send the groom away from the circle.

For the first lessons the use of the whip is unnecessary. In fact, it could even do harm, because it can result in the horse becoming over-collected and over-bridled. It can see the whip and will almost certainly hurry more than it should. So as not to over-collect the horse, always remember to give rein and, whenever it appears appropriate, make gentle, wavelike movements with the rein. The horse is now used to the tack and to having the outside rein round its leg; it no longer hangs on to the lunge-rein which pulled it to the inside of the circle. Now is the time for the trainer to watch the horse carefully. He cannot afford to make a mistake. I have already mentioned the importance of always being ready to give rein. However, this does not mean that the reins should drag along the ground.

In order to lengthen the rein, particularly at the walk, commence by making gentle, wavelike movements with the reins. In addition the hands must go up and then again, giving rein, go down to allow the reins to slide easily in the rings. If one increases this movement, always giving plenty of rein, and walks or runs (depending on the temperament of the horse) two or three steps towards the horse, it will enlarge the circle even if it has a tendency to lean towards the inside. Moving towards the horse's quarters will cause it to go forward; moving towards the shoulder, the horse will make the circle bigger; running clumsily towards the horse's head will make it turn round rather suddenly, particularly if the inside rein is too long and the outside rein too short. So far I have assumed that the horse is correctly positioned. In order to determine the size of the circle with the outside rein the body of the horse should be curved in line with the circle. It must be on the outside rein but must not hang on to it!

One would assume that any rider or driver with sense would recognize the importance of correct positioning. However, I have found on numerous occasions that this very simple principle is not observed, neither when working a horse in long reins nor when driving it. Until this important point is really understood and observed, long-reining as well as driving – particularly a team – can only be detrimental to all participants. Guiding the long-reins directly through the two large rings below the trace buckle is as wrong as holding the reins at knee level when riding.

In driving, correct positioning in turns is essential. This becomes most obvious when

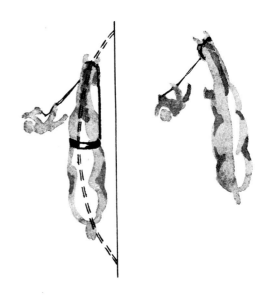

A horse being shown in hand with side-reins. (*Left*) It is being led on the left-hand side and, because the shoulder is pushed to the left, cannot break away to the right; (*Right*) shows the horse hanging on to the left-hand rein. In this position it can easily break away to the right; it is master of the situation driving a tandem or a four-in-hand round sharp corners or in an obstacle course in the show ring. When starting to work a horse on a lunge-rein the side-reins are usually even, but this must not be transferred to the work in long-reins. Here, correct positioning can be achieved immediately because the outside rein ensures that the quarters of the horse are not 'pushed out'. It is essential that reins and whip are always held by the same person. Only then can the necessary co-ordination between active and passive aids be established. This is of utmost importance in long-reining. Always observe the correct positioning of the horse and watch for the most advantageous sequence of the hind legs.

After the horse has been worked at a trot on both reins and has walked freely on a loose rein – naturally always correctly positioned – and has settled down, practise very carefully the changing of rein 'through the circle'. This is done by walking quietly, without altering the length or the position of the reins, towards any point on the outside of the circle (dotted line). This will lead the horse to the centre of the circle. As soon as the horse reaches the centre go quietly behind the horse, but do this carefully as most horses get frightened if somebody passes behind them and the now outside rein suddenly touches the other hind leg. For this purpose the present outside rein has to be gradually shortened twice, at the same time looping the rein to allow the change to be made correctly. As soon as the change has been introduced, let the original inside rein slip by about 3 m., thus turning it into the new outside rein. Give sufficient rein to allow it to go round the horse's hind legs but do not position the horse's head to the outside. Contrary to driving, when shortening or lengthening the reins on this occasion the hands should not be closed; the horse, then, does not get a jab in the mouth if it moves faster or differently than anticipated. Rein changes should only be made at the walk, always taking great care that the head is in the right position; this avoids mistakes and ensures that the horse is not disturbed in the mouth. A horse will only learn how to lean into the bend if the above is not observed.

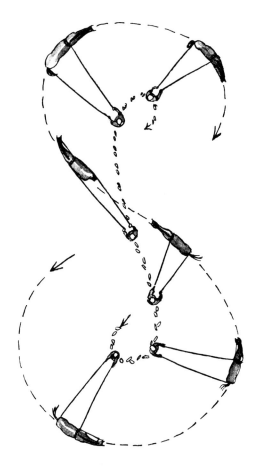

Changing rein in a figure-of-eight from one circle to another

If for instance, at the change of rein to the left, the horse leans to the left earlier than expected, do not think 'it is already turning too much'. Many bad drivers make this mistake. Long-reining shows up mistakes and their remedies clearer than any other exercise. Four-in-hand drivers whose leaders rush into a bend, particularly a right-hand bend, have not found the cause of the trouble and can neither long-rein nor drive correctly. Once they understand that the inside rein (whether long-reining or driving) can, and must, prevent the inside shoulder from leaning to the inside, they have begun to see the light. It is essential that drivers and harness horses realize the importance of the above, particularly when, after much experience, the change of rein is carried out at a canter. Should a horse succeed in turning round completely in long-reins it can be got back under control. After it has been turned back it may try again or may even rear up. However, it must never be allowed to get away with it. The horse cannot stay in this position and with this head carriage for any length of time. It has three alternatives; either to give in immediately, to walk backwards, or to fall over. If the rearing continues, pull the horse's head round as much as possible. It will not like this. If it walks backwards – on an ordinary lunge-rein it could get away – in long-reins it can only stay on the circle, particularly if the trainer is alert. Nobody would believe how fast an excited horse can run backwards, and with what energy and speed! Hold on to the rein, the horse will soon do as it is told. As it cannot get away from the rein it will, eventually, give in and stand. As soon as this is achieved give immediately as much rein as you can, and praise the horse. Then stand in front of it, pull the reins approximately half a metre forward at the snaffle rings and allow it to relax. Horses have excellent memories, and the running back is seldom repeated.

An excellent exercise to obtain immediate obedience from an obstinate horse is the 'tail to the boards'. Initially this should be done without using the whip. It is also a very good exercise for horses who are inclined to lean away from the spur or the whip or who do not want to turn right or left when in harness. However, like any other exercise, it must be started quietly and with patience. If an obstinate horse pivots round and winds the reins round its legs, no harm is done. Leave it for a while in its self-inflicted strait-jacket. It will soon realize that it is wiser to give in.

Once, a dangerous, tough old Irish gelding lost its bridle in such a fight. He ran to the door and although he allowed himself to be caught, it was impossible to get the bridle back on. As soon as somebody approached his head with the bit, the horse reared up and kicked. And how he kicked! I have never before or since seen a horse kick so much that one could hear his back and joints crack! In this situation the long-reins were a great help. They were doubled and then tied round the horse's front legs several times so that he could only move like a kangaroo. After a few unsuccessful attempts to get away the horse gave in and we were able to put on the bridle.

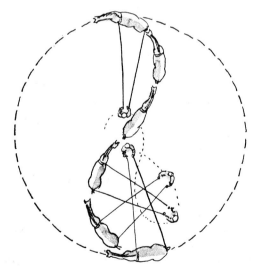 

Correct rein-change and path to be taken by a trainer within a circle

Incorrect rein-change within a circle

Who gives in?

The same method can be used for horses that rear up or kick when one tries to put on the collar. It is dangerous to go behind a difficult or temperamental horse until it has stopped kicking. It could lose a shoe and hurt somebody. Besides, no human is strong enough to hold it down. The same problem can occur when changing the rein through the circle for the first time. Of course, never let go of the horse. Instead, pull on one rein to get the horse back on the circle. This usually settles the matter very quickly.

When the training is sufficiently advanced, walk behind the horse, using a light driving whip, and work it in 'half paces' (very collected). This is a very good exercise for breaking horses to harness without using winkers – though putting a horse in harness without a winker bridle is taking the risk that the horse might run away. In any case, when driving a young horse in harness for the first time it should always be accompanied by a strong, reliable 'break' horse. A competent groom, holding a lead-rein which is attached to the cavesson

should walk alongside. Theory says that horses can see backwards as well as forwards. Practice proves this to be untrue – a horse will always

What to do when a horse rears

25

Creeping back

turn round when the bridle is taken off and the groom walks away to get its food! Anybody wanting to learn the correct handling of horses must first observe the basic rule of horse management – never approach a horse from behind without speaking to it first.

If you have horses in double harness without winkers the horse on the right-hand side will always peep to the left. For this reason many horses tend to hang away from the pole and, if they are even a little knock-kneed, will hit their right fetlock joint. This can usually be overcome by using winkers and it is one reason, among many others, why horses, whatever their temperament, should always be driven in winker bridles. Nevertheless, training should be in long-reins *without* winkers.

Force is inevitable to achieve absolute obedience. This means the horse has to learn the basic principles once and for all in a short space of time. If the horse suffers pain and discomfort, they are always self-inflicted. Thus long-reins, correctly applied, are invaluable in the education of a horse and impossible to compare with driving reins, even in effect. For example, you want to drive to the right, or round a right-hand bend. With its head positioned to the right the horse can break out to the left and cause havoc on the road. The driver must give in to avoid an accident. However, in the same circumstances in training, working in long reins, hold on to the right-hand rein, whether it is in an indoor

school or the exercise paddock. Never mind if the horse gets entangled in the reins or falls over. Persevere, the horse will give in eventually.

If you continue to hold on for a while, even after the horse has given in, it will remember that you are superior. In this way, even the most disobedient horse will soon become submissive. This is the basic reason for work in long-reins. No whip, no jabbing in the mouth – irresistible

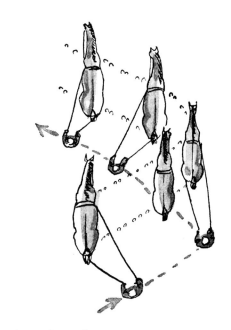

Quarters out exercise

26

leverage has achieved submission. The pains which caused the resisting horse to relent were self-inflicted. It is impossible to compare driving reins with long-reins because they lack the long-reins' main characteristic, the powerful aid of the outside rein round the hindquarters of the horse. I personally know of no better means of teaching a horse to react to rein-aids than the application of long-reins as described above. Leading the inside rein directly from the bit to the hand of the trainer has several disadvantages. Firstly, it has the same effect as an ordinary lunge-rein, i.e. it pulls to one side, which is of no use and does not apply when driving. Secondly, the horse's quarters will swing out and the horse will brush (hit its fetlock joints) in front as well as behind. Thirdly, it is impossible to change rein as frequently or carry out the excellent 'Travers' exercises (Head to the Wall), which are some of the best exercises to achieve complete obedience. It has been said that the power applied by the lunge-rein from the mouth directly to the hand of the trainer works at a right angle to the centre of the circle and that it is, therefore, 'unbroken and complete'. In theory this is correct. However, when a horse is disobedient – and this is the crux of the matter – the superior strength of the horse will also act 'unbroken and complete'. The indirect method, i.e. mouth – collar – pad, does indeed work against the movement, but so does each pull of the reins when riding or driving. It is definitely a mistake to assume that the effect of the long-reins is reduced because it is 'broken'. Nobody denies that due to the detour of the long-reins via the two rings it is impossible to give a horse a sharp jab in the mouth. In fact, this is a very good thing. However, pulling the rein hard and then holding on makes it impossible for a resisting horse to get away, despite its great strength, unless the trainer *allows* it to do so. As a result, even the strongest horse will capitulate within a few seconds, without being punished by the whip, which in most cases comes too late anyway.

Education and training without the whip, but making use of the considerable power of the

Tied up in the lunge

leverage of the long-reins – firmly applied and followed through at the right moment – are fast and effective means which no horse can, or wants to resist. It is a well-known fact that every horse has a difficult side to its nature. This can, for a number of reasons, become very obvious in long-reins. For example: take a high-spirited hackney who was ruined when he was broken to harness. He has a bruised bar on the right-hand side of his mouth. If you put him in harness, he will, at first, not take to the bit on the right-hand side for fear of pain. However, because he has spirit he will, after some 10 minutes, take the bit with a vengeance. The intention is to cure the mouth in long-reins. On the left rein, the horse's curved side, he goes perfectly. The horse is correctly positioned to the left and the right hind leg is kept in by the outside rein. If you try to work this horse on the right-hand rein he will arch to the right as much as he possibly can, naturally pushing to the outside. This is not because of centrifugal force, but because the curve is too acute and the horse goes over his outside shoulder. In such a case it is advisable to do away with the bit completely. This is the quickest way to heal a bruised bar. Use a cavesson, putting it on fairly low. Then attach the long-reins like draw-reins. However, if a horse with a sound mouth pushes away from the circle for no obvious reason, the most successful remedy is to work it first on the other rein for about half an hour; then work it at a walk,

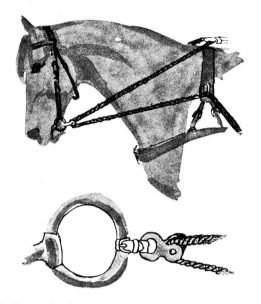

Rollers and string

Long-rein fitted to a cavesson

frequently changing rein, and in 'head to the wall' exercises.

Some say it is impossible to give sufficient rein in long-reins; and if it *is* possible, only too late. At the same time it is also said that long-reins ruin a horse's mouth. There is no logic to either statement. Should the long-reins not slide easily enough in the rings, use rollers and string (pulley system) instead of rings and reins. The many jabs in the mouth which occur with an ordinary lunge-rein when the whip is used, rather oppose these statements.

At the end of each lesson get the horse used to the touch of the whip. As soon as full confidence has been achieved, practise whip cracking, sounding of horns, sirens, drums, bells etc. This is a very important part of breaking to harness, because if a horse has confidence in his trainer many accidents can be avoided.

After these preliminary exercises attach the traces, which have been lengthened with ropes. Ask somebody to hold on to them, initially hanging on only a little, then harder, allowing himself to be dragged along. When the horse is completely steady put on a cavesson with a leading-rein and one half of the pair reins, maybe also knee-caps.

Breaking to Harness

A young horse should always be broken to harness with an experienced 'break' horse. Put the break horse to first, then stand the young horse next to the pole, talking to it quietly and put it to very carefully. Never forget to praise it, and give it titbits! The driver should then try to mount and dismount, sit on the right-hand side and on the left-hand side, take up the whip and move it. After this has been done ask the break horse to move off. The groom should walk alongside the young horse, holding on to the leading-rein. However, he must be careful not to disturb the horse in its forward movement. Should the horse show any sign that he is about to kick, the groom should pull hard at the leading rein, which is attached to the cavesson, at the same time speaking to the horse in a warning tone.

A swingle tree should never be used when breaking a young horse to harness because as soon as the break horse moves on the young horse will get a jolt on its chest and be pulled back. If a swingle tree exists on the vehicle it must be tied down.

When the young horse has settled down and has become used to the noise of the moving

28

A single Hackney horse to a viceroy wagon

Example of a single horse, English turnout, to a Spider Phaeton

Brook Acres Silver Nick to a viceroy wagon

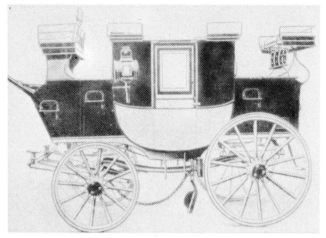

Private Drag

Tandem cart

Roof-top break

Gig

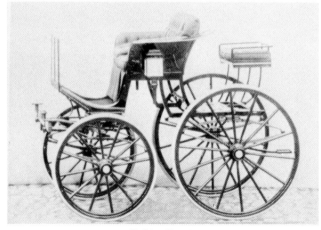

Spider Phaeton

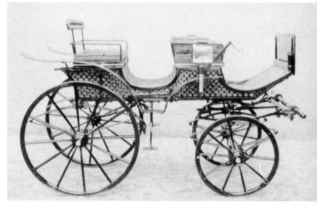

Hungarian carriage

German hunting cart

Mrs. Cynthia Haydon with Mrs. J. A. McDougald's team of Hackneys. Photographed during the 1974 World Championships

Mrs. Deirdre Pirie and her team of Hungarian horses

vehicle, continue the training on tracks and side roads, avoiding main traffic, in order to maintain the horse's attention. During the initial training period drive the horses at a walk, on a loose rein, then gradually increase the pace to a quiet trot, but only on good going, to improve the action. Give the horse several rest periods so as not to exert it. Avoid taking young horses on heavy going; the demands should only be increased slowly. Once the horse has proved safe in harness on firm, even ground, then work may be gradually increased, even to taking the horse on heavy going.

Keen, temperamental horses may get excited in heavy going, so do not try to overcome freshness and keenness by taking them on heavy ground. They will only want to go on even more. As a result you would have to shorten the reins repeatedly, the horses would become dead in the mouth and would only over-exert themselves. If a young horse initially tries to dodge its work, which after all is new to him, allow him just to trot along for a while. But aim to change to a quiet, settled walk in due course. In the early stages be satisfied if the young horse goes along willingly. Do not try to calm young, lively horses by allowing them to trot all the time. For the first few days, get rid of their freshness by long-reining or riding them. Unless a horse is used to harness work its shoulders will hurt from pulling the vehicle. This can easily lead to a bad 'moving off'. It is therefore advisable to drive young horses with a soft under-collar, and make it a rule always to check for sore shoulders when taking the horses out. For the first lesson in harness with the break horse give the young horse traces that are about 20 cm. longer, its reins being shortened accordingly.

6

Harnessing Up and Putting To

Before putting on the harness wipe the horse over, from the front to the back; then turn it round in its stall. Place the pad over your left arm and take the collar with both hands, wider part up. Then push the collar gently over the horse's head. Immediately behind the ears turn the collar in the direction of the mane and guide it slowly down to the shoulder. If the horse is nervous, or has a large head, take the hames off the collar, widen the collar over your knee and then proceed as above. Strap the hames back on to the collar, the hame strap going first through the inside hame and then through the outside hame, making sure that it can be unbuckled from the outside. The hame strap has three keepers, one fixed and two loose. The reason for this is to hide the point of the hame strap and also to ensure that the lead rein of a four-in-hand cannot get caught in it.

Next, put the pad on the horse's back and with the left hand pull the tail through the crupper. Take care that no hairs are caught between the dock and the crupper. Then put the girth through the martingale (breast-plate) but, for the moment, leave it fairly loose. Only when the bridle is on, do you tighten and fasten the girth. The belly-band is only buckled loosely and does not go through the martingale. If a pad is too narrow it will have a tendency to slip forward. As a result the girth is pushed forward to the elbow, where it will rub. Martingales and traces that are too short can also rub and neither sheep- nor deer-skin wrappings – so called 'dead cats' – can stop this. Back-band and tugs may slip forward but only when going downhill.

When in draught they should pull backwards so that withers and elbows are free from pressure.

After the harness has been put on, take the bridle in your left hand and lift it up to the horse's forehead. Then, passing your right hand over the horse's neck, take the bridle with your right hand at the poll piece and lift it up to the horse's ears. At the same time the left hand takes the bit at the mouthpiece and puts it in the horse's mouth, which is opened by pressing the left thumb on the bar. The right hand then pulls the bridle over the right ear, the left ear is pulled through by the left hand. Now straighten out the curb chain and hook it up, then buckle up noseband and throatlash. When the curb chain is hooked in correctly the cheek bars of the bit should form a half right angle to the mouth when the horse is on the bit.

The throatlash should be as loose as possible with its buckles on the outside, level with those of the cheek piece.

The noseband should be fastened so that the horse can still chew but cannot open its mouth. There should be sufficient room for two fingers to pass comfortably between the noseband and the jaw. The bit should neither rest too high (pull up the wicks of the mouth) nor too low (rest on the tushes of a gelding). Normally, it should be about the width of one finger above the tushes. For a horse with a medium-sized head, the bridle should fit if winkers and bit are buckled in the centre hole. Buckled shorter at the top and longer at the bottom the winkers would be too high, and if the reverse is done they would be too low.

After the horse has been harnessed, the reins are pulled through. First take the outside rein, which is the longer of the two, slide the hand down from the coupling buckle to pull it straight. Then lead it through the terrets on the pad and the collar – with a breast collar through the terrets of the neck strap – and buckle it to the bit. The coupling rein is led through in the same manner, but is not buckled to the bit. It is looped through the throatlash. Then pull the billet through from the back and push it through the loop. The handpart of the reins is fastened below the back-band.

It is very important that the reins are put on correctly. With horses coupled in the standard hole this would not matter quite so much, but very few horses are. Remember therefore, that the rein with the buckle at the end goes on the left-hand horse, the rein with the point on the right-hand horse. Observing this rule will prevent the reins from being switched. After the horses have been harnessed, tie them up in their box or leave them loose with a groom in attendance until you are ready to take them out for their drive.

Putting to

The vehicle stands ready with the brake on.

Unless the horses are absolutely quiet and reliable they must be put to individually. Lead the horses carefully out of the stable, watching them to ensure that the harness does not get caught up anywhere. If the horses are reliable and quiet, stand them in front of the pole and back them carefully making sure that they do not hit the pole end or the splinter bar. However, it is always safer to put the horses to individually, with the quieter horse first. Fasten the pole strap, initially quite long; then push the traces over the roller bolts or the bars, outside trace first.

Now bring in the second horse. Again, fasten pole strap, then outside trace and then inside trace. Now attach the coupling reins to the bits, coupling rein on the left horse to the bit of the right-hand horse, and the coupling rein on the right-hand horse to the bit of the left-hand horse.

Make sure that the reins are not twisted and that the rein of the more sensitive horse is on top. Then push the reins underneath the back-band of the left-hand horse.

Now the pole straps are pulled up so that, at the halt, the collars are not pulling away from the shoulders or, if a breast collar is used, this does not stand off at a sharp angle.

7

Taking Out and Unharnessing

Taking the horses out is the reverse procedure. Firstly, lengthen the pole straps, release the traces – inside trace first – unbuckle the coupling reins and put them through the throatlash as they were when the horses were brought out; finally, release the pole strap. The grooms then lead the horses away from the pole, walking backwards and making sure that nothing gets caught in the pole end. With a four-in-hand the leaders should not be taken away unless the wheelers are also free and ready to be taken away from the carriage. Lead the horses away carefully, because due to the winkers they cannot see sideways. Never release the outside rein or the girth so that the horse can run away or the harness become undone.

In the stable, lead the horses directly to their box or stall and then unharness in reverse order to the harnessing up. Firstly, unbuckle the outside rein, then the throatlash and noseband; remove the curb chain and put in a pocket, then take off the bridle. If the horse is nervous put on a halter and tie him up. Take off the reins and hang them up. Undo the girth and take off pad and crupper together by pulling the pad backwards so that the tail comes out of the crupper. With the pad over the left arm, release the tie rein – if one was used – and lift the collar to the narrow part of the neck. Now turn it in the direction of the mane and pull it over the head. If the horse has a big head it may be necessary to undo the hames. Pull the collar apart to widen it a little so that it can pass over the eyes without causing injury, then lift it off.

The harness must be fitted in such a manner that when all straps are correctly buckled – preferably in the centre hole – the points should not show much outside the well-fitting keepers.

8

Taking up the Reins

The reins are always taken up before mounting the carriage. They should always be 'measured' in accordance with the Achenbach instructions. The author of a book on driving argued against this some years ago. He was of the opinion that it is done much easier and quicker from the box seat.

Sensible riders adjust their stirrups and reins as far as possible before getting on a horse so that they can start off immediately. The same applies to the driver. With a couple of placid old nags in front of the carriage it may not matter much; however, with a pair of young, lively horses it is a very different picture. Also, where would the driver of a four-in-hand be, had he not sorted out the length of his reins beforehand!

Some so-called drivers often stand on the box. This is very wrong because the horses could move off unexpectedly, and the driver could be thrown back so that the poor horses get a jerk in the mouth. Should this happen with a four-in-hand the wheelers will push the bars and the crab into the hocks of the leaders. If you then have an inexperienced groom in front of your leaders who does not move out of the way quickly, an accident is unavoidable. Because the reins are neither in order nor at the right length the horses will move off at an angle and not in correct relation to each other, i.e. leaders and wheelers. They may run against the pillar of a narrow gate or against a door, having run over the groom first or, if he managed to jump to the side, crush him against a wall. Besides, not all gate entrances are flat; some may slope downwards, and have corners or open up into roads with heavy traffic. It would then be necessary to

stop the horses on the pavement. Just think what could happen with reins that are too long and disorderly, particularly with lively and excited horses.

It would take too long to give more examples. I only want to emphasize the importance of preparation before moving off. A bad move-off can lead to dangerous confusion, always because the reins are either not sorted out or are incorrectly measured, or both. There is no reason to be very pedantic about sorting out the reins when riding; it only involves one horse. If the reins are too short you can let the horse pull the reins out of your open hand. Furthermore, when riding, you usually move off at a walk. When driving, however, the move-off is very often at a trot, albeit sometimes unintentionally. A reasonably well-broken riding horse will move off straight because there are no reins which are too short to pull it sideways. In driving, everything is reversed: the hand must be closed; direction and speed depend, at the very same moment, upon accurate measuring of the reins.

To measure the reins when mounting from the left the driver stands one pace to the side of the pad of the left-hand horse, facing it. With his left hand he then pulls the reins from underneath the back-band. The right hand takes the right-hand rein between index and middle finger just behind the buckle and establishes a light contact with the horse's mouth. The driver then slides his right hand down the rein until his right arm hangs down the side of his body. This length of rein must be retained, but check that the rein is actually in contact with the horse's mouth and is not hooked up anywhere. The contact must be

Taking up the reins

very light so that the horse is not disturbed in the mouth. With his left hand the driver then places the left-hand rein between thumb and index finger of the right hand by the buckle and pulls it out until the two coupling buckles are level. He then pulls the left-hand rein out a further 5 cm. The right hand now passes the reins over to the left hand in such a way that index and middle fingers are between the reins, with the left-hand rein on top. He then lengthens the two reins by about 20 cm., applying the holds laid down in the 'standard position'. The measurements of the reins are dependent upon the type of vehicle used, that is to say the distance of the box seat from the horses. Before mounting the box, loop the reins over the left forearm so that they do not get caught up anywhere.

Drivers who intend eventually to learn how to drive a four-in-hand should get used to putting only the middle finger between the reins when the right hand passes them over to the left hand. This will be explained in greater detail when we discuss taking up the lead reins.

Taking up the reins from the right

If for one reason or another one has to mount from the right-hand side (this is normal in Britain because of the left-hand traffic) this need not cause any difficulty. Take the reins with your right hand from underneath the back-band. Stand between pad and hip of the right-hand horse about three quarters of a metre to the side. Now with your left hand take the left-hand rein and let it hang down through the whole hand. Then establish contact with the horse's mouth. Slide your hand down the rein until your arm hangs straight down. Hold the rein at this point firmly in your left hand. Now move with your left hand towards your right hand and take over the right-hand rein between index and middle fingers. With your right hand pull the coupling buckle (with single reins the splice) to within 5 cm. of the left-hand coupling buckle. Now let the reins slide forward about 20–30 cm., depending upon the distance of the horses from the carriage, and push your middle finger between the two reins. Pass the reins over to the right hand and mount. If the whip is in the whip-holder on the dashboard, pick it up with your right hand when mounting. The ends of the reins are hanging over your right arm. When on the box seat put your left hand directly in front of your right hand, pushing index and middle fingers between the reins and taking them over.

Taking up four-in-hand reins

To take up the reins from the left, the driver steps next to the pad of the wheeler, pulling with his left hand the lead-and-wheel-reins from underneath the back-band, and placing them over his left forearm. He then takes with his right hand firstly the right-hand wheel-rein and then the left-hand wheel-rein (as explained for pair reins) and passes them, already measured, on to the middle finger of the left hand and holds them there.

The lead-reins are then measured in the same manner, except that the measuring takes place from the splices, and the left-hand splice is pulled out 5 cm. over and above the splice of the right-hand rein. He must then check whether the leaders are standing in draught and if so, must shorten their reins by about 10 cm. If the leaders are standing close to the bars the lead-reins are lengthened by approximately 20 cm. The lead-reins, thus measured, are passed over to the index finger of the left hand which pushes between the reins. After the four reins have been lengthened by the amount required for the box (about 20 cm.), place the ends of the four reins over the left arm and mount, picking up the whip which was placed beforehand across the seat.

Taking up the reins from the right

Stand slightly behind the pad of the right-hand wheeler. Take the left-hand lead-rein between thumb and index finger of the left hand, establish contact with the horse's mouth and slide the hand along the rein until the arm rests at your side. Keeping in this position, place with your right hand the right-hand lead-rein between index and middle fingers of your left hand and push the splice to within 5 cm. of the splice of the left-hand lead-rein. Now pass the measured lead-reins into your right hand, with the middle finger between the reins. Thus thumb and index finger of the right hand remain free. Lengthening or shortening the lead-reins, depending on whether or not the leaders are in draught, are carried out as described before.

Now, with your left hand take the left-hand wheel-rein between index and middle fingers and measure it as the left-hand lead-rein. Then place with the right hand, the right-hand wheel-rein between middle and fourth fingers of the left hand. Pull the coupling buckle forward to within 5 cm. of the left-hand coupling buckle. Finally, the right hand passes the lead-reins on to the left index finger. All four reins are now in order and measured in the left hand.

To mount, the reins are passed back again to the right hand, and when you are safely on the box seat, the left hand finally takes them over.

Care must be taken that no rein slips before moving off, nor that anything is altered. To avoid the reins getting caught in the steps or on the dashboard, loop them over your right arm before mounting.

9

The Achenbach Method of Driving
(Preamble)

As mentioned in the first chapter, Achenbach's method is based on the English style of driving which he improved and refined. The English method of holding the reins had been adopted by driving clubs in existence in Britain, France, Holland, Belgium and North America, which proved its superiority. Particularly with the English method, the art is to temper the aids so delicately that they never work suddenly or too harshly.

Before going into the details of holding the reins and the various positions, the basic difference between right-hand and left-hand turns should be explained, as it is not observed by unskilled drivers. The horses of a cab driver, for instance, will rush into a right-hand bend and get slower in a left-hand one.

The turntable of the fore-carriage is located in the centre below the box. The driver is seated on the right-hand side of the box. When the horses turn to the right they come closer to the left hand (rein hand) of the driver, which is in front of the driver's body, and the horses move away from him in a left-hand turn. Take a point on the reins, say about level with the top of the tail, of the right-hand horse in a left-hand turn. If the horse then turns to the right, this point moves to R. H is the circular arch with the rein hand as the centre point. D is the circular arch with the king-pin in the centre of the turntable as its centre point. With a well-built four-in-hand carriage this point may even be slightly to the rear on the left-hand side of the driver.

Therefore, in a left-hand turn the horses move away from the driver which makes the reins shorter than they were when driving straight ahead. These shortened reins will make the horses go slower through the left-hand turn than when they were walking ahead. The reverse is the case when turning to the right. The reins are longer and the pace gets faster because of the unintentional lengthening of the reins. The sharper the right-hand turn, the faster the pace

The influence of the box on the rein length

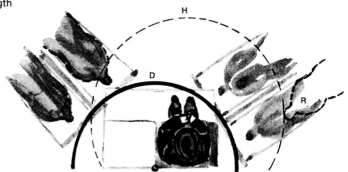

36

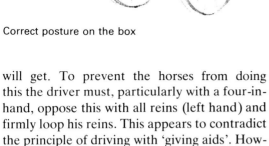

Correct posture on the box   Incorrect posture on the box

will get. To prevent the horses from doing
this the driver must, particularly with a four-in-
hand, oppose this with all reins (left hand) and
firmly loop his reins. This appears to contradict
the principle of driving with 'giving aids'. However, by pulling back the reins or shortening

them, they are only shortened by the distance
the horses come towards the driver in the turn.
This distance is approximately 20 cm., which
means that in a right-hand turn the reins
become 20 cm. too long and in a left-hand turn
they get that much shorter.

37

10

Exercises at the Driving Apparatus

To avoid any interference with the horses' mouths, all the various holds should be practised on the driving apparatus until they become automatic. Wherever possible ask a driver who knows the Achenbach method to help you. It is naturally easier to copy the holds than to teach yourself from a book. Making a driving apparatus for pair-driving is very simple. Attach a piece of string, about 1 m. long, to each end of a driving rein. Guide the two pieces of string through two loose rings which can be either attached to a board on the wall or even to the edge of a table. Hang an ordinary 2 lb. weight or a 2 lb. sandbag to each end of string. For practising the holds for four- or six-in-hand driving, the pieces of string must be guided over rollers which are set into a piece of wood, one above the other. Right from the start get used to carrying something in your right hand to simulate the whip – a stick or riding crop will suffice. It is much harder to get your fingers used to it later on. Tackle difficulties immediately; bad habits are hard to kill!

Working on the apparatus will soon give the novice the necessary confidence. However, he should not practise on his own. If he has no instructor, he should ask somebody to read out every hold to him, showing him the

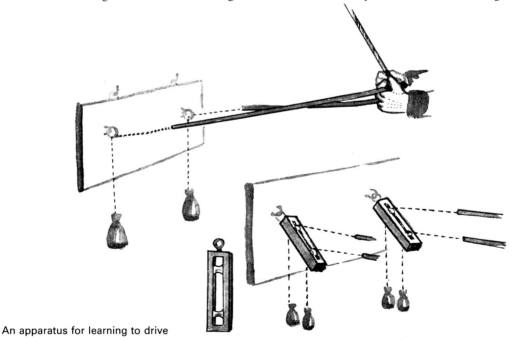

An apparatus for learning to drive

38

picture, until he remembers each one without looking.

If an instructor has a large number of pupils at the driving apparatus he must avoid army-type drill. Otherwise the pupils could get used to jerking movements and easily transfer these later to the actual driving. The driving apparatus should teach them how delicately the aids must act on the horses' mouths. Avoid routine! It is the enemy of good driving. Get your pupils to practise all the holds in random order, and never allow them to practise without a stick or whip in their right hand, or without gloves.

At this stage, some advice about gloves.

Any sport can only be done justice if all the equipment is in order. For a driver it is important that his gloves do not in any way impede the holding of the reins, or even make it difficult. The type of leather and the style of the gloves should be such that they prevent the reins from slipping. Suede gloves are therefore unsuitable; not only are they more slippery but they also soak up water if used in the rain. The most suitable gloves are made of a soft, pliable leather of medium thickness, like pig-skin or kid leather. They must fit comfortably; the fingers should not be too short or they will press on the fingertips, nor should they be too long because they could get between the reins when one applies the various holds. They should also not have pleats in the palm of the glove.

Always choose gloves with a button or press-fastener, but do not button them up. However, it is advisable to buy gloves with the button on the thumb side of the glove; it stops the rain from running into the glove when the hand is upright in the driving position. The seams of the gloves should be on the outside so that the glove can be easily repaired.

Exercises on the apparatus for single and double harness

1 Take up and measure reins.
2 Basic position, standard or driving position, schooling position and transition from one to the other.

3 Lengthen reins.
4 Shorten reins four different ways:
   (a) by moving the left hand to 5 cm. in front of the right hand
   (b) by sliding forward with the right hand and following with the left
   (c) for braking – by moving the right hand behind the left and then sliding the left hand forward
   (d) by sliding the right hand forward and lifting the left hand.
5 Lengthen and shorten one rein only, the so-called 'Filieren', which is a preparation for driving a four-in-hand.
6 Collect rein, give rein and give way by turning the hands.
7 Left-hand turn with two hands, left-hand turn with one hand.
8 Right-hand turn with two hands, right-hand turn with one hand.
9 Left about-turn with two hands, ditto with one hand.
10 Right about-turn with two hands, ditto with one hand.

Exercises on the apparatus for driving a four-in-hand or a tandem

1 Take up and measure reins.
2 Basic position, standard position.
3 Lengthen reins.
4 Shorten reins three different ways:
   (a) by sliding the right hand forward by 5 cm. and following with the left, again by 5 cm.
   (b) by moving the right hand behind the left hand then sliding the left hand forward
   (c) by sliding the right hand forward and lifting the left hand.
5 Straighten the leaders.
6 Straighten the wheelers to follow the leaders.
7 Lengthen the leaders.
8 Shorten the leaders without altering the wheelers.
9 Give way to the right:
   (a) with two hands
   (b) with one hand

(c) to halt on the right-hand side.
10 Give way to the left:
   (a) overtaking – with two hands
                  – with one hand
   (b) to halt on the left-hand side.
11 Left-hand turn.
12 Right-hand turn.
13 Acute turning to the left, or left about-turn.
14 Acute turning to the right, or right about-turn.
15 Halt on the right-hand kerb after a right-hand turn.
16 Halt on the left-hand kerb after a right-hand turn.
17 Practise the hold (position) which should get the leaders in draught in a turn, after a turn or up a hill.

The sequence of exercises for a six-in-hand or a tandem is similar.

When practising on the apparatus do not look down at your hands. Learn how to *feel*; a rider has to feel whether his horse is cantering on the right or left leg. You will never be able to drive in heavy traffic or in the dark unless this is strictly observed. Only on the driving apparatus can all the holds be taught and learned. There is no point in getting the horses confused and unsettled by wrongly-executed holds. At the apparatus the instructor can ask for holds to be repeated and demonstrate their effect by the movement of the weights. The pupil can practise the hold ten or even twenty times if need be, until it is correct, and no harm is done. At the same time he will learn and understand his instructor's phraseology, and the horses are not pulled about unnecessarily when driving.

Finally, I recommend practising the following both on the driving apparatus and later with the horses. It will help you to avoid hanging on to their mouths. These holds are made from the standard (driving) position: the left hand leaves the reigns and picks them up again about 20 cm. in front of the right hand; now take the right hand off the reins and put it back in front of the left hand in standard position. Then slide the left hand back to its original position whilst the right hand holds determinedly on to the reins. Practise this on the apparatus, making sure that the weights do not move; this means that when practising with horses or in driving, the horses are not disturbed in their mouths and will change neither pace nor direction. This should be practised over and over again, faster and faster, but as delicately as possible. It is a good idea to get so used to handling the reins that you can alter them almost without thinking.

It is also the safest method to develop a gentle and supple hand.

11

Driving a Single or a Pair

Both reins are held in the left hand separated by the index and middle fingers. The left-hand rein is placed over the index finger and the right-hand rein under the middle finger. Hold the left hand upright, the width of one hand in front of the centre of the body. This is the basic position from which all other holds are derived, whether the right hand is engaged in using the whip, saluting, or operating the brake. In short, this is the position when the left hand is forced to do the driving.

The reins must never be allowed to slip through the fingers. To shorten or lengthen them the correct holds must be applied. Turns are achieved by yielding with the outside rein, never by pulling the inside rein.

Side view of basic position of the hands

Before using the whip or operating the brake, the right hand leaves the reins completely, otherwise the whip could unintentionally touch the horses. A rider secures the reins mainly with the top fingers, including the thumb; in driving, thumb and index finger do not participate in holding the reins. The driver holds the reins with his third, fourth and fifth fingers. Thumb and index finger stay slightly open, ready to take over the whip.

Avoid falling into the bad habit of niggling and pulling at the reins to urge on the horses. If you do this you will never make a good driver.

We differentiate between three positions in holding the reins: the basic position, the schooling position, and the standard or driving position. However, if a turnout is in sudden danger, due to unforeseen circumstances, anything is justified to prevent an accident.

The schooling position

In the schooling position the left hand stands upright, one handsbreadth in front of the driver's body. The driving reins go down the hand of the driver, unlike riding reins, and are therefore secured by the third, fourth and fifth fingers, not thumb and index finger, which remain open in a slightly curved position. (This is also an important preliminary exercise for four-in-hand driving, where these two digits have a very special and important job.) Keeping thumb and index finger slightly open has the great advantage that their muscles, which run into the forearm, remain relaxed; this in turn allows a much more delicate and sympathetic operating of the left hand. The right hand, slightly opened,

Schooling position (from above)

with the whip held between the nearly straight thumb and index finger, is then placed lightly on the right-hand rein approximately 5 cm. in front of the left, the back of the right hand facing upwards. Now close third, fourth and fifth fingers of the right hand, thus holding the right-hand rein in the palm of the hand. Thumb and index finger remain in the original position, however, because the other three fingers have been closed; the whip now has a firm position in these three fingers with the additional support of the palm. The right hand is then turned into an upright position, at the same time pulling the right-hand rein about 5 cm. out. The right hand is now in front of the left hand, slightly to the right-hand side, with the rough side of the right-hand rein facing up. The whip points half left-forwards-upwards. Make sure that the right hand stays in this vertical position, and practise taking the right hand off the rein without causing unintentional change in direction or pace. Remember, however, that before the right hand is taken off the rein, the left hand must take in the 5 cm. let out earlier. This is done by holding on to the left rein with thumb and index finger, opening the other three, moving them over to the right-hand rein and the closing them again. In doing this the left hand moves exactly in front of the centre of the body. This is important as it will keep the horses straight.

Side view of schooling position of the hands

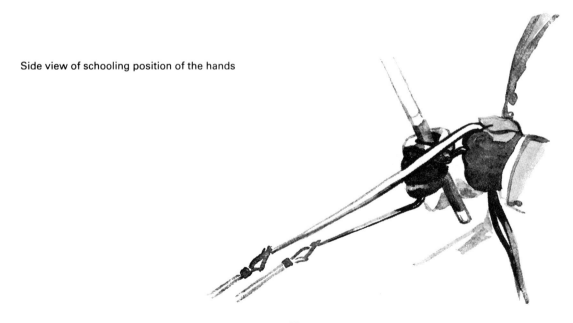

Standard or driving position

The standard position is the one used most. For this the left hand remains in the basic position. The right hand is placed in front of the left so that the right index finger encloses the left-hand rein from the top, and the three lower fingers close over the right-hand rein. The whip is held by thumb and index finger supported by the third and fourth fingers of the right hand. The little finger is not involved in holding the whip. When the right hand is in its correct position the whip will automatically point in the right direction.

Shortening the reins

There are four ways of shortening the reins.
1 The right hand holds on to the reins whilst the left hand is taken out and placed in front of the right hand, then taking up the reins as before. Thereafter the right hand takes up its position again in front of the left.
2 The right hand slides forward on the reins and the left hand follows.
3 For braking purposes: the right hand goes

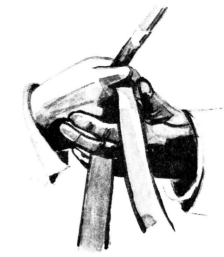

Shortening the reins

behind the left, taking both reins between index and third fingers. The left hand slides forward the required distance. The right hand is then taken off the reins, while the whip is transferred to the left hand in order to apply the brake.

Basic position with double harness

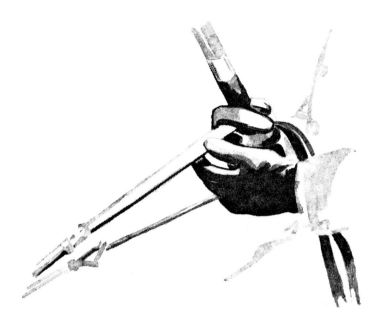

4 Slide the right hand 20–30 cm. forward on the reins and take them back. Raise the left hand to make room. This method is used when there is no need to use the brake afterwards.

'Filieren' – shortening and lengthening of one rein only

Shortening and lengthening of one rein as and when required is also a very good preliminary exercise for four-in-hand driving. By turning the right hand, the right-hand or left-hand rein is either pulled out of the left hand bit by bit by the required distance, or pushed into the left hand.

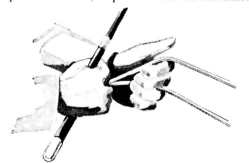

Shortening the reins – particularly suitable before braking

This is always carried out in the standard position. If the left-hand rein is to be shortened or lengthened, thumb and index finger of the right hand push in or pull out the necessary length of rein. For the right-hand rein third, fourth and fifth fingers take the right-hand rein and turn the hand either in or out, depending on the requirement. The left hand either releases the required length of rein or takes it up. Both hands must work in unison. 'Filieren' is the most artistic form of driving as it allows the most delicate and sympathetic transmission of rein aids. It is also an essential condition for four-in-hand driving.

Collecting and giving rein by turning the hands

Because in the schooling position the left-hand rein is over the left index finger, and the right hand is on top of the right-hand rein, turning of the hands will have different effects.

1 Turning the left hand anti-clockwise (little finger moving towards the body) equals easing the left-hand rein or giving rein.
2 Turning the left hand clockwise (back of the hand uppermost) equals collecting rein

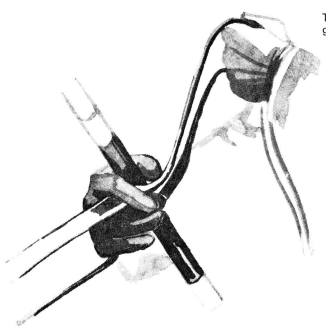

Temporary shortening of reins for an emergency stop

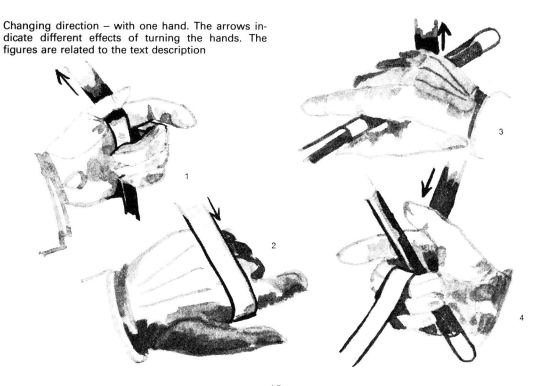

Changing direction – with one hand. The arrows indicate different effects of turning the hands. The figures are related to the text description (increasing pressure with the left-hand rein).

3 Turning the right hand so that the back of the hand is uppermost – easing the right-hand rein (giving rein).

4 Turning the right hand so that the inside of the hand becomes visible – collecting the right-hand rein (increasing pressure).

Bends and turns

Co-ordinating the positions of left and right hands as described in 1 and 4 results in a half right-hand turn due to the increased pressure on the right-hand rein and the easing of pressure on the left-hand rein. Co-ordinating 2 and 3 achieves a half left-hand turn, for instance, when overtaking (in right-hand traffic). Points 1 and 4 are applied to give way (again in right-hand traffic only; in left-hand traffic the opposite applies).

I would like to emphasise again – do not drive turns by pulling on the inside rein; do so by easing the pressure (giving rein) on the outside rein so that the horse on the outside can walk on freely and pull the carriage round the turn at the splinter bar. The horses should always be positioned 'into the turn' i.e. the horses' heads should not be pulled away from the circular arch, which always happens if horses anticipate the turn; they 'lean into the bend', rather than wait for instructions from the driver.

Driving turns in traffic, particularly right-hand turns, must always be introduced by reducing speed. To drive a well-executed and safe turn on slippery tarmac roads, fluently and without hitting the kerb, the horses must be collected. However, do not pull the inside horse round on the rein, it would only hang back in its collar and try to pull the carriage round at the pole chain (risk of slipping and over-reaching). Horses that hang back or lean into a turn do this because the driver has the terrible habit of turning quickly by pulling the inside rein.

A right-hand corner, driven at a walk or a slow pace with horses that are collected and

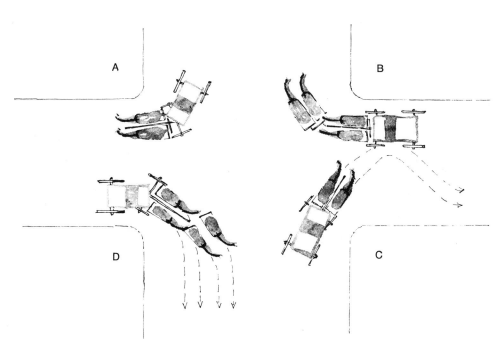

A and B. Negotiating a corner correctly. C and D. Negotiating a corner incorrectly

Right-hand turn – front view

Right-hand turn – side view

therefore on the bit, can be executed safely and beautifully, even on wet tarmac. Driving this same corner with a sweep to the left, then hitting the kerb and ending up nearly in the middle of the road, is not only contrary to the traffic regulations, but also unsafe and clumsy.

Turning to the right

Shorten the reins to reduce the pace to a walk, then slide the right hand about 10 cm. forward on the right-hand rein and turn both hands clockwise so that the backs of both hands face downwards. This means that the left hand has given rein, whilst the right hand has shortened the right-hand rein. Although this appears to be in contradiction to the demand that turns should be introduced by 'giving' the outside rein and not by shortening the inside rein, this is not the case; the position of the hands as described above is completely in accordance with the basic principle. As mentioned earlier, in a right-hand turn the reins will get about 20 cm. too long. To reduce the speed before the turn, they have been shortened slightly, but are still too long to drive the turn. By shortening the right-hand (inside) rein by 10 cm. and turning the right hand, the left-hand rein remains 10–15 cm. longer and, therefore, has an increased 'giving'

effect. The same would be achieved by shortening both reins by 20 cm. and then letting the outside (left) rein slide by about 10–15 cm. This would require more alterations of the reins, apart from having to use the right hand to pull out the left-hand rein which is in contradiction

A badly performed right-hand turn

47

to the principle of holding the reins. After completing the turn the right hand slides back 10 cm. on the right-hand rein, and both hands return to their original driving position.

To drive a right-hand turn in traffic, bring the horses back from a trot to a walk by gradually shortening the reins by about 20 cm. The horses must not hold back the vehicle in a turn.

Turning round to see whether the right-hand rear wheel will scrape along the kerb demonstrates bad driving and is *not* the way to drive a right-hand turn. The horses are not on the bit, the driver pulls the outside rein to avoid hitting the kerb and, as a result, the horses go over the inside shoulder and lean into the turn.

The Right about-turn

Right about-turns (U-turns) are prohibited in towns because they delay and endanger traffic. Even on very quiet roads they should only be made if the turnout has halted on the left-hand side. The turn must then be made at such an acute angle that the turnout does not exceed the centre of the road.

To execute a right about-turn shorten the reins by sliding the left hand 10–15 cm. forward along both reins. Reduce the speed to nearly a halt. Look to the right, signal to the right, and make sure that your signal has been acknowledged. Now apply the correct hold.

A right about-turn

With the right hand take the right-hand rein from the left hand and move it behind the left, thus shortening the rein by about 15 cm., then place the rein back in its original position between the third and fourth fingers of the left hand. The three lower fingers of the right hand then take hold of the right-hand rein in front of the left hand. Turn both hands clockwise as for the right-hand turn.

When the turn is nearly completed, with the right hand pull the shortened right-hand rein slowly out by 15 cm., then return it to its original position.

Right-hand turn with one hand

If the right hand is engaged in using the whip, saluting, or for a movement in a dressage test, it will be necessary to drive with one hand. Unless every turn, change of speed, and pace can be accomplished using one hand only, driving remains amateurish. Therefore, driving with one hand must be practised.

In order to drive with one hand, the reins must first be shortened sufficiently to ensure that speed and pace are maintained. The right hand is then taken off the reins. Make sure that the left-hand rein rests over the index finger directly in front of the knuckles. The right-hand turn is accomplished by placing the left hand in front of the left hip, turning the left hand anti-clockwise (i.e. to the left) so that the thumb is now pointing in the direction of the left thigh. Keep the left hand in this position until the turn is completed and you wish to drive straight ahead again. The same applies if you wish to drive a right about-turn with one hand.

When driving a right-hand turn with one hand, turn off half a metre later than you would if driving it in standard position. This avoids hitting the kerb.

Left-hand turns

In traffic all left-hand turns must be driven as wide as possible. Approximately 15 m. before the turn, the driver should look round and signal with the whip. Make sure that your signal has been noticed and understood. For a left-hand

Right-hand turn – with one hand

turn both hands are turned clockwise so that the backs of both hands face upwards. This results in reduced pressure on the right-hand rein and increased pressure on the left-hand rein which achieves both the left-hand turn and the positioning of the horses' heads to the left. The driver should always make sure that the left-hand rein lies close to the knuckles as it makes it easier to give the 'collecting' aids. If the reduced pressure on the right-hand rein is insufficient to achieve the turn, pull with your right hand about 5–10 cm. of the right-hand rein from the left hand, but slide the right hand immediately back to its old position. After the turn is completed, collect the length of rein pulled out earlier with your right hand. The right hand should never cross over and pull at the left-hand rein.

Left about-turns

For a left about-turn, the right hand pulls about 15 cm. of the right-hand rein out of the left hand. By turning the left hand inwards, the left-hand rein is slightly shortened i.e. collected. The right hand slides immediately back to its old position in front of the left hand. When the turn has been completed take the right-hand rein out of the left hand and shorten it gradually by moving the right hand behind the left. Slide the right-hand rein back between the third and fourth fingers of the left hand, which then closes the fourth and little fingers over it.

Left-hand turn with one hand

To drive a left-hand turn with one hand, the left hand is turned clockwise (back of the hand facing upwards) and, if necessary, is moved towards the right hip.

It stays there, without pulling at the reins, always ready to give rein immediately should it be required.

Left about-turn with one hand

For a left about-turn with one hand, drive close to the right-hand kerb and nearly stop. Now bring the left hand suddenly to the right, turning the hand clockwise (back of the hand

Left-hand turn

A badly performed left-hand turn

A well performed left-hand turn

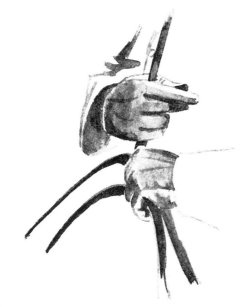

A left-hand turn – with one hand

facing up) and keep it there without applying any counter-pressure.

Remember, for all turns driven with one hand, whether right-hand or left-hand turns, the more the left hand moves to the outside, the smaller the turn. Therefore, the more pressure is applied in the opposite direction, the more effective it is. That is to say, to increase pressure for the left-hand turn – hand moves to the right; increase pressure for the right-hand turn – hand moves to the left. The more the left hand moves to the outside the more rein is given on the outside.

'Paraden'

(Halts and half-halts – temporary shortening of the reins to indicate to the horses that either a change in pace or speed is wanted or that a change in direction is imminent; in short, a change is about to be required.)

Any halt for which the driver has to lean back looks bad. With his own horses, a driver will soon know how much the reins have to be shortened for a halt. The four methods of shortening reins are known. Sliding the right hand forward, taking the reins and shortening them by moving backwards to the left hand – which lifts to make room – is used when a reduced speed is temporarily required; for instance, driving down a short slope in the road which then continues to be flat or even uphill.

Excellent exercises for the hands: left hand leaves the reins and takes them up again 10 cm. in front of the right hand. Right hand moves forward and takes up the reins in the standard position whilst left hand slides back immediately by 10–15 cm. Right hand follows and stops in front of the left. Keep repeating this. If you can do this on the driving apparatus without moving the weights or, when driving, without altering direction or speed, an easier life on the box seat has begun for you.

A driver must look ahead, think ahead and introduce his halts and half-halts accordingly. Only then will he be able to drive fluently.

Backing

Very few drivers realize the importance of the rein-back. If they are car drivers they probably accept it quicker. However, it must be mastered by every driver. Reining-back is very often part of a dressage test in four-in-hand competitions, and the method of reining-back is explained in greater detail in the chapter on four-in-hand driving.

Backing round a corner is more of a day-to-day traffic requirement. It entails placing the pole, and thus the fore-carriage, at an angle to the rear axle.

The rein-back should be executed with care and after due consideration. With well-trained horses the so-called 'flexing of the hindquarters', or preparing for the rein-back, is as useless as applying the whip. Using the whip for a rein-back only shows up a bad driver who is covering up for rough and faulty rein aids, blaming the horses for any mistakes. Before starting the rein-back, imagine the position of the pole from the point you want to rein-back to, or the point you are reining-back from. Only the greatest care and a correct plan will achieve a good rein-back and prevent bad mistakes and over-reaching.

51

The correct rein-back is done step by step, slowly, but without hesitation. Therefore, do not alternate between pulling at the reins and releasing them. If the horses run back you have pulled too hard; if the carriage is too much at an angle, you have not taken the peculiarities of your horses and carriage into consideration.

Once the angle of the pole has been decided upon and has been taken up, it is important to maintain this angle for the rein-back. If at all possible, take care that a rein-back is not made towards a bank or a ditch. Be patient and careful.

To stop the horses from rushing back, rein-back at intervals. That is to say, stop and try again after the horses have settled down completely. Always rein back as if your horses were shod with sharp studs. Take up the required position of the pole slowly and carefully and maintain it if at all possible. Changing the direction of the pole during the rein-back can easily lead to damaged coronets.

If one is forced to rein-back downhill or if there is a likelihood of the horses rushing back, apply the brake as well as giving rein. However, giving rein with the left hand is of main importance.

Moving off

To move off, always release the brake without noise (this is very often forgotten). The whip should, of course, have been passed over already to the left hand. Operating the brake with the whip still in the right hand could easily upset the horses, particularly the right-hand horse, as the whiplash could drop on its quarters.

Before moving off, establish light contact with your horses, and from this contact give rein. Make sure you give enough, so that your horses do not feel any resistance from your hand, as this would interfere with their moving off evenly.

Should it be necessary to use the whip, use it on the lazy horse the moment the rein is given, supported by saying 'walk-on'. Never start your team by 'clicking'.

Whilst still at the halt, do not collect your horses too quickly, otherwise a smooth moving-off with horses with sensitive mouths will soon be impossible. If the move-off is slightly insecure, take a firmer hold of the right-hand rein and give a little rein on the left as if trying to move off in a half right direction. As soon as the horses begin to move, return to the straight-ahead position.

The following method is very often applied when moving off with a four-in-hand. The right hand is placed on the two right-hand reins making the opposition point. At the same time 'give' with both left-hand reins.

Support the rein aids for moving off by saying 'walk-on'; your horses will know this word as an indication to move off or increase the pace from their work in long-reins. It must always be accompanied by giving rein. Once your horses have learnt that the giving of rein means going into their collars or increasing the draught, you may stop saying 'walk-on' as they now know that they must follow the reins.

If one wants to move off without saying 'walk-on' this can be achieved by shortening one lead-rein as if to loop. However, the left hand must give sufficient rein so that the leaders do not run against the bit.

Inattentive wheelers may require a touch of the whip as soon as the leaders move off, but apply the whip without making a noise.

Miss Araminta Winn driving Mr. and Mrs. Ted Rowley's team of Welsh ponies to a dog cart

Miss Sally Moore driving her father's pair of Gelderlanders to a Shooting Break

Commodore Chauncey Stillman driving his pair of Hackney geldings to a Lawton Phaeton

Mrs. Helen Southgate photographed at the Royal Winter Fair, Toronto

Miss Sydney L. Smith and her pair of Hackney ponies. Photographed competing in the dressage at Balmoral, 1981

Mr. Van Dijk with his thirteen-in-hand of Gelderlanders

Commodore Chauncey Stillman's Bay Hackney tandem, driven by Mrs. Cynthia Haydon at the Royal Winter Fair, Toronto

Mrs. Haydon, again, with Commodore Stillman's Hackney Unicorn to a game cart. Photographed at the Devon Show, Pennsylvania

12

Driving a Four-in-Hand

The basis for driving a four-in-hand is being able to safely drive a pair. It is important to remember that the reins must always be secure in the left hand and not allowed to slip, otherwise a team will never work in unison. The driver's insecurity will be transmitted to the horses and he will not be master for long. If, further, he has not learnt to drive with thumb and index finger open, they will not be ready to make the necessary opposition points at the right moment independently from the other three fingers. Before attempting to drive a four-in-hand, practise 'Filieren', i.e. shortening or lengthening of one rein bit by bit without taking the right hand off the rein; practise, first, on the driving apparatus, and when driving a pair. Unless a driver masters this easily he will never be able, when driving a four-in-hand, to bring his leaders exactly in line with his wheelers

or vice versa, which is absolutely essential for correct driving of a team.

When coupling the leaders, an experienced driver will always bear in mind the various temperaments of his horses and will balance out the work accordingly.

The leaders are harnessed up as explained in Chapter 6. If the long lead-reins are correctly secured all one has to do when putting to is to take the end of the rein, pass it through the boss attached to the throatlash and the terret on the pad of the wheeler.

The bosses are buckled to the back of the throatlash buckle before doing up the throatlash. The bosses must never be buckled into the buckle of the cheek piece because this would lift the cheek piece to the side and cancel out the advantage of the winker.

The grooms lead the horses to the carriage,

Correctly secured lead-reins when harnessing up and unharnessing

Rein ferret fitted (*at left*) correctly and (*at right*) incorrectly.

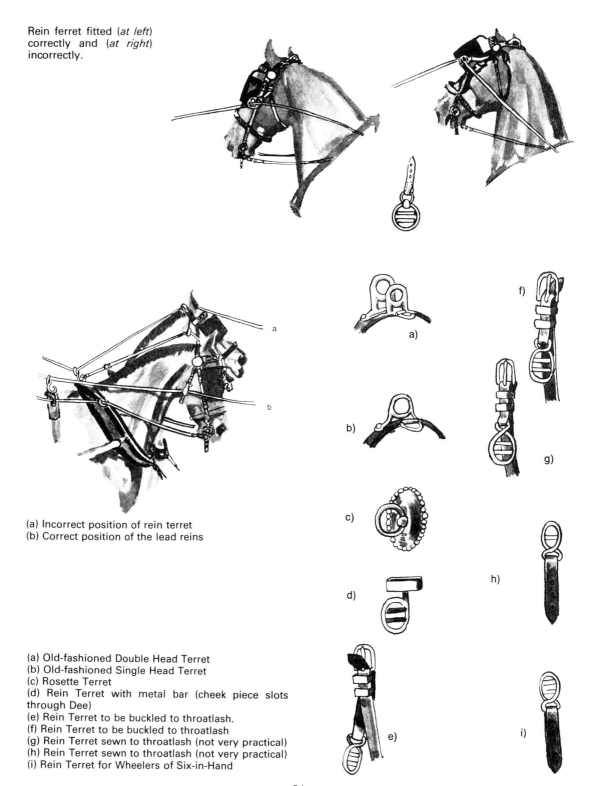

(a) Incorrect position of rein terret
(b) Correct position of the lead reins

(a) Old-fashioned Double Head Terret
(b) Old-fashioned Single Head Terret
(c) Rosette Terret
(d) Rein Terret with metal bar (cheek piece slots through Dee)
(e) Rein Terret to be buckled to throatlash.
(f) Rein Terret to be buckled to throatlash
(g) Rein Terret sewn to throatlash (not very practical)
(h) Rein Terret sewn to throatlash (not very practical)
(i) Rein Terret for Wheelers of Six-in-Hand

wheelers first. The wheelers are positioned alongside the pole and put to as described in Chapter 6. Then stand the leaders in front of the wheelers. Pass the right-hand lead-rein through the outside boss on the bridle and the terret on the pad of the right-hand wheeler. Then throw the rein across the back of the left-hand wheeler. The rein of the leader on the left-hand side is again passed through the bridle boss and pad terret of the left-hand wheeler. Then buckle the two lead-reins together. Now push all four reins behind the back-band, from the front to the back, and ensure that they are hanging tidily in even lengths either side of the back-band.

Although taking up the reins is carried out as described in Chapter 8, it is explained again here. It should be pointed out, however, that this description only applies when mounting from the left-hand side. Where it is customary to mount from the right the reverse applies.

Stand level with the pad of the wheeler, pull all the reins out from underneath the back-band, sort them out and hang them over your left forearm. Then take the right-hand wheel-rein between the index and fourth fingers of your right hand, establish a light contact with the mouths, slide your hand along the rein until your arm hangs straight down along your side and hold on to the point of the rein thus established. Then with the thumb and index finger take the left-hand wheel-rein and with the left hand pull the coupling buckle out 5 cm. further than that of the right-hand wheel-rein. The two wheel-reins are then passed over to the left hand in such a fashion that the right-hand wheel-rein is between third and fourth fingers and the left-hand wheel-rein between third and index fingers.

Now measure the lead-reins in the same way, starting with the right-hand lead-rein, and establish contact with the mouths of the leaders.

As the coupling buckle cannot be used as a guide for measuring the lead-reins, use the rein splices. Again, the left-hand splice must be 5 cm. in front of the right-hand splice.

The lead-reins are now passed from the right

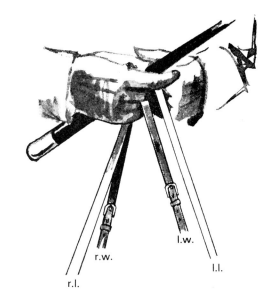

Basic Position Four-in-Hand: r.l. = right-hand leader; l.l. = left-hand leader; r.w. = right-hand wheeler; l.w. = left-hand wheeler

hand to the left, right-hand lead-rein between index and third fingers, left-hand lead-rein over the index finger. The position of the reins is now:

Left-hand lead-rein – over index finger.
Right-hand lead-rein and left-hand wheel-rein – between index and third fingers.
Right-hand wheel-rein – between third and fourth fingers.

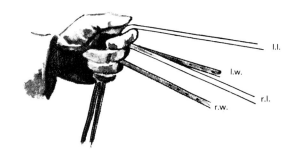

r.l. = right-hand leader; r.w. = right-hand wheeler; l.l. = left-hand leader; l.w. = left-hand wheeler

If, when the reins are measured, it is found that the leaders are in draught, shorten the lead-reins by approximately 10 cm. If the leaders are standing with slack traces, lengthen the lead-reins by about 20 cm. Do not instruct the grooms to move the leaders, either forward or back, as the movement of the pole or the vehicle could cause the wheelers to become restless or move off, and it is not only difficult, but also dangerous, for the driver to restrain a team from the ground.

As in driving a pair, it is necessary to adjust the reins according to the height of the box seat, which usually means lengthening them by about 20–30 cm.

Position of the reins when driving a four-in-hand

When driving a pair, three positions may be used; the basic position, the schooling position, and the standard position. For four-in-hand driving, the schooling position cannot be applied because the right hand is required to make the loops and pass them over to the left, and to relieve the left hand on a straight road by being in front of it in the standard position. From this position all opposition points are being made.

The position of the reins in the left hand, as described before, must be retained at all times unless it is deliberately altered by the right hand. It is also maintained when the driver uses the whip, or after having passed the whip over to the left hand to operate the brake, or for salutes.

In the standard position for four-in-hand driving the left hand is always supported and relieved by the right hand because the right hand is positioned so that it holds both right-hand reins (as the right-hand rein when driving a pair) unless it is required to make opposition points. By holding on to the reins firmly the left hand can also relax temporarily behind the right hand. This is done by pushing the third finger of the right hand between the left reins and closing the right hand, leaving the thumb free. The reins hang down on the outside of the left leg.

The whip is carried pointing left, forward-upward, as in driving a pair. Although, when

Resting the left hand

sitting on the box seat before moving off, the driver may think that the lead-reins are too long they must not be shortened. Provided they were measured correctly and did not slip, they will fit exactly once the horses are moving.

To rest the left hand for a while, hold on to the reins with the right hand. Then open the left hand and spread the fingers, but always keep the left hand immediately behind the right on the reins.

If, in exceptional circumstances, the left hand must be taken off the reins completely, the right hand should take over all the reins, but not as in the standard position. They must be taken as they were positioned in the left hand. For this purpose, place the index and third fingers of the right hand between the reins in front of the left hand. Before closing third, fourth and fifth fingers of the right hand firmly over all four reins, turn the left hand anticlockwise (back of the hand facing down). This lengthens the left-hand lead rein and slightly shortens the right-hand wheel-rein, keeping the horses on course instead of deviating to the left.

Lengthening all four reins at the same time

From the standard position, the right hand pulls out all reins the required distance. This can

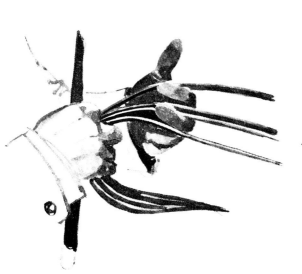

Shortening all the reins

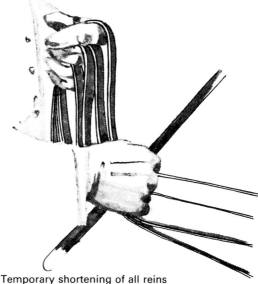

Temporary shortening of all reins

be done centimetre by centimetre or, if required, as in negotiating a sharp incline, by 15–20 cm. at once.

Shortening all four reins at the same time

This can be done three ways:

(a) To shorten the reins only slightly, slide the right hand along the reins in front of the left by no more than 5 cm. Close the right hand and follow with the left. If the reins are still too long repeat the movement.

(b) If the reins suddenly have to be shortened considerably, move the right hand behind the left, and with the three lower fingers of the right hand take all four reins. Then slide the left hand forward for the required distance. The whip will be held between the thumb and index finger of the right hand.

(c) To shorten the reins temporarily, as for a halt, slide the right hand forward on the reins and take them in by moving the hand backwards. The left hand gives way by moving up.

Shortening or lengthening of the lead-reins

If the leaders are pulling too much, or too little, the lead-reins must be shortened or

lengthened. To do this, pull the left index finger out from between the two lead-reins and place it under the right-hand lead-rein, i.e. between the right-hand lead-rein and the left-hand wheel-rein.

The two lead-reins are now resting one on top of the other. With the right hand, which is in front of the left, push these two reins either back into the left hand, or pull them out further, depending on whether the leaders are to be brought back, or let out. After the reins have been thus adjusted, the left index finger moves again between the two lead-reins.

Shortening or lengthening the wheel-reins

If the wheel-reins are to be shortened, this is achieved by either applying positions (a) or (b) (not c), taking in all four reins by the required distance and then lengthening the lead-reins as described above.

To lengthen the wheel-reins apply the reverse. Lengthen all four reins and then shorten the lead-reins.

Lining up the leaders

If the leaders veer to the right, in order to line them up properly, pull the left-hand rein out gradually with thumb and index finger of the

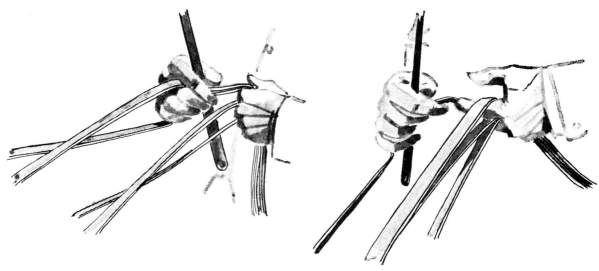

Lengthening the lead reins   Making an opposition point

right hand, assisted by the left thumb. If the leaders are required to move more to the left, thumb and index finger work in reverse order.

This method is already described in Chapter 11. Whether lining up the leaders or the wheelers – described hereafter – never shorten one individual rein behind the left hand.

Lining up the wheelers

If the wheelers are too far to the right, pull the right-hand wheel-rein gradually from the left hand with fourth and fifth fingers of the right hand, whilst thumb, index and third fingers hold on to the other three reins. Should the wheelers be too far to the left, open the fourth and fifth fingers of the left hand and shorten the right-hand wheel-rein with the assistance of the fourth and fifth fingers of the right hand which, going forward, gradually pushes it back. The right hand must remain in contact with the four reins.

Giving way to the right

Giving way to the right requires that the vehicle must move to the right-hand side (this is mainly done by the wheelers).

In order to achieve this quickly, both leaders and wheelers must move to the half-right together. It takes longer if only the leaders move to the half-right, followed by the wheelers.

Should it be necessary to apply the brake for a halt at the kerb-side, place the right-hand wheel-rein – in advance – over the left index finger.

Now take both right-hand reins as one rein in the right hand, give rein with the left hand, and both leaders and wheelers will go to the half-right. Now give both right-hand reins and take the whip over into the left hand. At the same time the opposition point on the right-hand wheel-rein by the left index finger ensures that the horses move to the kerb. Then use the brake.

Giving way to the left

In order to give way to the left, or to halt at the kerb on the left-hand side, take up with the right hand the left-hand lead- and wheel-reins by pushing the third finger between the two reins approximately 15 cm. in front of the left hand. Then close the hand. Move the left hand below the right, thus giving with the right-hand reins. To halt at the left-hand kerb, place both left-hand reins over the left thumb, pass the whip over to the left hand so that the right hand is free to operate the brake.

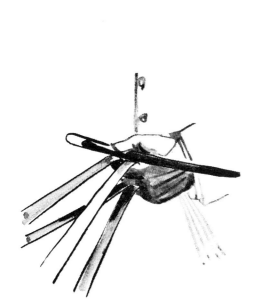

Small loop on index finger

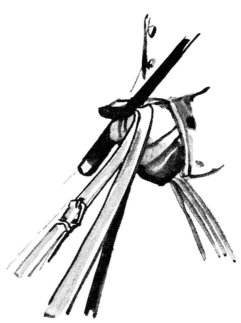

Giving way to the left

To ensure that the opposition point is not too harsh, move the left hand slightly to the left-hand side. However, should it not be harsh enough, move the left hand to the right and use the whip on the right-hand wheeler. Both vehicle and horses will then move to the left.

Turning by looping the reins

Prior to explaining the technique of opposition points for turning, it must be explained in detail why looping in pair-driving is paradoxical, while for driving a four-in-hand correctly it is an absolute *Must*.

59

Driving a Pair

Once it is fully understood why, in a right-hand turn, pressure on the right-hand rein must be maintained, and the pressure on the left-hand rein must be reduced, and why for a U-turn or an acute turn to the right, the right-hand rein is completely taken out of the left hand and very much collected, and why for similar turns to the left this same rein is let out considerably, it becomes obvious why, when driving a single or a pair, the holds for these turns, explained in Chapter 11, must never be replaced by looping the reins. In a left-hand turn, a pair will be pulled away from the driver by the pole strap, hence the extreme 'giving' of the outside rein. It would be utter nonsense to 'squeeze' the horses, which are being pulled forward by pole and pole strap, through looping the rein. It would be asking something they just cannot do.

Four-in-Hand

When driving a four-in-hand the rules are quite different. Firstly, in turns, the leaders should not be in draught (except on very rare occasions and then only very little); secondly, in a left-hand turn – unlike a pair which is coupled to the pole – the leaders are not moving away from the driver; thirdly, by placing the left-hand loop underneath the thumb initially a pressure is created. The leaders will start to turn – only start – now pull the lead-rein into as large a loop as is required. Remember, however, that this will not work quite as it did on the driving apparatus. Why not? At the apparatus the pupil sits still and pulls the weights towards him, whereas on the vehicle the driver will constantly be in a 'forward movement', which means he is getting nearer the leaders which have by no means been 'pulled back'. Therefore, in order to achieve the new direction, the correct positioning of the horses' heads, and to maintain contact – which would be lost if the leaders were not brought back – the driver must loop. Studying this in detail, one will realize that looping does not only shorten the inside lead-rein, but also the outside lead-rein, because the lead-reins run on the outside of the heads of the wheelers, and the outside leader moves away from the outside wheeler in every turn. By making large loops we achieve correct head positioning, a safe pace and slack lead-traces. The more the inside lead-rein is shortened for the loop, the more the outside lead-rein shortens automatically, and the slacker the lead-traces will become.

Left-hand turn

For a left-hand turn, particularly with a four-in-hand, take a wide sweep. If the road is free, it may even be driven at a collected trot.

Fifteen metres before the turn, check the traffic behind you and ask your passenger on the box seat to signal the left-hand turn. This saves signalling with the four-in-hand whip which might get too tangled up.

To ensure a wide sweep from the beginning, and in order to avoid moving the left hand unnecessarily far away from the right, place the right-hand wheel-rein on the top of the pointed left index finger. This is called 'opposition point on the index finger'. It means resisting the wheelers leaning into the turn. By pushing the left index finger a little underneath the right-hand wheel-rein, which shortens it slightly this opposition point should not disturb the wheelers. As soon as the leaders are level with the corner of the house on the corner (not the kerb) slide the right hand 15 cm. along the left-hand lead-rein (hand in upright position, rein between index and third fingers, thumb pointing up) and slowly place the loop under the left thumb.

The outside lead-traces should never 'push' the horses to turn. Should this occur, the loop was too small and the opposition point not strong enough. Make bigger loops in future. To make a second loop immediately is dangerous because the required 'resistance' is still lacking. With horses that have never been in a four-in-hand, do not apply 'resistance' (opposition) right away because the wheelers will not yet follow the leaders; on the contrary, they sometimes have to be led into the turn, and require the opposition

Left-hand turn – first stage

Left-hand turn – second stage

point only in the second half of it.

In a left-hand turn, the loop must be taken gradually so that the horses are not pulled into the turn. First make the opposition point with the left-hand lead-rein so that the horses understand what is required and begin to turn, then make the loop more boldly. Because of the first opposition point, the horses are expecting new instructions and will be ready for the turn.

If the driver has practised, and is careful, and is determined not to disturb his horses, even the most sensitive horse will soon gain confidence and go through the turn quietly, safely, and correctly positioned.

Should the driver wish to complete the turn with one hand, he must move the left hand more into the turn – i.e. to the left.

If the horses go too close to the left-hand kerb, grasp both right-hand reins with the right hand and increase the pressure; reduce the pressure on the left-hand reins but do not release the loop.

If the loops are too small, or were released too soon, the leaders will lean into the turn. This can be recognized immediately because the head positioning will be all wrong and the outside lead-traces will push against the hind legs of the horses.

Therefore, release the left loop slowly. This will stop the horses from hanging incorrectly positioned on to the outside rein. For instance, on a road well-known to horses, they may try to take the turns without waiting for your instructions. Never allow them to do so. They must await your command.

Release the last bit of loop only when the rear of the vehicle is parallel to the new direction. Then release the opposition point of the right-hand wheel-rein from the left index finger.

If there was no time to make the opposition point, this can still be done after the loop has been made, which must never be made hastily. It would pull the horses back, they would lose their contact with the outside rein and, on slippery ground, could easily lose their footing.

Right-hand turn

Many drivers dislike right-hand turns, particularly in traffic, the sole reason being that they cannot drive them properly. However, only two main conditions must be obeyed. Namely, drive it at a walk and move the hand 'into the turn'.

In right-hand turns particularly, the wheelers must follow the leaders exactly. Should the wheelers get too close to the right-hand kerb,

61

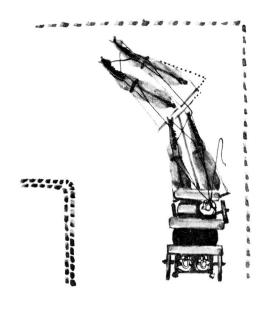

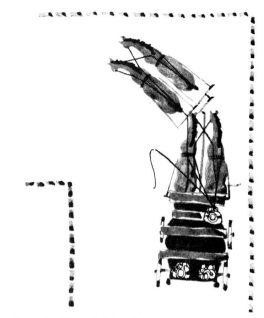

Incorrectly driven left-hand turn

Correctly driven left-hand turn

slightly pull out the right-hand wheel-rein. This avoids your hitting the kerb. On slippery roads the horses must be at a walk by the time they are three paces away from the corner. As soon as the forelegs of the leaders are level with the corner of the kerb, loop with the right hand approximately 20 cm. of the right-hand lead-rein under the left index finger. In addition move the left hand far to the right (into the turn). This slackens the right-hand wheel-rein and thus allows the inside wheeler to take the vehicle nicely through the turn. Only urge the inside wheeler on, or if necessary touch it with the whip, if it leans into the turn despite the slack right-hand wheel-rein. If the position of the left hand in front of the right hip is still insufficient, and there is a possibility of hitting the kerb, take hold of the left-hand reins with your right hand approximately 15 cm. in front of the left – with the third finger of the right hand separating the two left-hand reins – and provide 'oppo-sition' in this way. Give rein with the left hand by moving it below the right, but do not release the loop.

Only let the loop slide out when the leaders are safely in line with the kerb in the new direc-tion.

With practice the above opposition point can also be made with one hand by placing both left-hand reins over the left thumb.

Under normal circumstances the loop is released early in a right-hand turn and late in a left-hand turn.

The opposition point 'both left-hand reins over the left thumb' – unless the turn is driven with one hand – is usually made only if the right-hand wheeler is permanently leaning into the turn. This opposition point, however, forces it to pull through the turn correctly.

Acute left-hand turn or U-turn to the left

This must be carried out at a walk. Turn round, signal, opposition point on the index finger, small left loop. As soon as the horses have started to turn, larger loop. Then slide right hand along left-hand reins and carry out the turn by moving the right hand below the left, giving rein as and when required. As soon as the turn is three parts completed, let the left loops slide slowly underneath the right hand. Remember that the opposition point on the index finger must already be released when the second loop is made.

Acute right-hand turn or U-turn to the right

Execute only at a walk. Again, two loops are necessary. Shorten reins considerably before the turn. Hand into the turn, first small loop. As soon as horses start to turn, second large loop. When making the second loop, move the hand out of the turn. It will now become necessary to apply pressure on both right-hand reins with the whole of the right hand. However, leave the right hand half open to allow the loop of the right-hand lead-rein to slide, whilst the finger-tips still apply pressure on the right-hand wheel-rein – the aim being to remain as close to the kerb as possible.

Halting at the kerb after a right-hand turn

To execute a right-hand turn cleanly, without hitting the kerb, and to halt immediately after the turn parallel to the kerb, first ensure that the right-hand wheeler is attentive. Then move the left hand sharply into the turn and (with the whole of the right hand) take a large loop of the right-hand lead-rein and place it under the left index finger. As soon as the danger of hitting the kerb is over, move the left hand out of the turn (i.e. to the left) and release the loop quickly. Move the right hand, half open, (back of the hand facing upwards) on to the right-hand wheel-rein and, at the same time, let the loop of the right-hand lead-rein slide over the back of the right hand. This ensures that the vehicle will be placed absolutely parallel to the kerb.

Halting at the left-hand kerb after a right-hand turn

After completion of the right-hand turn, the driver must first look round to see whether the road is clear. He must then signal his intention to turn left. Now place both left-hand reins over the knuckle (second joint) of the left thumb. When the horses get close to the left-hand kerb,

Opposition point

Loop for right-hand turn

Giving rein with the left hand

Correctly driven right-hand and left-hand turns

make a small loop of the right-hand reins. Leave both left-hand reins over the thumb until the vehicle is parallel to the kerb. Then release the right loop, which must be done in such a way that the leaders (as well as the whole turnout) keep close to the left-hand kerb. Only then release both left-hand reins from the thumb.

Opposition points to get the leaders in draught, in and after a turn and when driving uphill

To enable the leaders to get in draught in turns, smaller loops must be made. Therefore, particularly in right-hand turns, leaders which are heavily in draught cannot be guided close to the kerb. Correct head positioning, however, must always be aimed for.

Should the four-in-hand suddenly be required to move half to the side and uphill or turn on to a muddy track, do not loop the inside lead-rein, but lengthen the outside lead-rein by 10–20 cm. to allow the leaders to get more in draught and turn. If the incline continues on the straight, also lengthen the inside lead-rein.

If the leaders do not respond straight away, and continue to let the wheelers do all the work, grasp the wheel-reins with the right hand below

the lead-reins and hold the wheelers back until the leaders are in full draught.

Hints on driving a four-in-hand

Rest the left hand as often as possible, even before it gets tired. It remains more sensitive and is alert when required.

When on level tarmac roads the leaders have nothing to pull, the traces are slack and should only 'carry' the bars. Once on the move, the weight of the traces and reins of four horses will keep the vehicle in motion.

Many drivers are unable to determine which horse is leaning on the bit. This cannot be felt. Watch the inside reins between collar and bit and you can see which horse is the culprit.

Look after your four-in-hand reins. Do not treat them with saddle-soap but use wax or a good quality leather polish. Your reins must not be slippery, rather a little on the sticky side.

Before each journey, the turntable of a vehicle with a perch must be cleaned and greased and, if the route is over dusty roads, this should be repeated even before the return journey is commenced. Therefore, ensure that grease is always carried. The pole of a vehicle with a perch runs underneath the springs. Depending upon the quality of the road, this causes the bars to rattle if the leaders are hanging back. This makes it easy at night to know whether or not they are doing their job.

Heavy rain will make the reins slippery. The only remedy is to wipe them with a moisture-absorbing cloth. Always carry one with you. Leather gloves are not very suitable in wet weather, so carry a spare pair of gloves which absorb water more easily.

Lining-up leaders and wheelers should be done by lengthening or shortening the left-hand lead-rein and the right-hand wheel-rein, i.e. the two centre reins. Do *not* use the right-hand lead-rein and the left-hand wheel-rein. This could easily get the reins in disarray.

Whenever necessary the brake must be used, otherwise the bars might hit the leaders, and the result could easily be four horses in full flight!

Before moving off, release the brake, give

sufficient rein so that the horses, particularly the leaders, do not run against the bit or you may risk inviting the horses to stop, go backwards or even rear.

If the leaders shy, do not punish them. Slow down to a walk and if possible move away from the cause of the trouble. It is a good idea in such circumstances to have the groom get down and walk with the horses, talking to them quietly.

When carrying out turns, the opposition of the outside reins must only be sufficient to determine the size of the turn. It must never be so firm that it positions the horses to the outside.

13

Driving a Tandem

The reins are handled as in driving a four-in-hand. However, tandem-driving where one horse is in front of the other presents certain difficulties which do not make it easy for a beginner.

The reins, which are much closer together, make turning more difficult, particularly if the turn comes unexpectedly and the driver is unprepared. Someone who is not used to holding his hand firm in a turn, will find it even more difficult to adjust the tandem reins. Usually, after having made the loops, the two outside reins have to be held with the right hand to enable the left hand to move forward.

The possibility that an unsteady leader may turn round is an added difficulty.

When driving a leader in long traces rather than a double bar one must take care that the lead-traces are slack, although the leader must be well on the bit. If the lead-traces are taut, the outside lead-trace will pull the vehicle into the turn.

However, the distribution of the work for the horses is much easier with a tandem than with a four-in-hand.

In tandem-driving two additional opposition points (apart from those used for driving a four-in-hand) may be used. Although they are useful, they have the disadvantage that the right hand is engaged. They do, however, ensure that the reins do not get mixed up.

The left-hand turn

From the standard position, slide the right hand 10 cm. forward on the right-hand reins, giving up the contact with the left-hand reins. Take the two right-hand reins as one rein, and pick up the left-hand lead-rein with thumb and index finger of the right hand to loop it for the left-hand turn. The loop may be made in several

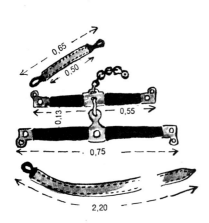

Double bar for tandem

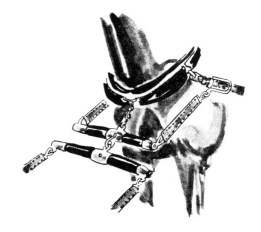

Tandem bars in position

stages; the left thumb, however, should not get in front of the right thumb.

The right-hand turn

For a right-hand turn, the traces of the leaders must be very slack. Move the right hand forward approximately 15 cm. on all four reins, releasing the left-hand lead-rein, but increasing the hold on the left-hand wheel-rein. Turn the left hand forward (so that the palm of the hand faces you). This lengthens the left-hand lead-rein and the leader will turn to the right. As the right-hand reins were not looped and the turn was achieved solely by giving with the left-hand rein, it is essential that both lead-reins had been shortened.

Driving a tandem safely and correctly can be extremely difficult with unsuitable harness. The leader may be driven either in long traces or with a double bar. Long traces have the disadvantage of pulling the cart into the turns if the lead-reins have not been shortened sufficiently. This is a particular risk if the wheeler is hitched to a bar which is only attached to the centre of the splinter bar, and pulls with chains from the axle. This will cause the outside wheel-trace to 'give' a little in turns.

Long lead-traces also present the risk that the lead horse, should it shy, hang back, or step aside, can get its leg over a trace.

Unsuitable tandem pads allow the traces to slide across the leader's back. Always fit a correctly-made tandem lead-pad.

The second method is by hitching the leader to the tandem double bar. This does, however, present two minor disadvantages: it hangs more or less on the neck of the wheeler and, when going downhill, could hit the wheeler's knee.

The tandem-cart or dogcart should be high off the ground – it gives a much better drive. Ensure that the cart is well balanced. The higher the wheels and the lower the body of the vehicle, the better the balance. If one is shaken about, the balance of the vehicle is wrong, or the belly-band has been fastened too tightly so that there is no vertical movement.

The tugs should not be fastened between

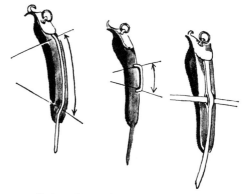

Incorrect (*left and centre*) and correct (*right*) means of passing traces through the loop on the pad of a tandem leader

shaft-stops that are screwed in or can be altered. They wear out and get loose. They should be secured.

If the tandem is driven in hilly country the vehicle should have a brake, and the wheeler, at least, should have a breeching. The buckles of the quarter-strap should be handforged and then plated. Buckles made entirely of brass or nickel will give at the first kick.

As the tandem-cart is built to carry two to four persons, the balance of the vehicle is adjustable by moving the seats. The buckle-pin

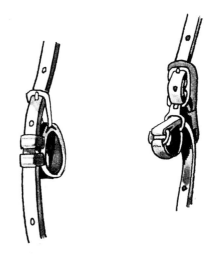

Tugs for (*left*) a two-wheeled vehicle and (*right*) for a four-wheeled vehicle (known as a 'Tilbury' tug)

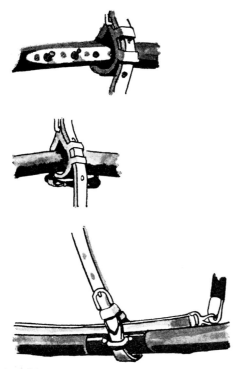

Shafts in tugs

of the tug-strap must have a certain amount of 'play'. The vehicle should never have 'front weight' when it goes downhill or 'back weight' when going uphill.

At the halt the groom stands at the head of the wheeler, holding it with his right hand by the cheek piece. The left hand holds the lead-reins, which are slightly pulled forward, in front of the head of the wheeler.

Taking up the reins is as for a four-in-hand. Measuring the reins is even more important than with a four-in-hand, as one must be master of the situation immediately.

The most suitable wheelers are short-limbed horses that are keen but with a reliable temperament. Wheelers usually tend to be lazy. The leader should be a horse of good conformation, with a lot of action, but one that does not shy.

The Unicorn

Two horses in the wheel and one horse in the lead. Pair reins and tandem lead-reins. Four-in-hand bosses on the inside of the throatlashes of the wheelers. Leader hitched to main bar. The lead-traces should be buckled in the first hole. However, this looks very unattractive and, therefore, it is better to lengthen the hitch of the leader by means of a shackle consisting of a strong ring and a strap, the width of a pole strap, between the crab and the main bar. At the halt the groom goes immediately to the head of the leader (the driver must lengthen the lead-reins) to ensure that the leader does not turn round if, for instance, one of the wheelers tosses its head and hits a lead-rein.

The Random

Three horses driven one in front of the other and hitched to a tandem-cart. High cart is essential. Harness and hitching as for a tandem. The reins are handled as described in the next chapter when driving a six-in-hand.

14

Driving a Six-in-Hand

Once you have mastered the art of driving a four-in-hand, driving a six-in-hand presents very little problem, providing you have never got into the bad habit of letting the reins slip.

In 1920, having returned from Hanover, where I had learnt how to drive a four-in-hand, I continued to practise to become more proficient. After a while I thought I would also learn how to drive a six-in-hand. So I wrote to Benno von Achenbach, whom I did not know personally at the time, and asked for written instructions. A week later I received a very detailed letter (his book had not yet been published). I started work immediately.

I had a centre pole made, pole straps (100 cm. long, 40 cm. when they were buckled),

a pole-carrier consisting of a leather-covered expander (rubber elastic) 50 cm. long with points to buckle to the inside trace-buckles. This expander carried the pole more flexibly for the centre horses. The pole can be attached to the crab by a ring, and on top of this go the bars for the centre horses. The reins for the lead horses – 10.20 m. long – a further set of bars, two bridle bosses, two more terrets with two slots for the centre and the lead-reins were yet to be obtained.

In the meantime I had my driving apparatus altered, by adding two pulley wheels so that I could now use it for six reins instead of four. I then started to practise, diligently following the instructions and sketches supplied to me by

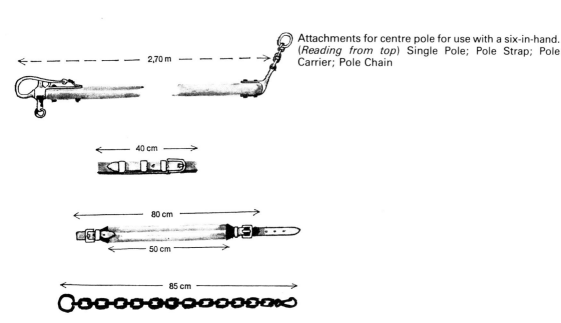

Attachments for centre pole for use with a six-in-hand. (*Reading from top*) Single Pole; Pole Strap; Pole Carrier; Pole Chain

2,70 m

40 cm

80 cm

50 cm

85 cm

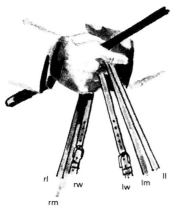

Basic position of reins for a six-in-hand (front view)—
rf = right hand leader
rm = right hand centre horse
rw = right hand wheeler
ll = left hand leader
lm = left hand centre horse
lw = left hand wheeler

Position of reins just before a left-hand turn

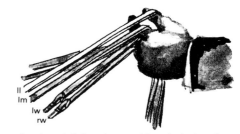

Looping for a left-hand turn with a six-in-hand

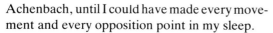

Side view of reins in basic position

Position of reins just before a right-hand turn

Achenbach, until I could have made every movement and every opposition point in my sleep.

It became very clear to me then how very important the driving apparatus is, because it avoids pulling the horses about unnecessarily.

When I finally mounted the box with carefully measured reins, everything worked like a dream. At least I thought so. I found out later when I drove through Berlin, sitting on the box next to the 'Master', that I still had a lot to learn. However, as this little reflection shows, even without an instructor, one can perfect one's driving if one is keen and follows accurate descriptions.

For six-in-hand driving the position of the reins is as for a four-in-hand, with the addition of the extra lead-reins.

Left lead over left centre (in a four-in-hand the left centre rein would be the left-hand lead-rein).

Right lead over right-centre (right-hand lead as for a four-in-hand); below, left wheel-rein.

As for a four-in-hand, right-hand wheel-rein on its own.

The position of the right hand is the same as in driving a four-in-hand.

The holds and opposition points are the same as for a four-in-hand. Where they require further explanation, these are given in the following.

Right-hand turn

If the right-hand wheeler does not pull through the corner sufficiently, as a precaution, lengthen the right-hand wheel-rein by 1 or 2 cm. – not so much, however, that the pole would deviate from the straight line.

As lead- and centre-reins are very close together it is not easy (particularly for anxious drivers) to get hold of the lead-rein immediately. To facilitate this, place the right-hand lead-rein over the index finger.

This overcomes the problem of getting hold of the wrong rein or taking both, the right-hand lead-, and the right-hand centre-rein.

Now make a loop of about 15 cm. in the lead-rein and place it below the index finger. Then take both reins, right-hand lead, and right-hand centre, and loop again.

When looping the reins, move the hand into the turn. (Naturally, prior to the right-hand turn, the reins had been shortened and the pace reduced to a walk.) The first loop is now twice as big as the second loop for the centre horses. The horses turn in a clean sweep. The centre pole has the advantage of providing a certain amount of resistance to the main pole so that the whole team cannot lean into the turn.

Now release the loops quickly, as with a four-in-hand. If necessary, use the right hand to support the sliding reins to prevent one of them dropping on to the quarters of the right-hand wheeler.

Remember: Right-hand turn – walk, shortened reins, large loops and, in the turn, left hand close to the right side of the chest.

Left turn

For a left turn, the left-hand lead-rein must be placed in good time over the first joints of the left thumb. The fist must be closed very firmly.

Then, first loop left-hand lead-rein; second, loop left-hand lead-rein and left-hand centre-rein under the left thumb. Release the loops more slowly than with a four-in-hand.

Centre horses too much in draught

Shorten the leaders and the centre horses by placing the four top reins (as with the leaders of a four-in-hand) over the index finger and fetch them all back. Then pull out the reins of the leaders as required.

Leaders too much in draught

Make a small loop with each of the two lead-reins and, in this particular case, let it drop behind the left hand.

Centre horses insufficiently in draught

Lengthen lead- and centre-reins together and then shorten lead-reins as described above.

Leaders insufficiently in draught

Pull out the lead-reins, one at a time.

Centre horses not in line (leaning out to the left)

Firstly, shorten the left-hand lead-rein, then lengthen the left-hand lead-rein and the left-hand centre-rein together.

Practical hints on driving a Six-in-Hand

Have the hand-piece of the lead-reins made 1 mm. wider than the reins themselves – they are easier to hold. Practise driving the right-hand turn at the walk. If the horses jog continuously the driver will never learn to execute properly a right-hand turn at the trot. To encourage the leaders to accept the reins immediately the loop is let out, do not bit them too severely. If sharper bits are required, put them on the wheelers or the centre horses. There is no need to take a wider sweep than usual with a six-in-hand. For instance, steer the leaders straight for the centre of a gateway. A six-in-hand shows any mistakes much more clearly than a four-in-hand: loops too small or too big, leaning of the horses into the turn etc.

Do not make opposition points with the three

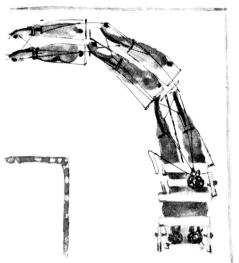

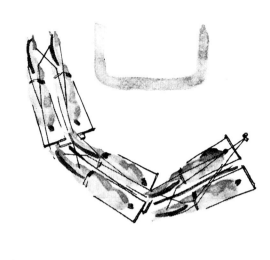

First loop too big, second loop too small. If the inside wheeler does not follow immediately, touch it with the whip

Correctly driven right-hand turn with a six-in-hand

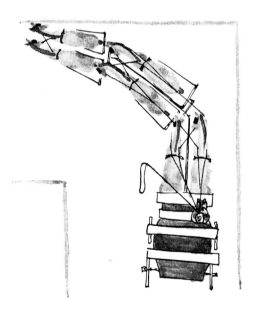

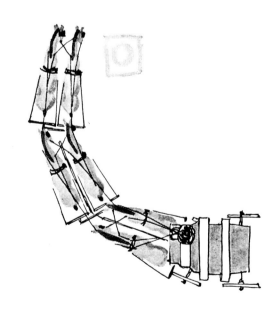

First loop too small, second loop correct – but unable to rectify what the first loop has caused to go wrong

Correctly driven right-hand turn with a six-in-hand

outside reins as the horses will not only be wrongly positioned but will also lean into the turn. Even in a left-hand turn, drive rather more into the turn and, if the left-hand wheeler hangs back, touch it with the whip. In a correctly driven turn, each pair (of a six- or, indeed, a four-in-hand) should 'move over' just enough, as if the inside horse was to go between the two horses in front.

Practise driving a six-in-hand at the walk, always observing strictly that the horses must be correctly positioned. Studying pictures of six-in-hands as well as their explanations can be a great help.

Unless you have two active and keen leaders there is no point in trying to put together a six-in-hand, because lazy horses cannot always be reached with the whip in turns. Many people will argue: 'If one cannot reach the horses with the whip one is entirely dependent upon their goodwill.' This is utter nonsense. In the end we are all dependent upon the goodwill of the horses whether riding, jumping, or driving. If horses shy, or if for example they do not want to pass a steam-roller, what good can the whip do? To punish them would only make them more frightened and they certainly will not pass a steam-roller the next time.

I cannot remember ever having used the whip on the leaders of a six-in-hand. Sensible drivers do not use the whip to get their horses on the bit, but teach them to accept the bit when breaking them to harness! Very few drivers practise this art, and yet it is so easy. Drive all corners, or turns, as slowly as possible, preferably at a walk. As soon as the horses come out of the turn into the new direction, give plenty of rein – without the use of voice or whip. Within a few days the horses will accept the bit gladly because they want the contact as much as a child, learning to skate, is glad of the assurance of a helping hand.

In turns, correct positioning of all horses is determined by the size of the loops. With a four-in-hand, as well as a six-in-hand, the additional touch of the whip on the ribs of the inside wheeler is sufficient. If the loops are too small the horses will get into the habit of leaning more

and more into the turn. A driver with little knowledge and experience may think: 'The loop was not too small because the horses are already turning too much.' On occasional drives in the country it is not too serious if the loops are too small. However, practising corners and turns, one after the other, will show that with large loops and, therefore, correctly positioned horses, the whole turnout will improve visibly, provided that all right-hand turns are driven at a walk. If one is unable to keep the horses at a walk and makes the loops so small so that a 'counter positioning' occurs, the team will be a very unattractive sight. The horses will jog or even trot in right-hand turns and the whole turnout will be in chaos. If the driver then makes opposition points with the outside reins the problem will get worse. Correct positioning, achieved through making large loops and driving at a walk, is the only infallible remedy.

On a flat, even surface the weight of the traces, the reins and the centre pole is sufficient to keep the vehicle in motion. It would therefore be wrong to have the horses in draught because the brake would have to be in operation all the time. All the traces should be slack, even those of the wheelers. However, when driving slightly uphill, or on uneven surfaces, this is a different matter. The reins must be sorted out in such a manner that all traces will be evenly tight and all horses are working – although the leaders should never participate too much in the work or the centre horses and the wheelers will become lazy and avoid theirs. It is a sign of bad coachmanship if the leaders do the work and the wheelers hang back. More details will be given in Chapter 24.

I would like to conclude my elaborations on driving a six-in-hand with the comments of a Swiss pupil of Benno von Achenbach, Major Barth, who writes in his book *Swiss Handbook on Riding and Driving*: 'Only after driving a pair of horses safely and confidently should you advance to driving a four-in-hand and then to a six-in-hand. Four- and six-in-hand driving is excellent practice for a driver. Adjusting and balancing the reins, which is difficult, will create a feeling for the horses, and observing the positioning and the draught will sharpen the eye. Those who call this useless play only demonstrate their ignorance of the demands which correct driving makes on the driver. If one has no intention ever to drive correctly and only wishes to pull one or even two horses about without any finesse, one need not drive a four-in-hand. But for somebody who wishes to drive dressage tests or, in any case, a professional whip and a driver who wishes to master the art of driving, these exercises are excellent, even if, later on, one is confined to driving only singles or pairs.'

15

Reining-back,
Hanging away from or Leaning
against the pole

The Rein-back

Reining-back is required more often than one expects. It must, therefore, be practised thoroughly. The rein-back must be executed in such a way that it does not unsettle the horses. Correctly executed, it forms part of the art of driving.

Many drivers spoil the rein-back by not giving it sufficient thought and by applying the opposition points too hastily. Whenever a rein-back is necessary – and there are many occasions where it is unavoidable – the driver must remember that the angle between front and rear axle, i.e. the turning angle, must be equivalent to the

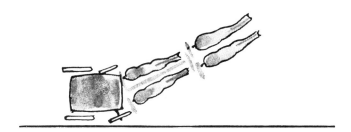

Reining back

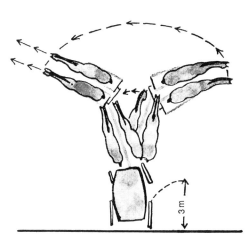

3 m

angle the two axles would have had, had he turned into the road he is in, from the road to which he is reining back.

Imagine this angle painted on the road. Drive from the right-hand side of the road half left, then turn right and halt in this right-hand curve. The pole is now pointing to the right. Now give calmly the aid to the rein-back by increased pressure on the right-hand rein – when driving a four-in-hand, small loop under the index finger and increased pressure on the two right-hand reins – the importance being that the position of the pole to the right-hand side is maintained. The horses should step back calmly until the rear wheels nearly touch the kerb. If necessary, lightly apply the brake. Now let the horses stand in this slightly right-hand curve, get the grooms to dismount and let them stand with the horses. Then, by increasing the pressure on the left-hand rein and giving the right-hand rein, lead the horses in small steps to the left. The pole now points to the left. Let the grooms mount.

With a four-in-hand, release the small right-hand loop and indicate to the leaders by careful 'nagging' with the left-hand lead-rein that they should move to the left in small steps. As soon as the leaders are facing the opposite kerb, apply pressure on the left-hand wheel-rein and get the wheelers to move step-by-step to the half left. When the pole points to the left-hand side, give rein and get the team to move forward.

To achieve a good rein-back praise your horses, talk to them and never be too hasty in applying your opposition points. Last, but not least, practise as many times as possible on quiet roads or lanes. If it is possible to rein-back into a side road, the intention must be to get the right-hand rear wheel in the turn close along the right-hand corner of the kerb.

Hanging away from or leaning against the pole

This can happen for various reasons. Apart from a one-sided stiffness on the part of the

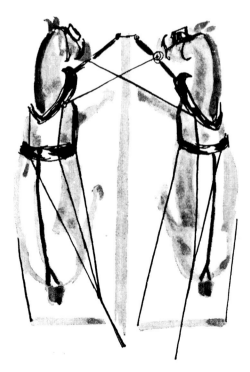

Hanging away from the pole

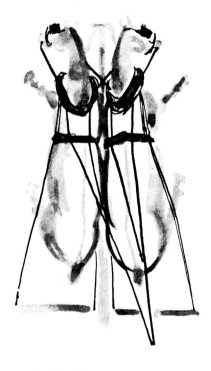

Leaning against the pole

76

Mrs. P. H. Northen driving her Welsh pony Marston Mirage

Mr. Clive Richardson driving the Ashworth Morgan Horse Stud's entry in a dressage competition

A coaching class at the Richmond Royal Horse Show

Mr. D. Nicholson and his team of Gelderlanders

George Bowman competing in the World Championships, 1980

Mr. Peter Munt returns from exercising Mr. R. Coleman's team of chestnuts

Colonel Sir John Miller, Crown Equerry, driving Her Majesty The Queen's team of Greys

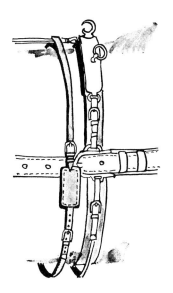
Strap with leather pad to prevent hanging away from the pole.

horse, it may be caused by wrong bitting, wrongly coupled reins, bad driving, steeply cambered and slippery roads, bad or missing studs or defective brakes. Very often several of these points coincide. Hanging away from the pole is the opposite to leaning against the pole. When hanging away from the pole the horse wants literally to get away from it, the more so the more taut the pole straps are. The pole straps will become taut if they are too short or if the driver 'brakes' with the reins instead of using the brake. Although the horses are held back, the carriage, and with it the pole, will still run forward and the horse is in the same position as a dog tied to a tree. Whenever hanging away from the pole occurs suddenly, stop, lengthen the pole

strap and, in this case – against all rules – shorten the two inside reins. The horses are now closer together and the lengthened pole straps are quite slack. The horses no longer feel restricted. If there is nothing to pull, use the brake to stop the vehicle from running forward. With careful driving the horses may regain confidence in a very short time. However, if horses have got into the habit of hanging away from the pole, switching them over may help. Another remedy is to use a leather pad with metal inlay and protruding pins.

This leather pad is attached to a strap which is buckled behind the pad. The thickness of the traces will keep the pins away from the horse until such times as the horse hangs away from the pole. The strap continues underneath the belly of the horses and above the pole.

Leaning against the pole may have similar causes, for instance on country lanes to avoid ruts or in fear of slipping. Again, stop, shorten the inside reins and drive without using the brake, thus trying to get the horses rather to hang away from the pole. Another remedy is to fit brushes to both sides of the pole level with the front legs of the horses. As soon as the brushes have cured them, lengthen the inside reins so that the horses straighten out.

Whenever hanging away from the pole or leaning against the pole could result from a fear of slipping, do not hesitate to drive your horses with studs.

In all cases where either of the above has become a habit, the easiest remedy is to change over the horses. This, in any case, is something that should be done more often as it stops horses from becoming one-sided.

16

The Whip and its Application

Depending upon the turnout, we differentiate between three types of whips.

1. The bow-topped whip for English turnout (full collar).
2. The Jucker or drop-thong whip for Hungarian turnouts or country turnout with breast collar.
3. The American buggy whip used for American fine harness horses and for trotting races.

The bow-topped whip is made of blackthorn, or holly. Shape, colour and hand parts may vary, but certain characteristics are inseparable from a 'decent' whip in addition to quality and condition. Particularly valuable are whips made from blackthorn with the bark still attached. They are very dark in colour. The ideal shape of a whip is thick at the hand-piece, tapering to the top. Unless the hand-piece is thicker and balanced by a metal sleeve underneath a leather cover, the whip will be top heavy. A well-balanced whip should not tire the driver, even on a long journey.

The general impression of a Gentleman's turnout is easily spoilt by a whip which looks as if it has never been hung up properly, but as if it had been standing in a corner.

The thong of a whip, whether for a pair or a four-in-hand, should always be of very thin, tightly-plaited leather. Silk lashes are unsuitable because they get easily caught in harness or equipment. They are, however, popular with some drivers as they make it easy to crack a whip. A good driver must remember, on the other hand, that a whip should not be used for cracking.

The stick of a whip, whether for a pair or a four-in-hand, should measure 1.5 m. excluding the bow-top.

Four-in-hand drivers should practise the use of the furled, four-in-hand whip even when driving a pair or a single.

The drop-thong whip is a straight, slim, flexible stick with two, button-like enlargements at the top. The thong is fastened between these two 'buttons' which allows it to move freely around the stick. The American buggy whip is a straight, slim stick without a thong, often bound with braided thread. It has been adopted from the trotting track, where it belongs, but is used in America for fine harness horses in single or double harness.

To keep a whip in good condition it must be hung up properly on a whip board and not stood in a corner. A whip should be hung up over a reel of about 12–14 cm. diameter.

Concerning the use of the whip, the following must be mentioned. The correct position of the whip results from the correct positioning of the right hand. The whip should point towards the left in a forward/upward direction. It should be held at the hand-piece with the butt sticking out of the palm of the hand by about 10–15 cm. If the whip is top heavy this distance must be increased. However, experience will soon establish the most comfortable position and when the whip is correctly balanced.

When driving, the driver should always carry

the whip in hand. When dismounting, it should be placed in the whip socket or laid across the seat. The whip should not be used to crack nor should it whizz through the air. This not only unsettles the horses, it is also not good style.

The whip should be used to urge on or to collect the horses and should be applied without noise. It should touch the horse where the leg of the rider would act, behind the pad. If rein is given at the same time, the whip urges on the horses, if the rein is shortened it collects them. In conjunction with a sensitive guide by the left hand, it also aids the positioning of the horses in a turn.

When moving off or urging on the horses, hand, voice and whip should act together, i.e. lengthen the reins, and at the same time call 'walk on' and touch the lazy horse with the whip. Of course, when the whip is used, the reins should only be held in the left hand. Never use the whip with the right-hand rein still in the right hand.

The whip is used with the whole of the right arm (not just from the wrist) by letting the thong touch the outside of the horse when the stick is in a near-horizontal position. The stick should not touch the horse.

The position of the driver's body remains unaltered; on no account should he lean forward.

The brake should be applied only after the whip has been passed to the left hand, otherwise the whip nearly always touches the quarters of the right-hand wheel-horse, causing it to jump forward.

'Brushing' with the whip (repetitive touching) is very wrong. Soon, the horses will no longer respond to the whip, and a sensitive horse will only get upset.

If a horse deserves punishment, hit it properly either on the shoulder or just above the elbow' never on the back or on the quarters because the horse may retaliate by kicking.

Never apply the whip between the horses, or on the outside horse in a turn – this would result in wrong positioning of the horses. In a turn only the inside horse should be urged on or touched

Whip reels and whips:
(1) Properly hung retaining the curve of the thong
(2) Incorrectly hung – too far away from the curve
(3) Incorrectly hung – too close to the curve of the thong. It is also wrong to tie the thongs of two whips together
(4) Dealer's whip
(5) Trotting whip

with the whip to achieve correct positioning. However, a novice driver should not attempt to do this as it requires very delicate co-operation between rein- and whip-aids.

It is unsightly if the carriage jerks every time the whip is applied. As an eager horse should always be bitted kindly, whereas the lazy horse should have a more severe bit with a corresponding longer rein, the lazy horse should be urged on as follows. Touch it with the whip at the shoulder, just in front of the pad; *at the same time* the left hand applies opposition relative to the contact with the bit of the horse in question. The lazy horse will acknowledge the touch of the whip by going forward; it will run against the collecting aid of the rein and accepts the aid because of the more severe bitting. The result – no jerking of the vehicle, and no upsetting of the keener horse.

Finally, a word on the technique of using the whip. Move arm, hand and whip sideways to the right, slightly upwards so that the stick is approximately 2 m. away from the horse. From this position bring the thong very slowly towards the right-hand ribs of the horse, increase the speed and hit. After the blow, leave the thong for a few seconds so that it comes away from the horse of its own accord and does not get caught up anywhere. Trying to jerk the thong away may break the whip. If necessary, apply the same procedure for the left-hand horse.

17

The Four-in-Hand Whip
and its Use

A driver who does not master the art of using a four-in-hand whip well and correctly should use it daily for at least three months, whether driving a single or a pair. Even then he will still find that he is not yet very expert at using a four-in-hand whip, but at least he will have learnt how to carry it correctly.

Driving with a four-in-hand whip teaches the driver to watch out for trees, street lamps, fences, gateways, etc., because the double thong can get caught and will break the whip if he hangs on to it.

Drivers practise the shortening and lengthening of the reins, going forward on the reins with the right hand etc., but do not observe how unsteady the whip has been. Watch what happens to the beautiful double thong after each turn, overtaking or giving way – and even worse after a rein-back!

If one has learnt to carry the whip steadily, however, it will always look tidy and there is no need continuously to try and catch it when driving a tandem or a four-in-hand; this only looks clumsy and insecure.

Carrying the whip and using it correctly is so subtle an art that usually only experts and 'connoisseurs' appreciate it. Regular use of a four-in-hand whip not only teaches the driver how to carry it correctly, but also how to use it on the wheelers. Every beginning is difficult. You will soon notice that 'stroking' or 'brushing' the horses with the whip is impractical. For instance, stroking the right-hand horse with the whip will wind the double thong round the stick as well as making ugly twists in the loop.

'Brushing' the left-hand horse will unfurl the double thong; add to this the risk that the thong may get under the horse's tail and you will begin to appreciate the problems.

With sufficient concentration, a four-in-hand driver can easily teach himself how to use the four-in-hand whip correctly – provided he takes the trouble to examine carefully where the horses can be hit easily without getting the whip caught in the harness, or vehicle parts, and

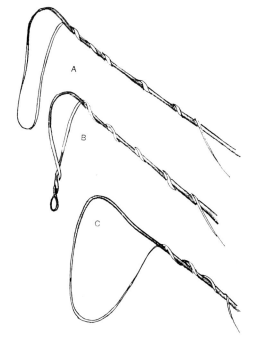

A A four-in-hand whip correctly furled
B A badly furled four-in hand whip
C Badly furled four-in-hand whip, but better than B

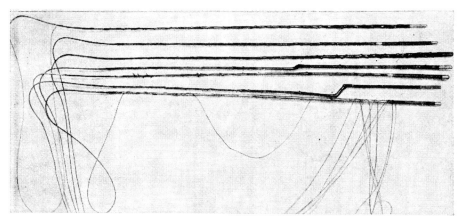

English holly four-in-hand whips

without interfering with the other horses and the passengers in the carriage.

For a 'gentle' reminder, touch the outside ribs of the horse once with the double thong. Touching the horse repeatedly (without 'brushing') will make the horse more attentive and the effect will last longer. To be more definite, strike a light blow. This should not be made from the wrist – and never tug the whip back. Lay on the thong without a noise so that only the horse that is struck will notice it.

To hit the left-hand wheeler correctly without leaning forward, push the hand-piece of the whip right into the palm of the hand. When using the whip on the left-hand horse, the danger that the double thong might get caught is much greater than when using the whip on the right-hand horse. Therefore, always remember to leave the thong for a few seconds, rather like casting a fishing line.

With difficult horses it may be necessary to hit one of the wheelers rather sharply on the neck to stop it leaning into the turn. Without the double thong this would not be possible.

After using a four-in-hand whip religiously every day, say for three months, one begins really to get to know it. It is no longer in the way and it becomes a pleasure to handle it correctly and well. Experts can see from a distance whether a driver is master of the art of handling a four-in-hand whip or whether he is so concerned with his horses, and such a novice, that he has no time to think of his whip.

The purpose of the double thong is to have a whip with a thong similar to that of a single or pair whip (despite the considerable length when it is unfurled) which can reach the wheelers as accurately and, if need be, everywhere, as an ordinary driving whip. As already mentioned, the stick of a four-in-hand whip is 150–160 cm. in length; the thong, including the bow, approximately 370–380 cm. Good English four-in-hand blackthorn whips are difficult to obtain, particularly with the good English lashes.

Catching the Thong

This is difficult to explain, but even more difficult to learn well enough to be able to execute it properly without interfering with horses or passengers. Only practice and a lot of patience will overcome this problem.

The initial exercises should be done without a whip.

Draw a large 'S', about 60–70 cm. high, on a wall. Then try to trace this 'S' with the tip of the right-hand thumb in reverse i.e. from bottom to the top. Start with the thumb at 'A', then go very slowly, slightly downwards, to the right, then up to 'B'. From then on move the thumb upwards to 'C', moving from the wrist, with increased speed, finishing sharply at 'C', and remain there for a few seconds. (When using the whip this will allow the thong to twist round the stick so that it can be caught.)

When the hand and arm movements – exactly following these instructions – are mastered, practised over and over again, checked and re-checked for shape and speed, take a short stick without a thong and practise again until every movement comes naturally. Only then start practising with a whip. Practise with closed eyes, it avoids the temptation of following the thong with the stick to catch it rather than throwing the thong carefully up on to the stick.

The basic position for this exercise is as follows. Hook the third finger of your left hand between two of your coat or waistcoat buttons and keep it there. Hold the right hand in front of the body, the arm bent at a right angle, the hand slightly turned inwards at the wrist so that the thumb points upwards to the left. At half-way point 'B', speed up the movement of the hand as if to turn the hand with a slight flick over to the right, i.e. back of the hand downwards. Arrived at 'C' the right hand must close firmly over the stick of the whip. At the last moment, tighten the muscles of the whole arm so that the stick comes to a sudden halt in its half-right, upwards position.

To be able to enjoy catching the thong when driving it is necessary to sacrifice 10 minutes a

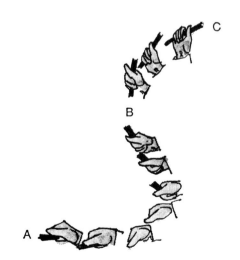

Practising with a whip

day for practising. Do this with closed eyes and without the whip, only to get the movement of the hand right. If a beginner practises with the whip straight away he will only watch the thong. If it happens to catch on to the stick he will be pleased. However, he has not learnt anything and his success was only a fluke. Catching the thong must not be a fluke, it must be caught correctly and the success must be guaranteed, otherwise driver, horses, and passengers will get nervous and frightened. Unless catching the thong has been practised slowly, time and time again, and without making a noise, the horses will get restless, and the thong may get caught in the dashboard or even in the reins. You could thus end up with a broken whip.

If, after long practice – strictly in accordance with the instructions – you are absolutely sure that the movements have become second nature, then practise with a proper four-in-hand whip either of blackthorn or, if this is not available, with a fairly flexible stick and a light thong. Do not get hold of the whip at the butt as this would be unnecessarily tiring, but let the butt stick out of your right hand by about 25 cm. The lash of the whip, however, should only show by about 10 cm.

The preliminary practice should have been so thorough that there should now be no temptation to follow the thong with the stick. The thong must fly back of its own accord and wind round the stick.

The procedure is as follows. Because of the slow movement of the hand the centre of the thong will fly upwards in a half-right direction. As the centre of the thong is now flying upwards, supported in this by the increased speed of the movement, the centre of the thong will fly against the suddenly motionless stick and will wind itself around it.

So much for the catching of the thong. The stick is now in a half-right, upwards position and the thong is flying against it from underneath – provided the stick was held firmly. The middle of the thong, hampered in its flight by the stick, will furl around it three or four times in two different 'threads', a right-handed thread at the

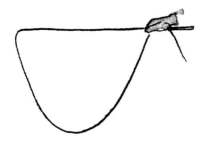

Slow the hand movement so the thong will fly upwards

The thong flies up and then around the stick

Taking the thong off the stick

top and a left-handed one at the bottom. The top thread must be retained. Now bring the whip carefully back so that the right hand is again in the standard position and tip the whip nearly horizontal. With thumb and index finger of the left hand take the centre loop of the thong, but without destroying the thread at the top. As the left hand, when driving, must remain in front of the centre of the body to maintain the direction, it cannot move towards the left to 'pull out' the lower thread. The right hand, therefore, must move the stick to take the lower thread of the thong off the stick. If the top of the thong – at the bow – is not furled round firmly, maybe only twice or three times, hold on to the end of the thong with the left hand, whilst the right hand describes three circles from the wrist with the stick and loop, so that the thong winds itself a few more times round the stick. The right hand then passes the whip over to the left, takes the lash and winds it three times – without looking – loosely round the butt end of the whip in the direction of the top thread, i.e. to the right. For this purpose the whip must be held lightly, otherwise the nicely-caught whip will get into disarray.

If, although the whip was caught correctly, it has only been possible to get the thong on to half of the stick – this sometimes happens in strong winds, or because of troublesome horses – do not try to rectify it straight away. Drive with the whip as it was caught, until you get the time to throw the thong again. If necessary, completely unfurl the whip, and repeat the process of catching and furling it.

Using the four-in-hand whip

The 'double thong' is obtained by catching and furling the long thong of a four-in-hand whip. It is applied as a pair whip – without brushing – i.e. laid-on between hip and pad or, for more forceful effect, on the foreleg just below the hame tug. The best way to practise with the unfurled four-in-hand whip is from the vehicle, but without horses. Instead of the horses place four chairs in front. Then think: what, how, and where you wish to hit, and remember where the whip might get caught up. The whip must be applied quietly and should not be used so clumsily that the thong gets caught under the wheels of the vehicle or the feet of the horses. Therefore, practice is essential.

To hit the leader, the four-in-hand whip must first be unfurled, on the right-hand side, without making a sound. Once the right hand has released the lash, the thong will drag along the right-hand side of the vehicle. To hit the right-hand leader, describe a large circle with the whip in the opposite direction to the wheels and then throw the thong forward, close to the ground, as if to hit an object standing about a metre to the half-right in front of the forelegs of the right-hand leader. Apply the four-in-hand whip quietly and deliberately with the whole arm, and never jerk it back.

To hit the left-hand leader the whip is again unfurled on the right-hand side. Then push the stick of the whip through so that the butt rests in the palm of the hand and, carefully, throw the thong over the horses to the left-hand side. Make a large circle with the whip, opposite to the movement of the wheels, and try to hit the corresponding point on the left next to the leader. Hold the whip to the left for a moment until the wheelers have passed the thong. Then bring it back carefully to the right-hand side with a movement as if to hit the right-hand rear wheel; at the same time move the bow of the whip slowly to the left. This will cause the thong to drop on the right thigh, or below the right arm, where it is easily picked up by the right hand. Now move the right hand over towards the left thumb which gets hold of the thong as close as possible to the right hand. Open the right hand slightly and then move the stick towards the right as far as the right arm will permit, thus pulling the thong which is held by the left thumb out of the right hand. Repeat this movement once, which will bring the end of the thong into the right hand. The whip is now ready to catch the thong.

For a tandem I recommend a whip with a stick slightly longer than 145 cm. so that the double

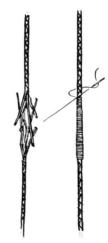

thong does not touch the high wheels – their sharp rims can easily cut through it.

To put on a new tip, cut the leather strips in different lengths. Then, starting at the top, wrap strong, waxed cotton round the thong about 5 or 6 turns, then upwards, wrapping the cotton round the thong very closely and tightly. Now secure the thread with a knot and pull it twice through the thong with a needle.

The easiest (but most inelegant) method of catching the thong is to hold the stick and the end of the thong together in the right hand and lift it to slightly above the horizontal.

Now describe downwards a half-circle on the right-hand side, next to the right-hand wheeler, so that the stick hits the thong – which will wrap itself round the stick and is quickly ready for use on the leaders.

If the leaders are keen horses which do not often require the whip, the lower 'thread' of the whip is unfurled and the double thong used like an ordinary pair whip. This method can also be used to catch the thong of a drop-thong whip provided the stick is fairly stiff and the thong pliable (waxed) – not vice versa as is commonly found. Needless to say, this will also require a certain amount of practice.

If the leaders are lazy and one or both wheelers rather impetuous it looks pitiful if a driver tries to move on the leaders by shouting at them. This may succeed once or twice, but the chances

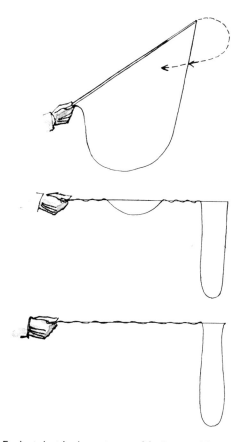

Easiest, but inelegant way of furling a whip

In order to be able to drive well and comfortably, it is essential that the leaders have learnt to seek contact with the bit, i.e. they must move forward as soon as the driver gives rein without him using either words or whip. The easiest and safest way of teaching this is by driving slowly through the turns, but getting the horses to trot on immediately after the turn by giving rein, without using the voice. Naturally, the unfurled whip must be ready for immediate use so that even the laziest horse knows, and does, what is expected of him.

A four-in-hand driver must always ensure that his whip is in first-class condition. The lash must be kept pliable by occasional wiping with a greasy rag. The bow of the whip (the joint between stick and thong) and the upper, thicker part of the thong should not be greased. When hanging up the whip take care that it is hung directly over the whip reel, and that the thong hangs down straight and smoothly, and is not furled round the stick.

Whips should not be dyed.

Bad catching of the whip, and furling the thong too many times round the stick, can easily twist the thong and may break it. If you wish to be considered a good and capable four-in-hand driver this must never happen. Correct handling and care of the whip is one of the rudiments of four-in-hand driving. Remember the dangers to your whip; as well as the possibility of it catching under the horses' feet or the wheels of the carriage, it can also get caught in trees, street lamps, doorways etc. Therefore, always keep your eyes open!

are that the wheelers, which hear the calls much more clearly, will become even more impetuous and unsettled. A four-in-hand driven by somebody who does not use the whip correctly is not a pretty sight.

18

The Hand of the Driver

If, many years ago, one had taken the time to stand for about half an hour at a street corner watching various drivers handle their horses, one would have been amazed. They were tugging and pulling and always moving their hands about, the only exceptions being drivers of trade vehicles whose horses were tired and knew the route.

Any horse, even a carthorse, will work much better if driven quietly. Most drivers who pull and tug at the reins only do so from sheer habit.

When driving blood horses a steady, attentive and sensitive hand is the 'conditio sine qua non', particularly if the horses are driven in curb bits or are still suffering from bruised bars. The more severe the bit, the more careful and sensitive the hand must be.

Driving plain cheek only 'guides' (directs) the horse, not collects it, because plain cheek works without leverage. The more severe the bit (first or second slot) the more collected or flexed the effect. The third slot should be avoided because of its considerable leverage. Driving in a snaffle one may be able to say 'round with you!' With a curb bit it is more like saying 'please, be good and turn right.'

Because the art in driving with curb bits lies mainly in the lightness of the contact with the horses' mouths and the 'giving of rein' – the desired head positioning is never achieved by pulling one rein – continual movement of the hand would only cause blood horses, which are very sensitive, to become increasingly unresponsive. A steady, attentive and sensitive hand, always prepared to give rein, is therefore essential.

The sensitivity of the driver's hand does not lie in the wrist. On the contrary, this must be firm, because the hand must be kept tightly closed to stop the reins from slipping. Therefore, the term 'to drive from the wrist' is utter nonsense. The sensitivity of the driver's hand lies in elbow- and shoulder-joint. With high vehicles, it even involves the driver's body from thigh to chest. With a high vehicle, the horses are more below him than in front of him, and this necessitates his hand covering a distance of more than 50 cm. if, for instance, the horses should suddenly stop or shy. A flexing of the wrist, which covers only a few centimetres, would in such circumstances be insufficient.

'Giving rein' plays an extremely important part in achieving a sensitive hand. To be able to give rein, it is very often necessary to reduce pace. Doing this on a straight road, however, would lose time. Therefore, collect the horses before each corner and shorten the reins, thus reducing the speed. Then take the turn by giving the outside rein carefully (not throwing it at the horses) at the most collected trot possible. When in the turn, neither speak to the horses nor use the whip, but give with both reins and the horses will steadily increase the pace again, without jerking. Driven in this manner the horses will become more responsive and attentive and, if they have learnt to follow the reins, will immediately increase their pace on a straight road if sufficient rein has been given.

With determination, everybody can improve his hand just as anybody eventually can learn how to ride a bicycle without putting his hands on the handlebars. The hand must become a tool that carries out the instructions of the mind. A thoughtless driver usually hangs on to the reins like somebody learning to ride a bicycle hangs on to the handlebars; it does not hurt the bicycle, but a horse will become dead in the mouth. The hand becomes 'hard' if a driver does not give serious consideration to the fact that the steel bit – and with a curb bit supported by the leverage – will press on nerves, gums and periosteum. A considerate driver, who collects his horses before each corner or fetches them back on the straight, will give rein hundreds of times in the course of a journey to take the pressure off the horses' bars and give them a chance to become refreshed and remain responsive.

Consider the above carefully, remember it when driving, act accordingly, and your hand will improve. In time the horses will go better for you and a whole new world in driving will open up.

It is much more difficult to give rein on the straight, and retain the same steady pace, than it is to do so in a turn. From my long experience in teaching, I found that the easiest way to learn how to give rein on the straight is with keen and willing horses. Remember the possibility of bruised bars, try and relax both elbow- and shoulder-joints, as well as leg muscles, holding the reins just a little lighter without increasing the pace. Thinking of this all the time has an improving effect on your hands as well as on your horses. Should your horse have only the slightest hint of a bruised bar keep thinking: 'Careful, bruised bars. Can I hold the reins even more gently?' To take the pressure off the bars, with quiet horses use a snaffle bit, or a curb bit with broken mouthpiece. If the horse is very sensitive and high-spirited, use a rubber snaffle with puller strap.

19

Auxiliary Reins and Equipment

Auxiliary reins are any reins which, apart from the ordinary type, are used in the schooling of a horse and are only a temporary measure; the same applies to any other auxiliary equipment.

Auxiliary reins and equipment are not allowed in competitions for driving horses. This follows the opinion that a well-trained team of horses should be presented to the judges without unnecessary trimmings, similar to the presentation of a hack.

The top rein (bearing-rein) is mentioned here first, because in Germany we are of the opinion that it should only be used for training. However, it is widely used in England and America. From the point of view of making work easier for the horses, it will never get our approval unless it is used in a tolerant manner.

Nevertheless, the usefulness of the bearing-rein in training a horse cannot be denied. In the hands of a driver who knows what he is doing, the bearing-rein can be useful as long as he discontinues using it once it has served its purpose. However, one should have the loop stitched in front of the bearing-rein hook so that, if need be, one can influence one side more than the other.

There is no objection when, in training a four-in-hand or a tandem, all horses are driven in a bearing-rein because one horse carries its head too low, or is overbent. However, the bearing-rein should be such that the horses can carry their heads normally. This means whether in riding or driving, that the poll should be the highest point and that the horse's nose is slightly in front of the perpendicular. This position, of course, is only when the horses are not in heavy

Cruel application of a bearing-rein

Bearing-reins incorrectly applied – too tight

draught. Bearing-reins that are too severe are cruel.

If the bearing-rein is used to set up a horse, short bearing-rein drops should be used and not the longer chain type which one so often sees. They are useless and ugly. If chains are used, the bearing-rein is not 'in contact' and may get caught below the rein terrets on the collar. An incorrectly applied bearing-rein causes horses to toss their heads as they seek relief from the continual pressure. Leaders of a tandem or four-in-hand may get a jab in the mouth and are tempted to canter. In particular, the bearing-rein with pulley continually used, can be cruel.

In heavy draughts the bearing-rein is a great hindrance. In order to be able to pull a heavy load, a horse must be able to arch its back and stretch its neck. The bearing-rein achieves the opposite effect.

The martingale or standing martingale has the opposite effect to the bearing-rein. It is used for horses which carry their heads too high; it is buckled to the girth, runs between the front legs and is then buckled to the noseband, thus regulating the head carriage. It is used to stop a horse that occasionally tosses its head from disturbing the other horse as the reins are crossed between the bits. A martingale is advisable in training the wheelers of a four-in-hand or a tandem where there is a danger that the outside bar of the bit may get over the lead-rein.

Side-reins

Horses that lean on one rein very often tend to get their heads over the pole. They either 'lean' on the outer rein or 'hang' on the inner. If they lean on the outer rein, they do not want to bend on the curved side, which means they usually hang away from the pole. From the box seat, the picture is the same if the horse 'hangs' on the inner rein.

To remedy this, use side-reins. At the same time the use of a bearing-rein is urgently recommended; however, this should not be used to set up the horse but only to carry the bridoon bit.

The side-rein, a strap about 1.5 cm. wide,

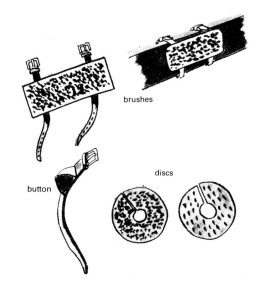

Aids for correcting bad habits. Brushes (*top*), button (*left*) and discs.

with a short buckle piece at one end, and a longer one at the other, is buckled to the bridoon and the back-band or the trace-buckle on the curved side of the horse. It should be buckled short enough so that the horse will step back at the halt. This will be the correct length when the horse is on the move. If a horse resists being put to harness with the side-rein already buckled, the groom should attach the side-rein *after* the turnout is on the move. The purpose is to get the horse to the pole and stabilize its position by trying to relax the stiff side. This requires a certain amount of patience. Try also a touch of the whip on the outside ribs or even the shoulder to get the horse to the pole. If the horse has been trained in long-reins to whip-aids, it will soon understand what is expected.

On slippery tarmac roads, release the side-reins and replace them either with a trace brush or trace button.

A 'trace brush' is considered as auxiliary equipment. It should touch either the shoulder or the rump behind the pad. The skin of a horse at the shoulder is sensitive; therefore do not drive for more than 15 minutes with a carefully fitted trace brush, to avoid bare patches. It is also possible to use buttons, about 4 cm. in size, made from hard wood tapering down to a point. They are buckled to the same places.

Avoid using discs with bristles or pins intended to stop a horse from leaning one-sided on the bit. They only cause more pain. If the horse is one-sided, check the mouth – a bruised bar could be the cause.

Try to avoid fixing side-reins in the stable. This may cause accidents. Due to the discomfort of the side-reins, a horse could creep back, try to lose its bridle, get caught in something and break it. If side-reins *have* to be put on in the stable, do not, afterwards, leave the horse on its own; always have a groom close by.

It is also important to watch the activity of the mouth and prevent the horse getting its tongue over the bit. This can become a very bad habit. If a horse gets its tongue over the bit, use either a tongue-strap or a tongue-band, made of a doubled 2.5 cm.-wide linen ribbon. Attach to one end a buckle and to the other a leather point. The strap should be 35 cm. long, plus the buckle, and the leather point 12 cm. long with 7 or 8 holes.

The strap is placed round the tongue and then buckled under the lower jaw.

Initially, buckle as loosely as possible, but if necessary tighten a little more, making sure that the tongue does not hang out of the mouth. Then put in a thick snaffle bit and give the horse sugar, salt or carrots to get it to chew on the bit. Use the tongue-strap in training, until the horse has lost the habit.

20

The Brake and Its Use

Police regulations stipulate that every carriage must have a brake. This regulation is not always obeyed yet correct driving in traffic *without* a brake is impossible. Remember, too, that using the brake is kinder on the mouths and the legs of the horses. This sentence alone, covers a whole chapter in the art of driving.

Occasions when to apply the brake:

1 At each halt.
2 When driving in traffic, particularly on slippery tarmac roads. Even on flat roads the carriage pushes at times and the brake should be used slightly, so that the horses' mouths and the breechings do not have to hold the carriage; otherwise the horses are disturbed in the mouth, the head position suffers and the horses are tempted to lean away from the pole.
3 Going downhill the brake should be used only to the extent that the horses are out of draught.
4 When giving sudden rein aids. (Prior to using the brake, the whip must be passed to the left hand.)
5 When reining-back for the purpose of getting the pole in the correct position.

The brake should be used as quietly as possible, particularly when moving off. The horses should not move off because they hear the release of the brake, but because of the releasing rein-aid.

Apart from the brake-shoe, there are three different types of brakes which are essential in mountainous country, particularly when heavy loads are carried. The brake-shoe hangs underneath the carriage and is used on steep downhill roads. In countries where there is right of way to the right, the brake-shoe must be put under the right rear wheel, otherwise the rear carriage could slide dangerously to the right.

Brake blocks are usually made from white beech wood, because they make little noise;

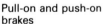
Pull-on and push-on brakes

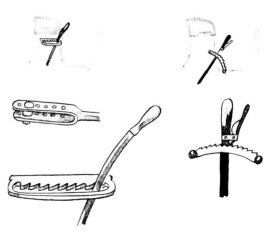

hard rubber, poplar, lime or willow wood are also suitable.

The three types of brakes include, firstly, the brake that is pulled back. This is in every respect the most practical. When the brake is on, it is not in the way, and if used, the 'backward pull' also affects the rein hand (left hand). Secondly, there is the brake that is pushed forward. Here the body is more inclined to lean forward and to give rein. This, however, should be avoided.

There are also situations when the box seat has to be mounted from the right-hand side, in which case a brake that is locked would be in the way. Thirdly, there is the spindle brake, which always reacts too late, particularly at sudden halts. On the other hand, it allows delicate grading and is particularly suitable in the mountains. With the pull- and push-brakes, the tension must always be checked as both types of brakes can easily jump out of the ratchet.

21

Driving Bits

There are numerous bits that have been developed to master the horse. It would take too long to name them all. Therefore only those that have been proven will be mentioned here.

Many bits used in agricultural or working turnouts are against certain animal protection laws. Even snaffle bits, which are normally harmless, have been produced with sharp edges, saw-like indentations, and double joints with hinges which cut the gum with their sharp corners.

The purpose of bitting is to give each horse its suitable bit. Experimenting is better than 'going by the book.'

Normally, the bit should lie about a finger's width above the tushes, or, with mares, where they are supposed to be. With sensitive horses, one should place the bit a little higher, but it should not pull up the corners of the mouth. For horses with bad mouths put the bit lower.

The kindest bit is a snaffle, particularly a hollow snaffle, because it is lighter in the mouth. It is used for breaking to harness and for long-reining. As a double-ring snaffle it is also the traditional bitting for a Hungarian turnout.

The unbroken rubber snaffle, the gentlest bit, is used mainly to correct, or cure, sore or ruined mouths. (Saliva dribbling from the mouth is a symptom of bruised bars. Examine the mouth carefully.) With bruised bars, the snaffle should be placed so that it does not hit the bruised place. Also use myrrh ointment as a soothing treatment.

The rubber snaffle, in conjunction with the puller-strap or a rubber curb with the puller-strap, is a combination very often used for horses with bad mouths. The narrow strap which lies below the nasal bone acts as a 'brake'.

The reason for thorough training is to get horses with good mouths. Therefore, for exercise and training purposes, a snaffle bit should be used, even when driving in full collars. Only use a curb bit when the horses are well broken, and for reasons of style. The latter is important, because a turnout should always be in correct style. If one horse has been accustomed to being driven in a snaffle, a broken Liverpool bit can be used to match the others driven in Liverpools. (The same applies with elbow bits etc.) To bit the horse more severely may cause problems.

Special noseband for a pulling horse (puller strap)

The horse could toss its head or go behind the bit. Therefore, before each public appearance, harness and bitting should be well tested.

The most popular curb bits are the Liverpool and the Elbow bit. They are particularly suitable for country turnouts with full collar. It is unsightly, however, to see country turnouts driven with a curb bit at a horse show if, in addition, the driver uses old-fashioned nosebands and buckles, the cheek bars of the curb bit stick out like elephants' tusks.

When buying new bits make sure that the top arms of the bit are turned well to the outside to avoid rubbing the horse's cheek and causing discomfort. If possible, use hollow bits – they are more gentle because of their thickness. Very thick, full bits are a good alternative, but hollow bits are lighter, and therefore preferable. It is better to buckle a thick, hollow bit more severely than a thin, full bit plain cheek.

In the following, we deal with the various possibilities to finding the key to a horse's mouth – whether by method of bitting or application of the bit. Horses with sharp bars (lower jaw) and thin tongues are usually prone to bruised bars. However, if they are of good conformation and of reasonably easy temperament, they will rarely suffer from bruised bars. The position of the bit – high, middle or low – is of great importance in driving. For instance when driving a tandem or a four-in-hand, it is impossible for the whip to be as effective as a rider with his weight, legs and spurs.

The steady position of the curb in the mouths of pairs or teams depends largely on the movement of the rein terrets on the inside of the collars. The higher the action, the more movement of the collar. If the terrets are fixed, the next horse is being disturbed; if they are free, they absorb the movement.

If the bit is low in the mouth most horses will get their tongues over the bit, and may then develop this habit. The observant driver will notice this immediately as the horse will suddenly drop its head and then go behind the bit. When bitting eager horses, always watch the work of the pulling horse before shortening the rein. Normally it is sufficient just to shorten the rein of that particular horse. Severe bitting, in addition to causing pain, will worry the horse. It cannot pull its load and, as a result, the excitement and pulling become worse. The art is to find the cause of the problem and the remedy.

Even with improved or correct distribution of work, a horse can pull with a weak driver. One is forced to look for the answer. There are four methods to correct horses with ruined mouths: firstly, a steady, kind hand; secondly, the broken mouthpiece; thirdly, the Segundo mouthpiece; and fourthly, the Howlett mouthpiece with the high port. Methods three and four are only suitable for drivers with sensitive hands.

These bits are a great relief to dead mouths and sore curb-chain grooves. The curb chain is kept away from the sore point by using a chin-strap which is attached to the throatlash by means of a strap. If the position of the bit has to be very low to achieve the intended fit, use a rubber tongue-strap which, apart from serving its purpose, will also stimulate the activity of the mouth. The chin-strap has to be buckled fairly short because it is much more elastic than the curb chain. When a bad mouth has been completely cured it is recommended to use a curb bit with a roller type mouthpiece.

This is very mild and does not rub, even if the mouth is completely dry, as it rolls upwards with the leverage of the curb arms, whereas a fixed mouthpiece would rub. Should the horse still hold on to the bit, try the Segundo mouthpiece, buckled plain cheek; it should never be buckled more severely than double cheek. If this does not work, place the curb chain with the chin-strap very high.

Should this type of bitting, even with careful guidance, not be suitable, try the Howlett bit, but again, only plain cheek, or at the most double cheek. In this case, however, the curb chain must be fairly short to stop the high port from injuring the roof of the horse's mouth. Both the Segundo and the Howlett bit can be placed low, as there is no danger that the horse could get its tongue over the bit. The noseband should be low, and if necessary, buckled slightly tighter than normal. With some horses a lip-strap (with a Buxton bit) works miracles; with other horses the puller-strap, which can be used with a four-ring snaffle but not with every type of curb bit.

Some horses are obviously 'one-sided'. This shows not only in the mouth, but they also hang away from the pole or lean against it. With such horses it is justified to buckle the bits 'one-sided', that is, one side more severely than the other. The apparent difference in the sides of the mouth is because horses are naturally not straight, although the degree of 'unstraightness' varies with each horse. A horse that is stiff on the left-hand side, is curved on its left-hand side, and 'hollow' on its right-hand side from head to tail. Such a right-hand hollow (soft) horse should be bitted very mildly on the right-hand side as this has a guiding effect. Assuming one is driving a single, the horse should go right if the right-hand rein gives a stronger indication than the left-hand rein. The milder the bit is buckled on the right-hand side, the more 'guiding' effect is achieved and correspondingly less 'collecting' effect. If one tries to 'guide' on the mildly-bitted right hand, there is a chance that the horse may turn to the right. However, if one bits the horse severely on the right-hand side, the effect is collecting rather than guiding. As a result the horse does not turn right but bends more to the right without following the guidance of the reins.

If you have keen horses and they are all bitted plain cheek, the weight in one's hand would possibly be too much. Therefore, bit the horses on their curved side more severely. It achieves a less 'guiding' influence on that side. This is important as any horse in harness will always lean into a turn with its curved side (at least it will try), as the spur of a rider is missing. However, bitting the horses more severely on the curved side gets them more collected than guided. Exceptions only occur if the driver, in conjunction with the severe bitting and the whip, grabs the reins on the curved side, thus stopping the horse from dropping its head and relenting, and pulling it by force to the other side. Persisting with this treatment achieves nothing but bruised bars. However, if one halts, bits as mildly as possible, maybe drops the bit one hole, and tries to achieve some position (and bending) on a long rein, one has won the battle with a kind, coaxing hand.

Very often so-called 'pump' bits are used (these are bits where the mouthpiece moves on the two side bars). These are sometimes suitable for ruined and bad mouths, but only in conjunction with a very short curb chain. Standing still, the mouthpiece slides down completely, so if the curb chain is considerably shortened, it will be in its normal position shortly after moving off, when the mouthpiece will slide up. As soon as it has reached the top it must *not* drop down again, or the horse will catch hold of the bit and lose any feeling. If, however, the curb is adjusted so that the bit is upright, the horse will relax with a driver with sensitive hands, while at the same time the mouthpiece will slide down on the bars, thus bringing relief to those places which have been under pressure. The driver should now realize what has happened, and understand why the horse suddenly goes behind the bit, so when the horse relaxes, the driver should not shout at it or chase it on, but should be thankful. A 'pump' bit should therefore not necessarily be disregarded for bad and ruined mouths, particularly if a lady is to drive such horses. The whole process is, however, only a cover-up, the purpose being to get some relief for the driver's hand. If the curb chain with these pump bits is fixed in such a way that the bars of the bit are at a half right angle, they will drop back as soon as the turnout is on the move and all sensitivity of the mouth is lost, the tongue turns blue, and driving is painful for both horse and driver. The tongue and the bars of the mouth can become jammed together like a piece of paper in a closed jack-knife. 'Pump' bits, like any other bit with movable bars, wear out very quickly if they are cleaned with sand, and can pinch the corners of the mouth until they bleed; when worn, they should be replaced immediately. A temporary remedy is to cover the joint with tape.

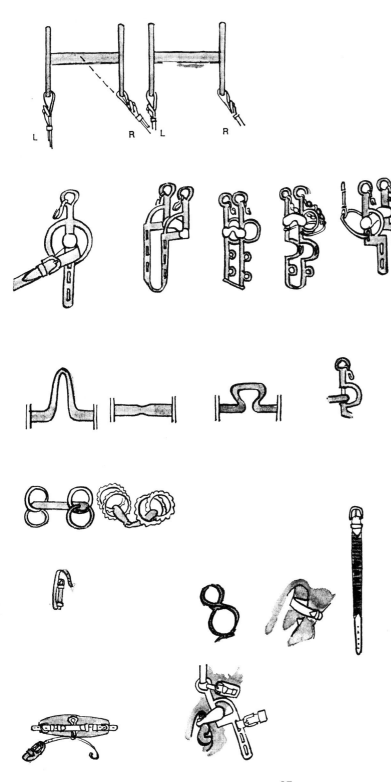

Driving bits and aids. Reading left to right, *1st column*: The Liverpool Bit. If one shortens rein L it acts on the left jaw; Rein R, however (imagine the draught extended), acts more on the centre of the mouth, and only more at R when the horse moves its head slightly to the outside (in this case, to the left); *2nd column*: Liverpool, Elbow, Tilbury, Buxton, Puller Strap; *3rd column*: Howlett, rolling-mouthpiece, Segundo, bit with sliding mouthpiece; *4th column*: four-ringed snaffle; *5th column*: connecting strap, tongue strap, cross strap; *6th column*: chin strap, snaffle mouthpiece

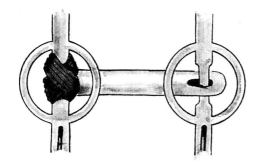

Temporary repair of worn-out pump bit

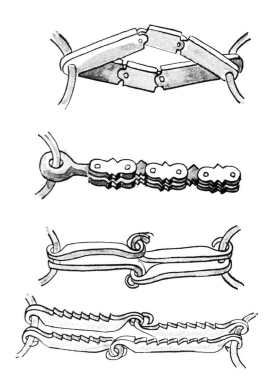

Some cruel bits

Driving 'bottom bar'. This experiment should be tried out on the human leg before deciding to place the rein in this most severe position

If, in addition, the inside rein is not buckled immediately below the mouthpiece around the bar (i.e. double cheek), but is buckled single cheek, or even cheek bar (the first slot), the inside bar, particularly with a Liverpool bit, will turn with its front part towards the upper lip. This is neither comfortable for the horse, nor does it look nice. All this can be avoided with a fixed mouthpiece. With the fixed bars of Liverpool or Elbow bits buckled single cheek, the pressure on the inside will not be as great as on the outside unless the horses of a pair or a four-in-hand point their heads slightly to the outside. Therefore it is possible to control each horse individually even with the English reins. If one does not want this effect, do not buckle plain cheek but round the bar, i.e. double cheek which creates less leverage. And if this is not desirable, for instance with a horse that is overbent, do the same, but buckle above the mouthpiece.

The width of a curb bit is correct if the mouth piece does not show on either side. The straightened-out (to the right) curb chain lies in the curb-groove level with the mouthpiece, the hooks pointing to the outside so as to avoid lip injuries.

With double ring snaffles, it should be mentioned that the mildest effect is achieved by buckling the cheek piece through both rings. Buckling it to the inside ring is the normal procedure, and buckling to the outside ring has a slightly more severe effect.

Driving 'bottom bar' is a most severe position. Try this on your own shin and you will find that the bit presses on the bone, so imagine having to suffer this pressure for half an hour. I believe this would convince anybody. Pressure creates counter pressure, the nerve is pinched, the mouth becomes dead, the horse has bruised bars and the pulling gets worse.

To complete the picture, the following curb bits – with bottom bars – should be mentioned: Tilbury, Buxton and closed Elbow bit. These should only be used with bearing-reins because otherwise there is the danger that the horses may get hooked up in the crab or elsewhere. I mention this at the end because we usually drive without bearing-reins.

22

The Coachman

Care of horses, harness and carriage, as well as cleanliness in the stables, depend on the coachman. Therefore only employ someone who has been recommended, and only keep a coachman who has proved reliable after several spot checks.

If you are an accomplished horseman and driver, train the coachman yourself. You are then assured that everything is done correctly. Pay him well, and if he works satisfactorily do not be mean with praise. The well-being of your horses depends on it. Always employ someone who loves animals. Careful training can be undone by a coachman who is rough and impatient. The owner of a team depends upon the reliability of his coachman. He holds a key position.

How few, however, meet these requirements! Therefore, only employ a coachman, if he is not personally known, on the basis of written references, and arrange a trial period to have a chance to test him thoroughly.

The difficulties in finding a good coachman are manifold. The old type of Gentleman's coachman is dying out and the young of today are more interested in motor cars. Riding and driving academies which held courses for new coachmen before the war, only do this nowadays to a very small extent. There are no state-owned institutions which demand proof of a coachman's capabilities. Any car driver, who is responsible for the lives of other people, has to pass a test before receiving his driving licence. Is not a coachman also responsible for the lives of his passengers?

What requirements must a coachman fulfil? Regarding character, he must be punctual, sober, careful, honest and industrious as well as being a horse-lover. As a driver, he should at least know the basics of modern driving; he must be conversant with correct harnessing; he must be a good groom, have a certain knowledge of shoeing, and know what to do in cases of colic, lameness, soreness etc.

Any driver of a good team, who wants to enjoy his horses, should therefore strive to learn from books enough to be able to supervise his coachman and, in conjunction with him, to improve the stable. He should give his coachman the opportunity to further his knowledge and maintain his interest by making available suitable literature.

H.R.H. The Prince of Wales driving a pair of greys

H.R.H. The Duke of Edinburgh with H.M. The Queen's team of Bays in the Dressage Phase at the Famous Grouse World Driving Championships at Windsor in 1980

Mr. Sanders Watney, President of the British Driving Society, driving his team to the Red Rover coach

Mrs. C. Thibeault driving her own team of Appaloosas

Mrs. Tom Ryder with a pair of ponies to a George IV Phaeton

Mr. John Richards, Chairman of the British Driving Society, photographed with his team of Welsh Cobs competing in the Holker Hall Driving Trials in 1980

Mr. Robert Weaver's Hackneys and the Yorkshire Hero road coach

Mrs. Bernard Homer's Morgan horse and Basket Phaeton

The Canadian-bred Welsh ponies of Mrs. Kenneth Wheeler, driven by Mr. James Wolcott

Mrs. Cynthia Haydon with Mrs. J. A. McDougald's team at the Royal Windsor Horse Show

23

Formal and Stable Livery

It is impossible to foresee how much modern times will influence style in the sport of driving. One thing, however, is certain; driving has moved from the towns into the country.

Whether town or country turnout, each will more or less retain its own particular style. This applies in any sport. Each discipline has its own written and unwritten laws. How far they cover liveries in town and country will be dealt with in the following.

Town livery

Coat and breeches. The coat is knee-length, tailored, single-breasted with six buttons, and four buttons at the back (two at the top of the pleat and two at the bottom). There are pocket flaps on the hips. The material should be matt, the colour black (to go with blue or grey trim), blue (to match dark blue trim), green (only with green trim), brown (only with brown), beige or sand-coloured with any trim. The lining should always be the same colour as the coat. The breeches are of white buckskin (with flap in front), and are pulled over a board for cleaning and drying. The breeches should be put on in such a way that the buttons are on the front of the shin and show 4 cm. above the boot.

Boots. Black calf-hide without spur-holders. Boot tops should be made of polished brown leather. Pink or beige boot tops are not as suitable because they mark; white celluloid (bone imitation) 'sleeves' should not be used.

Waistcoat. Either black and white or black and yellow, vertically striped, with sleeves. The waistcoat should not show.

Collar. Rounded corners, not joining at the front, with white stock tie.

Coachman's top hat. (Not a Gentleman's top hat). Should be firm and stiff, with a narrow ribbon at the base and the brim trimmed with ribbon. (The Gentleman's top hat has a wide ribbon.)

Cockade. Black patent leather, only for Ambassadors in the colours of their country.

Livery overcoat. Longer than the coat (should cover the knees), of the same colour as the coat, double-breasted, and with pocket flaps. May have a velvet collar of the same colour as the overcoat.

Summer coats and overcoats may have coloured collars. Black coats may have red, light blue, green or yellow collars; blue coats, no brown or green; green coats, no blue or brown; brown coats, red or yellow. Beige or buff overcoats have either collars of the same material or velvet of the same colour.

Coat of the second coachman or footman

As for coachman, but without pocket flaps, finishing a good hand's width above the knee. Six buttons in front and six behind.

Country or stable livery. Single-breasted coat, three or four buttons, trousers or breeches. For the coat, whipcord or covert-coat material is the most suitable, either in medium grey or 'pepper and salt' colour. Trousers or breeches of the same material. Leggings (gaiters) may be either of fabric or leather. No chauffeur's buttons, but bone or stone-nut buttons. The coat should have either one slit at the back or one on either side; lace-up boots, white stock tie, coachman's collar. No top hat, but bowler. Never velvet or military-style caps. Unsuitable for country liveries are plain-coloured liveries of grey, blue,

Coachman dressed for winter (*left*); summer (*centre*) and in a raincoat (*right*).

Groom in livery

Country and Stable dress

brown, yellow, green and black material with coloured collars and polished buttons. Livery gloves for both town and stable livery are light brown (tan) or natural-coloured leather.

The coachman in action

The position of the coachman or driver on the box seat is explained in Chapter 24. Many coachmen have the bad habit of keeping the left shoulder back. This can be avoided by placing both feet, closely together, to the right; the toes, however, must not show above the footboard. The whip should be carried, not left in the whip socket.

When his employer approaches the carriage, the coachman – looking straight ahead – salutes by touching the brim of his hat with his right hand. If his master wishes to take the reins himself the coachman waits on the ground and salutes standing in front of the horses. The reins are, of course, secured under the back-band. After his master has taken up the reins and mounted the box seat, the coachman moves away from the horses, mounts the carriage and takes his seat. With a four-wheeled vehicle (for instance, a Phaeton), this is on the rumble seat at the back; with a tandem or dogcart, diagonally behind his master, facing backwards; with a four-in-hand, on the left-hand side behind his master, facing forwards. If the coachman drives out on his own he sits on the right-hand side. However, if he is waiting for his master and only keeping the horses on the move until his master resumes the reins, he sits on the left of the box seat, passing the reins over from this position.

24

Driving in Town

A novice driver who has only learnt how to drive on quiet country lanes will not know what has hit him when he takes out blood horses for the first time on tarmac. 'Tarmac' in this context does not stand for road surfaces but for town streets with their numerous noises and hazards. Heavy lorries, cars, trams, parked or on the move, watching out for tram-lines, remembering the traffic regulations, the necessity of having to apply the brake frequently, in addition to the increasing restlessness of the horses – everything is there to make a driver nervous and tense. However, although such hazards make great demands on the driver's capabilities, they must be overcome, and this can only be done with practice.

When I moved from Hanover to Berlin I drove with the 'Master' (Benno von Achenbach) for months through Berlin's busiest streets. We drove pairs, four-in-hands and even six-in-hands, starting with a pair in Moabit and the Tiergarten and then extending our driving practices to the busier areas, finally driving with all types of turnouts along the Potsdamer Platz, the Friedrich Strasse, Leipziger Strasse and the Gendarmen Markt. And we were not driving nags! Eventually I even drove high-spirited hackneys through Berlin to the Sportspalast in the Potsdamer Strasse and also competed in marathons right across Berlin. I therefore believe that my experience permits me to repeat Achenbach's views as written down by his teacher, Edwin Howlett, in his book *Driving Lessons*:

'I enjoy driving on the road, which I have done a lot and wish to continue, but in learning how to drive, one lesson in town is worth more than 50 miles on the road.'

Let us stay for a while with tarmac or asphalt as a road surface, the kind normally met in towns. In itself it is not slippery; on the contrary. After heavy rain or a shower, the roads are clean from the greasy slime of motor oil, dust and sediments from the exhaust pipes of cars and lorries, and one can drive with an ordinary flat shoe without danger of slipping. On a dry day, however, this could be quite the opposite. The most suitable type of horseshoe for driving in town is one with a rope inlay, or one with a cork or wirebrush pad. On greasy or icy roads it is important that the horseshoe itself has little contact with the immediate surface, but that certain points penetrate through the grime and ice and gain a grip on the non-slippery tarmac or asphalt. For this reason Mordax or Widak studs are used nowadays.

For driving in town, expert shoeing is essential; further details are given in Chapter 39.

If it is necessary to take young horses out of a narrow driveway on to a main road make sure that your reins are accurately measured in your left hand, ready to take over the whip, if it is necessary to apply the handbrake.

Another requirement is the cleaning and greasing of the turntable of the carriage, particularly if the carriage has a perch. A dirty and dry turntable is bad for the nerves of both horses and driver. Therefore, never take a journey without prior cleaning and greasing of the turntable.

Remember also that the reins must be correctly measured. Moving off, particularly with a four-in-hand, can be dangerous without correctly-measured reins. You could be right in the middle of heavy traffic before you have sorted out your reins and got your horses under control. Unmatched reins or reins that are too long indicate a 'bungler'.

Once on the road, keep your horses at a walk for the first few hundred metres. It gives you a chance to take a critical look at your turnout. Are the reins buckled correctly? Is a trace twisted? If the horses' heads are pulled together it shows that either one coupling rein is wrong, the outside rein is on the inside, or even both.

Should it be necessary to stop and make adjustments to the harness, drive close to the kerb, apply the brake quietly and halt. Then get your groom to dismount to make the necessary adjustments. With a four-in-hand both grooms get down, one to hold the leaders whilst the other attends to the adjustments. Before halting, never forget to turn round and signal with the whip by holding it high in a vertical position.

Always drive correctly and in accordance with traffic regulations and drive as close to the kerb as possible.

Driving correctly in traffic, signal with the whip not only before turns, but also when wishing to cross the road or halt on the opposite side. Make sure your signal is seen by both the following and the oncoming traffic. If you wish to turn, prepare for this gradually; reduce the speed, and drop further behind the vehicle in front. Do not stop suddenly; it is neither comfortable for your passengers nor for your horses. When driving in town pay attention at all times if you want to avoid collisions. Even keeping a proper distance behind the vehicle in front requires concentration and should not be done clumsily so that another vehicle can slip in the gap or, even worse, cut right in front of your horses. Always leave enough distance between the vehicle in front so that, should a car or another carriage cut in front of you, you still have room to manoeuvre. If you have to cross tram-lines, try and find a place where they are level with the road surface and cut across them at nearly a right angle.

Horses that travel the same route every day require advance warning if you intend to alter that route. Reduce the speed considerably and indicate that something unusual is going to happen. In the turn, as always, give with the outside rein, do not pull the inside rein.

Moving off on a slippery road with one lazy and one keen horse is often difficult. Calling to them may cause the keen horse to jump into its collar and it could slip and hurt itself. Hanging on to the reins is not going to help, particularly if the keen horse is bitted fairly severely. The easiest method is to touch the lazy horse quietly with the whip and let it start off on its own for a split second. The keen horse will follow immediately and settle down quickly because it did not hurt itself in the move-off.

Overtaking in town is also difficult because many points have to be taken into consideration. Apart from the condition of the road, one must assess one's own speed, that of the vehicle to be overtaken – bearing in mind that its driver might increase his speed – and, thirdly, the speed of any oncoming vehicle.

All these elaborations concern driving techniques in traffic. However, it is essential to know the traffic regulations and how to act on them.

25

Traffic Regulations

As traffic regulations may vary from country to country it is recommended to study these in the countries concerned.

Hand and whip signals. Reading from left to right: turning left; turning right; going forward; pulling up

26

Long-Distance Driving

After the chapter on Driving in Town it would seem natural to write a chapter about driving in the country. However, very little could be added to that which has been said in Chapter 24. Traffic regulations in town also apply in the country, but the difficulties experienced when driving in town diminish. It must still be remembered, however, that accidents usually occur where they are least expected because drivers get careless and inattentive.

Heavy traffic, particularly in the country, holds danger for young horses. Cars and lorries are more likely to drive at speed and then brake suddenly. Quick reactions are therefore of utmost importance. Crossroads and bends may be difficult to survey and lanes may be narrow. Never be tempted to drive at a fast trot on narrow, winding roads, and never in the centre. Motorists are inclined to drive fast in the country and cut corners.

Longer journeys on the box seat to enjoy the countryside – being away from the stable maybe for days or weeks at a time – require adequate preparation. Nothing can give more pleasure than such a journey, but without thorough planning and reconnaissance nothing can be more miserable.

As far as private luggage is concerned, it is better to take several small pieces of luggage than one large trunk.

For horses and carriage the following equipment should be taken: a breast collar lined with roebuck skin; a soft, open under-collar; some pieces of felt, which should have a small strap at either end, to be attached to the collars in case of sore or swollen shoulders. Also: greasing can, hoof oil, blacksmith's tools, spanner, studs, thread-cutter, spare shoes, hoof-picks, brake-blocks, traces, pole straps, hame strap, kidney-link, snaphooks, screwdriver, corkscrews, first-aid kit, stable rubbers, towels, chamois leather, sponge, brushing boots, bandages, veterinary box, buckets, candles and a quantity of rags.

All this is packed tidily in a suitably strong belly-band. For big horses, the side with the two purchasing a vehicle a traditional English car-

It is also advisable always to take a spare whip, preferably a jointed one.

The distance of the daily journey depends on the weight of the carriage (including the number of passengers), on the type of horses used and, of course, on the route, i.e. whether it is in flat or undulating country. The average speed is determined by the speed of the slowest horse in the team. At the walk the horses should move with a long, relaxed stride and the trot should be lively, but steady. A good average speed is approximately 12 kph (5 minutes per kilometre). If the horses start sweating and get out of breath the speed is too fast. Alternate between trot and walk. After an hour or so stop in a sheltered place and, particularly on very hot days, give them water and a little sugar or glucose.

When planning your daily distances do not be too ambitious. Study the map in great detail bearing in mind stabling and accommodation available. Make a thorough reconnaissance of the route; diversions, roadworks and even strong, head-on winds may throw overboard any plans you have made. At every halt check your horses' feet for stones, loose shoes, brushing marks, cuts etc.

When driving a four-in-hand, it may be possible that one horse needs nursing along. This can be done by adjusting the reins and thus distributing the load more evenly, or even by taking one horse completely out of draught. However, this can only be done in the wheel. Put the horse you want to nurse on the off-side of the pole where it has less to do – it is the nearside wheeler which has to pull the carriage back to the camber of the road after each 'giving-way'. To ensure that the off-side wheeler is only 'taken', loosen his pole chain or pole strap and adjust the coupling rein so that it is completely out of draught. This, however, will result in the carriage having a tendency to run to the off-side as the nearside wheeler is now pulling more. On the other hand, we do not want the nearside wheeler to have to straighten out the carriage from the pole strap; this would put too much pressure on his shoulders. The thoughtful and considerate driver will therefore take his leaders slightly to the nearside, but only enough to allow a little slack in the nearside pole strap or chain. Thus the leaders compensate for the one-sided pull of the pole. It is recommended to put brushing boots on the hind legs of the leaders even if they normally go without. Nursing one wheeler can also be done by moving its swingle bar one hand further to the outside – thus increasing the leverage. The other horse then will have to work more to keep the pole straight.

Study your horses in detail and you will know their capabilities. Spirited horses can do longer distances in a day than quiet ones. I would mention here the marathons arranged by the Aachen Horse Show. They used to cover approximately 180–200 kilometres in three days. Agreed, these were specific stamina tests, but one should expect to be able to do about 40–50 kilometres a day at a suitable speed with adequate stops.

I would also mention that a long-distance drive through quiet lanes in the country offers the best cure for ruined or highly-strung horses, and the best way of getting to know horses you have just acquired. With a sensitive and considerate hand, the horses will soon relax and accept the bit.

A considerate driver will always bit his horses as mildly as possible, particularly for long-distance driving. If this is not possible on the first day, it will become easier as the days go by. Never forget to talk to your horses. The influence of the human voice cannot be underestimated. Use the long-distance drive as an education for your horses. Teach them to follow the reins by alternately increasing and reducing the pace; give them variety and they will remain alert and follow your rein aids more attentively.

When driving in mountainous country it may be necessary to use the brake-shoe. This was dealt with in Chapter 20.

27

Types of Turnouts
and their Styles

Everything in life has reason, and no style has suddenly been invented; it has developed over the years from experience. The styles of the various countries must be viewed in this light. However, mixing traditional with novelty is most definitely not 'in style' and will be noticed immediately by any expert. No man with sense would wear a coloured waistcoat or a red tie with a tail-coat. It would be as ridiculous to mix Hungarian-type turnout with English-type.

Over the years, four types of turnout have emerged: the English, the American, the Hungarian and the Russian. Only these four will be discussed. Of course, depending upon the requirements, each of these styles has very plain and also very luxurious carriages and harness. All four were developed in times when horse-drawn transport dominated the roads, and cars were not even thought of.

Nobody knows what the future will bring to the roads, but the sport of driving will always remain. Ever since the horse has entered the service of man it has had its place; and it will retain its importance in riding and driving for pleasure.

With the changes in social structure in the world, it must be assumed that privately-owned 'Town Turnouts' will disappear and, should the odd one survive, will take on a much plainer look. Coachmens' liveries with top hats will no longer be seen and will be replaced by a more practical dress.

It would therefore be wrong to advise new driving enthusiasts to go in for a town turnout. Driving enthusiasts as well as their horses will enjoy driving in the country. The whole emphasis of driving will move out of the towns to country areas where there are breeders of good 'light horses', who will seek recognition of their work in competitive driving.

After this diversion, back to the various types of turnout.

28

The English Turnout

The English-style turnout is entirely based on practicality. 'Handsome is as handsome does', say the British. Harness, carriage fittings and accessories have been developed on that basis over decades. Other countries, with their craze for using novelties, have tried to make harness and build carriages, but still have not produced anything better. The carriages they built (particularly the French) were unnecessarily heavy, with the centre of gravity in the wrong place; the harness was extravagant and made of light-coloured and often even multi-coloured leather. On the other hand, the well-known English carriage-makers made theirs in the traditional style, as light as possible and with beautiful lines. The English harness-makers were also practical. They made all those parts of the harness which are susceptible to strain really strong. The collars, for instance, depending upon the purpose intended, were always made correctly shaped and were well-padded – they fitted the shape of the horse's neck. A good collar should fit closely round the horse's neck and, when in heavy draught, its front rim should not press on the horse's throat.

In the main, our German traces and reins are too weak, and the buckle-tongues are so thin that they tear the holes; back-bands and tugs for dogcarts are too light. For a heavy carriage, the wheel-trace must be approximately 43 mm. wide.

As far as harnessing-up is concerned, we in Germany tend to pull up both pole straps and traces too tight. The horses are thus fixed in a vice, which results in pressure and pain on the withers. The reason given is that this ensures

Full collars. Reading from left to right: correctly shaped English collar, incorrect German collar; anatomically right English pointed collar; German round collar

that the horses work more evenly. It is plainly obvious, however, that one cannot drive like that on a slippery road. Should one horse hang back and slip it is bound to fall down, because it is being pulled over by the other horse. The English, on the other hand, practical as ever, put to very loosely, and even a layman can see from the traces which horse does the work; he can also tell from the pole, because the pole always points to the lazy horse. A keen horse turns its nose towards the outside, whereas the nose of the lazy horse is turned towards the inside, i.e. the pole-head.

I would like to explain in detail why it is nonsense to put horses tightly to the carriage. Assuming we drive on a flat road with a good surface, where the carriage rolls of its own accord, there is no point in having the traces tight and giving the impression that the horses are in their collars. If driving a four-in-hand, why should the leaders pull when there is nothing to pull? Should the wheelers pull the carriage on top of themselves just to have the traces tight? How are the wheelers to stop the carriage when it is necessary to halt, if the leaders are pulling them? It is essential to put the horses to loosely, to be able to observe their work and the reaction of the carriage. It makes it possible to see whether the wheelers are in draught and when the leaders should share the work, for instance when going uphill with a fully-loaded carriage. Only then is it possible to drive well and with due care for your horses. They should be bitted as kindly as possible and the contact between horses and driver should not be heavier than the weight of the reins. The leaders should not be tied together, and the wheelers should be able to move freely between the traces and pole straps or chains when the carriage rolls along easily on the flat. With a six-in-hand the advantage of slack traces on wet tarmac is even more obvious. If the two lead pairs have tight traces, the poor wheelers have to hold back the carriage all the time, because the weight of eight traces, four bars, and the centre pole, are more than enough to keep even a loaded carriage on the move. Driving cor-rectly is only possible with loose traces and pole straps; anything else would be paradoxical.

Let us now consider correct harness in detail. English harness, whether it is used for a park, town, or country turnout usually has full collars. The principles of properly fitted harness have already been explained and the following will complement those explanations.

The Bridle

Although we in Germany do not encourage the use of bearing-reins, they are discussed here because they form an integral part of the English harness. The bridle as used for a town or park turnout consists of:

1. The Face-Piece. Its purpose is to give a uniform impression of the horses from the front if their face markings are not exactly alike. It covers up a white star or white hairs.
2. The Winker-stays. To serve their purpose best they should be forked and flat.
3. Rosettes or Bosses to hold crests or mono-grams.
4. The Browband. Shown in the sketch as made from patent leather, rolled at the top and the bottom to form a channel which holds the browband chain.
5. Winker-stay Buckle which connects the face-piece and the winker-stays to the crown or head-piece.
6. The Throatlash. This must be loose enough so as not to impede the horse's breathing. The buckles of the throatlash – for presen-tation reasons – should be at the same height as the buckles of the cheek pieces. If the throatlash is too short to achieve this, exchange it for a longer one. When driving a pair, ensure that the outside buckles of both throatlash and cheek piece are at the same height.
7. Winker or Blinker. The eye of the horse should be just above the centre of the winker, that is between the middle and upper third. The winker should fit square on to the cheek piece i.e. it should not be shaped, because the top corner could press

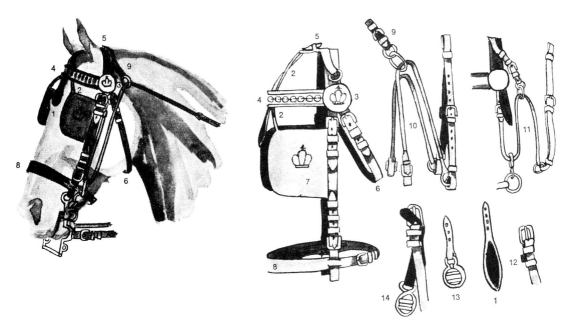

Correctly fitted English turnout bridle. Numbered parts are discussed in the text

on the horse's temple. If the winkers are not fitted correctly they can rub the eye which is very painful for the horse and has often been the cause of run-away turnouts.

8 The Noseband. It must be movable on the cheek piece, both up and down, because otherwise the bridle would not fit every horse. Its purpose is to hold the cheek piece close to the horse's head so that it cannot see behind the winker. The noseband should also stop the horse from opening its mouth. Horses which have adopted this habit are always very difficult. Correct adjustment of the noseband is of great importance for comfortable and pleasurable driving. The old-type nosebands, which do not slide up and down and are too wide, are useless and should be replaced or altered.

9 Bearing-Rein Drop. The very popular chain-type bearing-rein drops are, because of their length, ineffective in setting up a horse. They are out-dated and useless.

10 The Plain Bearing-Rein. The purpose of the bearing-reins is to set up a horse. They

should only be used by experienced drivers and are most suitable in the training of carriage horses. Their reason in farm turnouts is to prevent horses from eating during work.

11 The Pulley Bearing-Rein. Both bearing-reins use a bridoon snaffle which goes in the horse's mouth a little above the curb bit. The pulley bearing-rein has an additional narrower billet fitted into a point below the point of the throatlash, and thus does not show when the bearing-rein is not used; it is hidden in

12 a Keeper at the back of the throatlash.

13 Ring with two rollers to take the four-in-hand reins to stop the lead-reins from twisting. This ring or

14 Bridle terret is buckled from the rear into the buckle on the outside of the wheelers' throatlash. The lead-reins are put on the outside so that they shorten in a turn.

For some time, fashion has preferred rounded corners and lines on carriages and har-

111

Incorrect bridle — everything wrong and in bad style

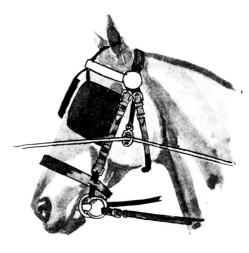

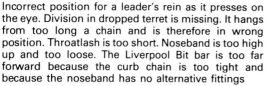

Incorrect position for a leader's rein as it presses on the eye. Division in dropped terret is missing. It hangs from too long a chain and is therefore in wrong position. Throatlash is too short. Noseband is too high up and too loose. The Liverpool Bit bar is too far forward because the curb chain is too tight and because the noseband has no alternative fittings

A well fitted bridle with correctly adjusted winkers. Dropped terret is properly buckled on. The noseband is fully adjustable, with three different adjustments on the inside — which assures proper pressure on the bit in the mouth

Noseband: (*left*) inside view with three different fittings for a cheekpiece; (*right*) outside for a modern noseband.

ness. Thus, winkers, buckles and browband chains have been rounded. As far as winkers are concerned, I would like to say a little more as there is so much nonsense said and written about them. Provided they are fitted correctly, winkers are a great safety precaution for carriage horses. For instance, suppose you have two horses of different temperaments, one keen and one lazy or nappy – if it is necessary to touch one up with the whip, without winkers it will see the whip coming and is likely to kick. The same applies with traffic coming from behind. Without winkers the horses get advance warning, shy, and probably do something like kicking. With winkers, the chances are that the traffic has passed the horse before the horse got a chance to do anything. Winkers also protect the eyes of the wheelers from the lead-reins. In addition, they ensure that a competent driver can touch any one of his horses with the whip

without the others even noticing it, and the pace and steadiness of the team does not become interrupted.

For the reasons explained above, expert driving and correct distribution of work (whether in double harness or with a four-in-hand) is impossible with blood horses unless they wear winkers.

As far as suitability and taste is concerned, if harness is properly cleaned, neither winkers, pads nor collars need be of patent leather. In fact, for a country turnout, patent leather is unsuitable with the exception, perhaps, of coloured, patent-leather browbands. In bad taste are winkers which have the inside lining made of yellow leather.

Let us now study in detail a set of traditional harness for a single horse, correctly made, giving the appropriate terms for each item and how to fit the harness properly.

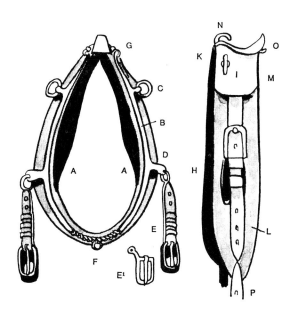

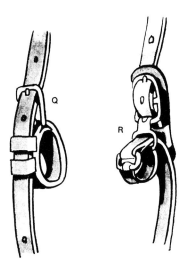

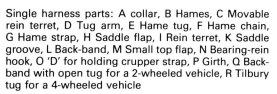

Single harness parts: A collar, B Hames, C Movable rein terret, D Tug arm, E Hame tug, F Hame chain, G Hame strap, H Saddle flap, I Rein terret, K Saddle groove, L Back-band, M Small top flap, N Bearing-rein hook, O 'D' for holding crupper strap, P Girth, Q Back-band with open tug for a 2-wheeled vehicle, R Tilbury tug for a 4-wheeled vehicle

113

1 Winker-stays.
2 Browband.
3 Winkers, well made and correctly fitting.
4 Noseband, again well made and properly fitted.
5 Elbow curb bit.
6 Cheek piece.
7 Sufficiently loose throatlash. Both the buckles of the throatlash and the cheek piece are level.
8 Hame strap. For a single they should be buckled from the left, i.e. the point of the hame strap should point to the right.
9 Hame with movable terret. The hame has a hook at the end to hold the hame chain.
10 Pad. This will be held in place by the back or crupper strap. It must not be allowed to slide up the horse's withers because, apart from being unsightly, it will cause soreness. If the pad is not in the correct position, shoulder and front of the horse are not shown to best advantage.
11 Hame Tug.
12 Tug for two-wheeled carriages.

13 Kicking strap. This should pass over the horse's loins; if it is too far back or too far forward it will not serve its purpose.
14 Crupper.

Brass fittings on harness are not only the most practical but also the most beautiful. Brass-mounted harness gives a much warmer impression than nickel, argentan or even silver.

In order to understand the importance of correctly putting to, let us now compare the foregoing example with that of a horse in single harness, badly put to. It is the classic example of how things should not be.
1 Head Terret. Only to be used with the wheel-set of a set of four-in-hand harness, and in any case now out of fashion. For single harness a head terret is superfluous and in bad taste. The crown piece of the bridle does not require decoration.
2 With a carriage horse the forelock should always be underneath the browband.
3 Rosette – should hold a crest or monogram which is its only purpose.

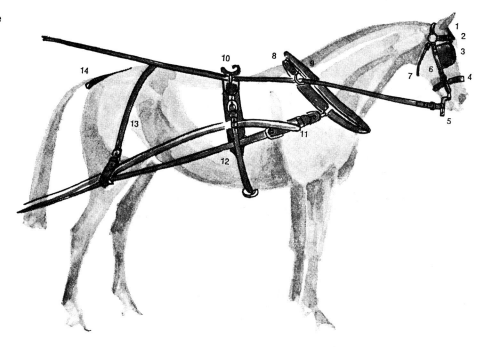

Horse in single harness. (See text for explanation)

4 Winkers – are much too high and would rub the horse's eye and temple.

5 The noseband – apart from being ugly, is incorrectly made and incorrectly fitted. It cannot move up or down, is much too big, and sits much too high.

As a result the bars of the bit are at an incorrect angle.

6 The bearing-rein as shown here is of no use whatsoever. In any case, bearing-reins are not used with breast-collar harness. The purpose of a bearing-rein is to set up a horse; it is of no use if the bearing-rein swivel is too low and the bearing-rein itself is too long.

7 The rein as shown here is pulled firstly under the bearing-rein, and then over it, before going through the terret on the pad. The turnout would be greatly improved if the bearing-rein was removed and the mane was pulled properly.

8 The reins should be spliced, not buckled, and should be made of brown or natural-coloured leather.

9 False martingale or breast-plate is useless with breast-collar harness.

10 The shafts are too long for the horse and bent too much; also the eyes and chains attached to the points of the shafts are incorrect, ugly and of no use.

11 The coloured under-pad serves no purpose and does not enhance the turnout.

12 For a two-wheeled vehicle, Tilbury tugs are incorrect; the tugs to be used should be strong, open tugs in which the shafts have some play. Tilbury tugs are used with four-wheeled vehicles.

13 The whole turnout looks untidy because all the points are too long. They should be shortened by a harness-maker. In addition, some keepers are missing, in particular on the girth and the belly-band.

14 Correct single harness should have a driving saddle. Furthermore, the breast collar is incorrectly made. It only requires a single neck strap, not a forked one. Also it is fitted too high and therefore presses on the wind-pipe of the horse.

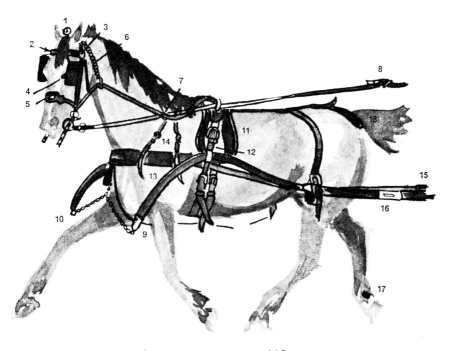

Single harness, with everything wrong! (See text for explanation)

15 The trace tug should be attached to the breast-piece, not at the end of the traces, which are at least one hole too short. As a result the saddle presses on to the withers rather than taking off the pressure.

16 The kicking-strap is pulled through the Dee which should be used for the breeching. It therefore lies too far forward. The Dee for the kicking-strap is further back on the shafts so that the kicking-strap passes over the horse's loins.

17 Brush or kick marks probably because the horse is badly shod.

18 The crupper should be sewn to the back-strap and the back-strap should be short enough to stop the saddle from slipping forward on to the horse's withers.

The breeching

Normally, a full breeching is not used for a single harness turnout. However, as there may be occasions when the use of a breeching is advisable, the various types are discussed as follows:

A – Breeching suitable for sporting vehicles when used for single harness, for instance dog-carts, tandem carts, gigs.

B – Full Breeching which combines the breeching with a kicking-strap. It is used for vehicles like a Coupé or a Victoria.

C – Kicking-strap.

D – Shaft-strap.

E – Back-strap.

F – Crupper.

G – Back-strap buckle.

H – Trace Carrier.

I – Decorated tandem shaft-strap, neither correct nor practical.

K – Breeching body.

L – Breeching strap.

There are a few general remarks which I would like to make. Hame top-eyes, hame draught-eye, and hame-clip should be made of steel or brass-plated steel – preferably steel, since brass-plating peels off when metal rubs on metal.

The saddle must be wide and well padded so

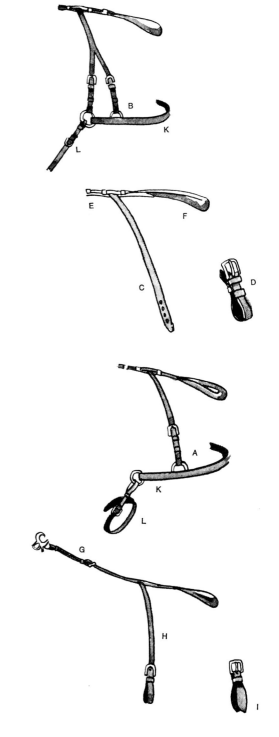

Different type of breeching

116

that pressure on the horse's withers is impossible. Even on a two-wheeled vehicle, if the shafts are very curved, Tilbury tugs may be used; however, for a dogcart, tandem cart or gig, open tugs should be used.

The buckle of the shaft-strap should be steel and then plated, not made solely of brass because solid brass buckles would bend. The purpose of the shaft-strap is to hold the traces close to the shafts.

The trace-tugs (hame-tugs) for single harness should be short, and the buckles should be in front of the saddle or pad. Traces should never be fixed to the hames and buckled at the end.

The following carriages are suitable for single harness:

Two-wheeled: dogcarts, gigs and Tilbury Gigs.

Four-wheeled: buggy, show wagon, Duc, Ladies Phaeton and Spider Phaeton (Duc or George IV Phaeton).

Coachman-driven: Victoria and Coupé or Brougham.

With two-wheeled vehicles it should be noted that it is better to have the shafts too wide than too narrow. From the pad (or saddle) to the point, the shafts should not be shaped too much; this is not only unsightly, but they also break easily should a horse fall. The point should be covered with either a brass or burnished steel cap. Never tip a two-wheeled carriage backwards for storage purposes, and ensure that the rear step never has a sharp point. The metal fittings on the shafts must always be safe; for instance, the shaft stops should not be screwed in, but welded and riveted on to a metal plate firmly secured on the shafts. The shafts should always have breeching Dees, either black or brass-plated. If a swingle tree is used, the best method of attaching this to the splinter bar is by leather straps. Two-wheeled vehicles ride more comfortably with high wheels and with the body of the vehicle close to the axle. The higher the seat above the axle the more difficult it is to keep the cart balanced. When putting to, ensure that the girth is tight but the belly-band comparatively loose so that the shafts have a certain amount of free movement in the tugs. A gig or Tilbury Gig is usually only well balanced with two people; if used by one person, the seat is lifted higher than normal to place a little more weight behind the axle. A two-wheeled vehicle is correctly balanced if, in motion, the tongues of the tug buckles 'float'.

With a two-wheeled vehicle, slightly sloping lines are preferred, i.e. the shafts should be at a slight angle (the lower point being nearer the carriage) when it is attached to the horse.

If at all possible, do not fit the whip socket to the dashboard.

With some dogcarts, balancing is achieved by moving the body on the undercarriage. They are fitted with four rails and the body is moved by turning a handle. The brakes of a dogcart should be so placed that they can be operated by the driver and not by the groom who sits behind.

Pair and Four-in-Hand harness

Always ensure that the hame straps can be adjusted from the outside; the same applies to the noseband. The bridle of a double harness is the same as that of a single harness, except that the rosette or boss should only be on the outside of the bridle. This ensures that the bridles do not get mixed up.

Let us look at this in more detail:

1 False martingale with drop, used for town harness. The drop usually carries a crest or monogram.
2 False martingale without drop suitable for sporting and country turnouts.
3 Hame tugs suitable for Pair and Team harness.
4 Tug buckle with pad-strap buckle.
5 Kidney link.
6 Kidney link ring.
7 False belly-band (strap and buckle).
8 Pad with girth and belly-band point for pair harness and the leaders of a four-in-hand.
9 Wheeler pad with centre terret, back-strap (buckled into a Dee on the pad), crupper strap and crupper. The crupper is sewn on to the crupper strap (not buckled).

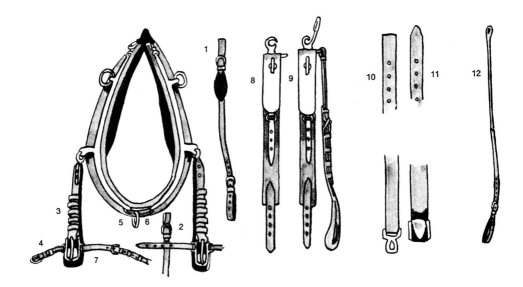

The right type of double harness – with a full collar

10 Inside lead-trace (straight) and steel cock-eye for a four-in-hand.

11 Outside trace of set of pair or wheeler harness and running-loop fitting (curved square metal fitting and tag).

12 Standing martingale used for horses which toss their heads. The girth passes through the loop; the martingale is then guided through the kidney link and finally fixed to the noseband.

The outside traces should always be made approximately 2 cm. longer than the inside traces because the inside traces run parallel to the pole, whereas the outside traces are always slightly at an angle, and thus cover a longer distance. With lead-traces, those on the outside should be 5 cm. longer. This stops the bars from hitting the main bar.

A correctly fitted double harness will consist of:

1 Well-fitted winkers.
2 Winker-stays.
3 Winker-stay buckle.

4 Rosette or boss.
5 Throatlash.
6 Cheek piece. With a pair, the buckles of cheek piece and throatlash should, at least on the outside, be level.
7 Curb bit.
8 Noseband. Correctly made and well fitted. To be buckled for the left-hand horse from the left and for the right-hand horse from the right, i.e. the points pointing to the inside.
9 Pole strap (for Gentleman or owner-driver, pole chains).
10 Pole head.
11 False Belly-Band.
12 Hame strap, correctly fastened, buckle end on the outside. This makes it easy to undo in an emergency.
13 Hame draught eye or anchor pull.
14 False martingale.
15 Hame tug.
16 Pad strap and buckle attached to the Dee on the hame-tug buckle.
17 Kidney link and kidney link ring.

118

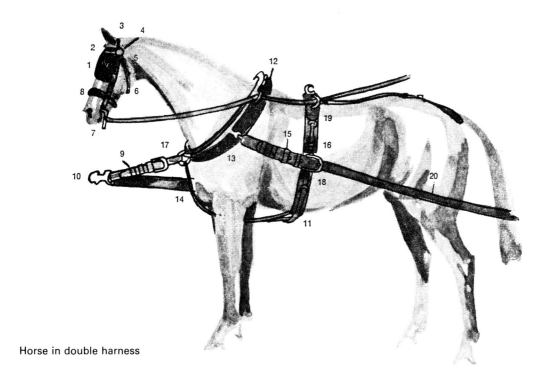

Horse in double harness

18 Point for false belly-band.
19 Pad.
20 Trace.

When ordering collars for a four-in-hand of medium-sized horses, 53–56 cm. collars would probably suffice. However, it is always advisable to get a harness-maker to take the correct measurements. Also order a number of kidney links in various sizes which allow collars to be slightly adjusted.

If, in addition, you have a few false collars, or collar pads, you are fitted for almost any eventuality. The false collar is fitted under the collar and secured by four straps. For single harness the kidney link is replaced by a hame chain. Hames that are hinged at the bottom are impractical – they cannot be adjusted; also, they can be dangerous because the hinge can become worn and work itself loose. The pad must fit the horse, otherwise it can slide forward and the girth will rub. The use of roebuck or sheepskin to overcome this is both unsightly and impractical.

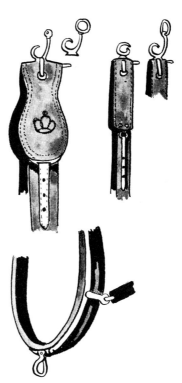

Pad Terrets. Hinged hames and an egg-shaped collar, not suitable

119

The bearing-rein hook on the centre of the pad should be fixed and not screwed into the pad; if it is screwed it will get worn and twisted, which is particularly dangerous if the centre terret is attached to it, as it could drop out quite easily, and then hang on the lead-rein.

It is suicidal to use a crab which can be screwed on to the pole-head. People use them because they are easy to remove when a carriage is used for both a pair and a four-in-hand. However, a pair can be put to a vehicle even if it has a four-in-hand crab. The crosshead of the pole-head should be free to turn upon the stem.

Collars used for horses pulling heavy loads like a coach or *char-à-banc* should have a groove at the bottom of the inside curve to take the billet of the false martingale which, for safety reasons, should be passed round the collar and then through the kidney link. It ensures that should the hame strap break, the hames do not fall off and the horse is still attached to the pole.

The hame clip should be visible on the outside hame tug to show off the brass, nickel or silver plating. However, it should be hidden in the inside hame tug and only the flat heads of the rivets should be showing. This has the advantage of making it quite easy to differentiate between inside and outside, even if belly-band and girth are buckled either side. It is uneconomical to have plated hame clips on both sides because the inside tugs can rub against each other, particularly with the leaders which are not separated by the pole, and the plating would peel off.

When cleaning collars, it is important that the hames are taken off. Then it can easily be seen whether the very important hame straps are still safe. Amongst other essential spares, each carriage should always carry a long, well-oiled hame strap with a large number of holes, and a rope, and both should be tied together with thin but strong string, which always comes in handy if something should break.

To ensure that the points of the false martingale and of the pad-strap stay in their keepers (these can easily come out), they are usually put

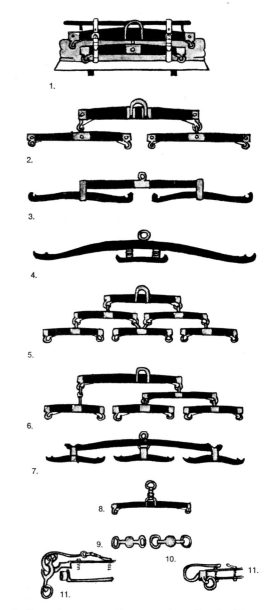

1. Spare bars correctly secured on Coach, (Char-a-banc and Mail Phaeton)
2. Lead bars, English style
3. Lead bars, Hungarian style
4. Lead bars for continental type Mail Coach
5. Suitable lead bars for Five-in-Hand Coach
6. Lead bars for Five-in-Hand Coach, not recommended
7. Lead bars for Five-in-Hand, Hungarian style
8. Lead bar for Unicorn
9. Pole end for pole strap
10. Pole end for pole chains
11. Pole crab for English turnout

120

The zig-zag line often seen with breast harness

A good straight line when English full collars are used

through full buckles compared to half-buckles used for every other part. It is also advisable to have five keepers on both the girth and the belly-band. For big horses, the side with the two keepers should be on the outside, and for small horses the side with the three keepers. This ensures that at least on the outside everything looks neat and tidy, and the points only just show from the last keeper.

With full-collar harness it is wrong to pull the girth between the hame-tug buckle and its leather underlay. Furthermore, if the harness fits, and is suitable, this is pointless because full-collar harness always has a belly-band. For slowing down and holding back the carriage, collar, back-band and false martingale are usually sufficient. Sometimes, because a horse has got too fat, the pad slides forward. Should this happen, it would be wrong to shorten the hame tug; it would be better to get a saddler to slightly widen the tree of the pad.

Hungarian harness does not use a belly-band or false belly-band and the hame-tug buckle has no Dee at the bottom. Regrettably, with Hungarian turnouts the horses are put to very tightly, which results in the pole being pulled upwards. In addition, the leaders are too much in draught and, therefore, continually pull the end of the pole downwards on to the neck and shoulders of the wheelers. This then pushes the tug buckles up, even if the girth strap has been pulled through between the tug buckle and the underlay. To give the impression that the direction of the draught is correct, a special strap is buckled into the tug buckles of the leaders. This prevents the breast collar from riding up and pressing on the leaders' windpipes. To help correct the 'zig-zag' line of draught, the four-in-hand crab is fixed underneath the pole.

If a Hungarian turnout is put to and driven correctly, the line of draught should not be broken, the leaders should never be in draught when there is nothing to pull, and the wheelers should work easily in their breast collars. To achieve this, the lead-reins must be buckled shorter than usual to the frog. If the girth, or back-band, has been pulled through the trace-buckle, the movable splinter bar of Hungarian vehicles, which is so practical, has no purpose whatsoever. The most important point of any turnout is that it must be both practical and correct.

Compare a Hungarian turnout with an English turnout which is correctly put to – provided the leaders are sufficiently big the line of draught is perfectly straight from the hame tug of the leaders via crab and pole to the axle.

When buying new, it is advisable to ensure that the splinter bar or the swingle trees – including the lead bars – are wide enough to protrude 5–10 cm. over the widest part of the vehicle. This is not only more comfortable for the horses, it also makes it easier for a beginner, as it gives him a guideline as to whether or not he is able to pass through a narrow gateway.

Wide splinter bars and lead bars, however, require traces of different lengths. With a fixed splinter bar, old traces will always tear on the outside, because in most cases the outside trace is not 2.5 cm. longer than the inside trace, and horses that go close to the pole are nearer the inside roller bolt than the outside one. The outside lead-traces should be 5 cm. longer than those on the inside. Because of the different lengths, it is important that the traces do not get mixed up. Therefore, it is advisable to have the inside trace blunt at the front and the outside trace pointed. For Hungarian harness, leather-covered rope traces are most suitable as they are the only ones which stay untwisted on the wooden swingle trees.

With English turnouts, all traces lie flat against the horse – the lead-traces as a result of the hame tug, the cock-eye, and the hook with safety spring on the bars (with a tandem the spring cock-eye), and the wheel traces to the fixed roller bolts.

Safe methods of fixing pole chains

For country turnouts, all steel parts such as chains and furniture on bars and pole, are painted black. However, spring cock-eyes, cock-eyes, and pole chains are polished. Always ensure the pole chain is fixed and secured.

The most suitable crupper straps, apart from those for the lead horse in a tandem, are those which have two means of adjustment. The top part of the back-strap is doubled (except for country harness), whereas the lower strap is made of single leather with a large number of holes. For the top part, one hole is sufficient which should be placed so that the point only just shows under the last keeper. This avoids the lead-rein getting caught. For the leader of a tandem, a martingale-type back-strap is more suitable because, even in turns, the reins cannot get caught. Cruppers which are buckled to the back-strap are not as practical because the tail hair can get caught in them; they also leave a mark at the root of the tail, which shows.

Some harness-makers fit pole straps which have a hinged tongue. I warn everybody not to use these. They can work loose and create highly dangerous situations. If a horse should fall, and the pole strap is too tight to be undone, there is no need to use a knife to cut the horse free. Unbuckle the hame strap and everything will come loose.

Different types of attachments for traces

122

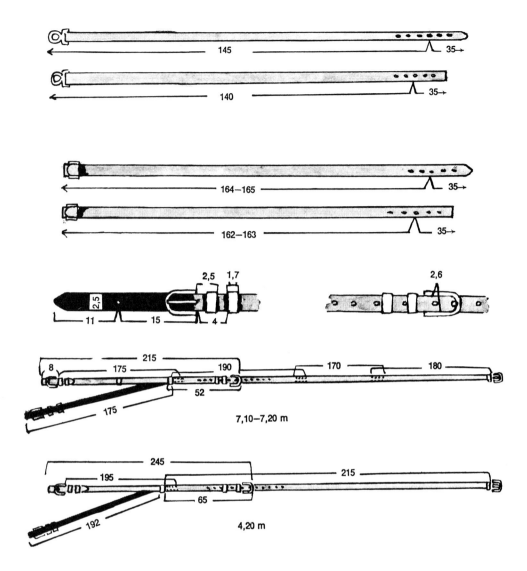

Measurements of traces and reins for tandems and four-in-hands. Note the inside trace is 5 cm. shorter than the outside trace, and also has a blunt end. Reading from the top: lead traces for an English turnout; wheel traces for roller bolts, outside and inside; lead rein with 11 holes distributed over 40 cm., total length of lead rein 7.10–7.20 m.; wheel rein with a total length of 4.20 m.

Following the above instructions will establish a certain good style. To complete the picture, make sure that everything matches. Rounded winkers, pads and buckles, for example, complement a carriage with rounded lines. Curved and square lines in one turnout are not 'stylish'. The same applies to the liveries etc. Brass-mounted harness should have brass buttons on the liveries; buckles and fittings should be of the same shape and material.

Nickel-plated steel fittings, argentan bits and curb chains are cover-ups and tempt staff to clean badly. They should therefore be avoided.

Hungarian-type harness (breast collars) on big, 'cold-blooded' horses is not good style. Bow-topped whips are unsuitable for a Hungarian turnout.

The 'driving crop' is of American origin and is only suitable for a long tailed horse put to a Trotting Sulky. Docked horses in English harness, even if driven to American vehicles, should always be driven with a bow-topped whip. The same applies to a two-wheeled vehicle. With very few exceptions two-wheeled vehicles are never put to in Hungarian or American style.

With curb bits, i.e. in English turnout, always use coupling reins. Hungarian turnout uses only snaffles and Hungarian ('Vienna') reins. For a pair of Trotters use English reins, if necessary with hand loops, which have buckles without pins.

For a German country turnout with breast collar use cross-reins.

Vehicles for English Turnout

Classical English pair carriages for the owner-driver are listed, from the heaviest to the lightest: Mail Phaeton (which can also be used for a four-in-hand); Demi-Mail Phaeton; Stanhope Phaeton; Spider Phaeton; four-wheeled dogcart. The choice of the carriage depends upon the type of horses available. Small horses of cob-type to a Mail Phaeton (this has a perch) are as unsuitable as Oldenburgers or large Hanoverians are for a Spider Phaeton – unless they are shown in a pair competition for

A bad turnout

'working harness horses' which is not judged on style of turnout. The principle must be that horses and carriage are in proportion. When purchasing a vehicle a traditional English carriage can hardly be bettered.

Study the accurate construction and beautiful lines of English carriages. Compare them with a bad turnout in which the box seat is too high. The driver would lose his balance if one of the horses were to stumble. He would require a safety belt. In the bad turnout above the browbands are as wide as halter browbands, and the horses are put to too tightly.

The ultimate carriage for a four-in-hand, English style, is the coach. Despite its height, it drives and rides extremely well because it runs, due to the solid under-carriage, very smoothly. Because it has such a limited lock the load will always be distributed over four points, lying far apart. This is not the case with vehicles which have a full lock – in a landau, for instance. In a sharp turn, a landau gives the impression that it is turning over, the reason being that, in the turn, the load is only supported in three places.

Britain has two types of coaches: the Road Coach and the Private Drag (Park Coach). They are basically the same except for the rear seats. On a Road Coach, where the seats could be booked, the rear seat is a large bench resting on solid wooden supports. The coach is painted in gay colours with the names of the first and last station of the route usually painted on it in large

Mr. James Robson driving his tandem in the dressage at Holker Hall, 1979

Mrs. C. Dick driving Mr. R. Wilcox's Tandem of Welsh Cobs

Mr. Joe Moore driving his team of Gelderlanders. This team was sold to the United States in 1980

Miss K. Bassett and her team of Skewbalds competing in a marathon

Colonel Sir John Miller, driving, with Colonel Sir Michael Ansell. At the invitation of H.R.H. The Duke of Edinburgh, Colonel Ansell drew up the first set of F.E.I. driving rules in 1970

Mr. John Parker driving the Norwich Union team of greys to a Demi-Mail Phaeton

letters. The Road Coach carries a guard who blows the horn to keep the road clear. With a Drag, there are seats for only two liveried grooms at the rear, and the head coachman blows the horn only when it is absolutely essential. The guard of a Road Coach stands up when blowing the horn whereas the coachman of a Drag or a *char-à-banc* remains seated.

With a four-in-hand the head coachman sits on the right, the groom or footman on the left. When the coach stops, both jump down; the coachman goes to the right-hand wheeler, the groom passes the horses on the left and stands in front of the leaders. If he has to hold the horses, they are held either at the cheek pieces or the cross-bar of the bits, never at the reins. When he is ready to move off, the driver signals with his head or by word of command, and the grooms acknowledge this by touching their hats. The driver should never move off without warning.

Before moving off, the head coachman, standing at the head of the right-hand wheeler, must check that the right-hand lead-rein is not lodged under the swingle bar, under the bar of a Liverpool bit or under the terret of the wheeler. The groom, passing along the left-hand side of the horses, checks on the left-hand side and then mounts the coach quietly and correctly at the same time as the coachman.

Other carriages correct and suitable for a four-in-hand are the *char-à-banc*, the Mail Phaeton, the Brake and the Wagonette.

The great advantage of carriages with a perch is that the pole always remains at the same height, namely 1.10 m. in front. It therefore never hits the wheelers if they are loosely put to. On carriages without a perch, the weight of the lead bars pushes the pole-head down. As a result the collars press on the top of the horses' necks and the lead bars can hit their front legs. The pin which fixes the pole to the carriage should be sewn to a piece of leather so that it cannot get lost.

I would like to mention here a few further details about putting to a four-in-hand.

When a four-in-hand is put to, the lead-reins should be secured to the outside hame terret. This is the safest method; even a horse harnessed up in the stables cannot step on the reins.

After the lead-reins have been pulled through the terrets and fitted to the outside of the bit, they are secured as follows: with the right hand, take hold of the rein above the coupling buckle and slide forward to the first rein splice. Follow with the left hand to about a hand's width from the right hand, and hold on to this point. The right hand then slides further forward towards the end of the rein to the next splice, which is placed on top

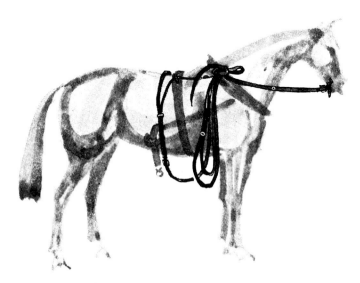

The way to secure reins when harnessing or unharnessing

of the first splice held in the left hand, making a large loop. The right hand then places a second loop of the same size into the left hand, so that there are three relatively thin layers of flexible leather in the hand. The right hand folds over this 'triple' rein and pushes it upwards through the hame terret. Then, with the right hand take the end of the rein and push it above the terret through the innermost layer. The rein is now firmly secured but can easily be removed. The same procedure is adopted when taking out the reins.

Always fasten the outside traces first. If the inside trace is attached first the horse can move away from the pole, which could break the back-band strap and the pad. The screw heads of lead-traces as well as the swingle bars must point upwards. This is a safety precaution since it becomes immediately obvious if a screw has worked loose. When buckling the traces, ensure that the inside traces are used only on the inside because they differ in length from those on the outside. It is therefore advisable to have the inside traces blunt at the front to make them more easily recognizable.

When putting to, make sure that the brake is locked so as to stop the carriage from moving and thus frightening the horses. Never tighten the pole chains by force or by lifting the pole. The wheelers must work, with correctly measured reins, in their proper places and must be able to move freely. The traces should be short, but not so short that the horses are too close to the footboard, because at a fast trot or canter they could hit the splinter bar, or even the wheels, with their hind legs. Always watch for this, especially if you do not know the vehicle and if the splinter bar is close to the wheels. Before moving off remember to check that all harness parts are correctly fitted, that the reins are properly pulled through and not twisted, and that bits and curb chains are placed as they should be for the individual horses.

Let us now turn to the tandem.

It is only possible to drive two horses, one behind the other, from a high cart, i.e. from a tandem cart, a gig, or a dogcart. With the last

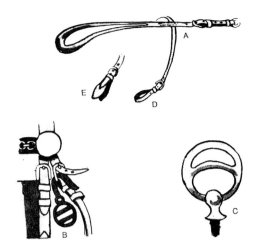

A Martingale-type crupper strap, B Tandem rein bridle terret, C Tandem rein pad terret, D Trace carrier, E Incorrect to have decoration on trace carrier

two, however, it is essential that they have high wheels. The tandem cart is of course the ideal cart for a tandem. It carries four people comfortably. For a stylish tandem the horses should have presence and action, good fronts, carry their ears well and have a high tail carriage. This is particularly important for the leader.

Now a few hints on harness and carriage.

The leader of a tandem should have a small 'saddle' without tugs. The crupper strap preferably should be a so-called 'martingale' crupper. The loin strap with the trace carriers lies just in front of the hip and is sewn to the back-band. The trace carriers are made like the end of a martingale so that the lead-rein cannot get caught.

The lead-rein is 7.20 m. long and made from four pieces spliced together.

The lead-traces are 3.30 m. long. The leader may go in a breast collar. This is particularly correct if he is driven in a snaffle. Using Buxton bits with a complete bearing-rein is very American. The bridle of the wheeler has terrets with two cross-pieces for the lead-reins. If the wheeler has a tendency to toss its head, it can be fixed with a breast-plate (martingale) that goes to the nose-band. This avoids jerking the leader in the mouth. However, this is only a temporary measure. Try to find the cause of the head tossing. It is often due to the bridle rubbing at the temples (winkers too high or too short). Also, if the lead-rein terrets are either *on* the boss, or just *below*, they can cause pressure-points as the reins run across the middle of the winkers, and, in turn, press against the outside eye.

The position of the terrets has changed over the years. The best method is to attach them with a small strap to the throatlash, buckled in from the back; do not buckle them to the cheek piece. The keepers should be big enough to hold two points.

The hame terrets must be movable and should lie flat; the saddle and tugs should be strong; the saddle cushion must be well padded and high and the tree chamber should be well away from the withers. The kicking strap or the cross of the breeching should lie behind the hip. The length of the wheel-traces depends on the type of cart used.

The hame-tug buckles have continuations with eyes pointing forward and downward where the lead-traces are hooked. The wide girth is lightly padded and has a loop through which the belly-band is guided. The belly-band should never be tight, or it may pinch. However, it must be especially strong and wide and must still slide easily in the saddle. Tugs, buckles and loops

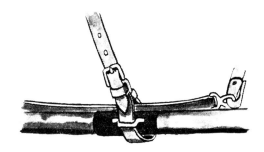

Attachment of kicking strap to shaft and wheel trace to bar

must also be strong. The terrets are shaped like a half moon so that the wheel-reins can be properly threaded through. In a pony tandem, both ponies are usually shown in breast collars.

A double bar may also be used with a tandem. This, however, requires a lot of cleaning work, and is, with well trained horses, unnecessary (although it is very good for uphill bends and very acute angles; downhill, it causes pressure on the withers). The lead bar measures 75 cm. and the other 55 cm. (the distance between the two, 12 cm.); the little chain measures 25 cm., the short traces with hook, 65 cm., the relevant lead-traces, 2.20 m.

Bars and fittings should be strong but as light as possible. The lead-traces are then ideally placed when turning; with the bar only attached to the centre of the travers, they lie adequately. Without a bar, however, they lie badly.

For tandem carts, 'Mail' axles are highly recommended because of their strong but narrow naves.

For safety reasons the following check-list is absolutely essential.

Examine and check the position of traces, bars, girths, reins, bits. Check wheels and axle stub ends; they must have a little play to be able to run freely and easily.

The whip socket should be either next to, or behind, the box seat cushion but never attached to the dashboard. If the driver wants to put the whip down he should not have to lean forward – he would not only lose contact with the horses but would also place too much weight on the

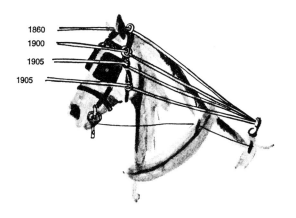

1860
1900
1905
1905

Differing positions of bridle terrets throughout the years

Types of carriages suitable for the owner to drive. Reading from left to right. *1st column*: Park Drag (four-in-hand) and Stanhope Phaeton (pair); *2nd column*: char-a-banc (four-in-hand) and Spider Phaeton (pair); *3rd column*: Brake (pair and four-in-hand); *4th column*: Mail Phaeton (pair and four-in-hand); *5th column*: Demi-Mail Phaeton (pair).

Types of carriages (*continued*). Reading from left to right. *1st column*: Ladies Phaeton (single and pair) and Gig (tandem and single); *2nd column*: Duc (single and pair) and Buggy (single); *3rd column*: Tandem Cart; *4th column*: Dogcart (tandem and single); *5th column*: Tilbury (tandem and single).

Types of coachman-driven carriages. Reading from left to right.
1st column: Omnibus (pair and four-in-hand); and Coupe d'Orsay (single and pair);
2nd column: Barouche (pair) and Coupé (single and pair);
3rd column: Landau (pair) and Victoria (single and pair).

forelegs of the wheeler. This could be dangerous on tarmac or on downhill roads.

A correct tandem cart should never have a rein bar, pneumatic tyres, a box-seat lamp or a rein-carrier. The handle of the brake must be handy for the driver; so must the attachment to adjust the seat, so that he can balance a front weight caused by braking, by moving back the box-seat. When driving down a very steep hill it is easiest to balance the vehicle by getting the groom to stand on the rear step. This gives sufficient weight to the back to allow hard braking without putting the weight on the wheeler.

Whether driving a four-in-hand, a pair, a single or a tandem, the Gentleman driver should always wear an apron. This protects the clothes from the reins which hang down on the left-hand side. In the summer the apron can be of light, or covert-coat, material. In autumn and winter a warm blanket should be used.

And what about suitable harness-makers? Correct, and in accordance with modern requirements, harness was supplied by companies which followed the Achenbach principle.

29

American Turnout

In general it can be said that the American turnout has developed from the English style. However, harness and vehicles have so many typical American attributes, that an 'American style' must be recognized.

This style is considerably influenced by the American Trotting sport. No vehicles are lighter, and no harness is thinner or more simple, than the genuine American ones. A long-tailed 'Roadster' horse with very light harness, put to a Buckboard, Runabout, Road Cart or Rockaway, four- or six-seater, shows the characteristics most clearly.

Hackney pony to a show wagon

The lightness of American carriages results from the very light hickory wood which is used to build them.

For tandems and four-in-hands, the Americans drive English fashion. However, there is a typical American style of driving for singles and pairs. The reins cross in the upright left hand, the right-hand rein runs downwards and the left-hand rein upwards. When driving a roadster the right hand takes the right-hand rein either between index and middle fingers or with the whole of the right hand.

The driving crop is used only with the pure American turnout. With an English turnout the bow-topped whip is used.

Availability of suitable horses is one of the basic conditions for driving, and America has breeds of horses which are equivalent to the superb English breeds. The American hackney can match the English hackney for excellent action.

Typical of the American turnout is the pole strap in the form of a 'Jocke' – yoke. With their very light vehicles and harness the Americans use very light collars, especially for shows. They make the horses' fronts appear longer, being very narrow and cut very far back at the top. This, however, makes them prone to pressing on the withers.

30

The Russian Turnout

The traditional Russian style of harness differs considerably from that of the West. Although in earlier days, foreigners living in the large cities of the vast Russian Empire brought English and Hungarian turnouts into the country, neither made any impression on the tradition-conscious Russian people. It can therefore be assumed that the typical Russian turnout has been retained in the country to this day.

Before the First World War one occasionally saw Russian turnouts belonging to Russian diplomats in Berlin or, in the big German Spas, turnouts belonging to wealthy Russian visitors.

The Russians differentiate between plain harness – only small amounts of metal furniture with the round undecorated 'duga' (central wooden arch) – and the traditionally richly-decorated Troika harness (Jamtschik), used with the wide, metal-studded duga. With owner-driven carriages, the coachman always sits next to the master.

In Russia, cruppers and crupper straps are not used; tails are not pulled, but are allowed to grow full and wide. The old Russian turnout consists of four types: a single; a single with a 'Galopin' on the left-hand side like a Troika, which only adds the right-hand horse; the Troika; and the tandem, which is only used in the country.

In our opinion, Russian carriages and sleighs are small compared to the very well-fed horses and rather portly coachman which accompany them. It is the pride of the Russian to see his stallions fat and fiery, and they always look as if they could go much faster with their light load, if only the coachman would let them. The harness has no winkers. The horses of the gentry very

rarely walk; they are allowed to jog – it makes them look more fiery.

The reins are held with arms stretched out, thumbs upwards, and are very often twisted round the hands. Although whips, and hitting the horses with the metal buttons of the reins (where leather and hemp join), are prohibited, the metal buttons are still sometimes used to urge on the horses.

Singles and pairs driven 'Russian Style' are always at the trot. The Troika has a trotter in the centre, with a 'Galopin' on either side. Most descriptions of this turnout refer to the 'heavily tied-back Galopins'. However, this is not quite correct. The driver of a Troika holds four individual reins in his hands. The trotter obviously has its right-hand and left-hand reins. The 'Galopins' are tied by means of thin straps (buckled through both snaffle rings) to the junction of shaft and duga. The 'Galopins' have only one rein (on the outside), and they turn their heads as far to the outside as the tie-straps allow. The right-hand 'Galopin' goes at a right-hand canter, and the left-hand 'Galopin' at a left-hand canter. The driver holds the two right-hand reins in his right hand and the left-hand reins in his left hand. Basically, only the trotter is driven; the 'Galopins' follow their contact with the tie-strap. The 'Galopins' should carry their heads low, whereas the head of the trotter is set high with a rein which runs through a ring at the top of the duga. The traditional Russian harness has practically no buckles. The straps are wrapped round the shafts and the duga, and the ends, tapering down to laces, are pushed under the last four wrappers. The harness of the trotter has no traces. Collar, duga and shafts are 'connected' in the real meaning of the word. The strap running from the axle to the point of the shaft might be a type of trace. The classical bit is the snaffle with flat, usually plated, rings. The Russian whip is very similar to a hunting crop. If it is carried at all, it hangs over the right arm.

The Jamtschik turnout is very colourful.

31

The Hungarian Turnout

The English normally use four horses only for big and heavy carriages, and only put horses to as a four which have been well trained in double harness. In coaching days, teams of four were the means of transport on the many good routes in Britain. Now, four-in-hands are no longer used for this purpose but merely for pleasure. In Hungary, however, four-in-hands are innumerable and they are nearly always driven to very light carriages. This is necessary because of the 'heavy going' in many parts of the Hungarian terrain – either the sand is so deep that two horses cannot manage, or clay sticks to the wheels after a heavy rainfall, and again makes the carriage too heavy for a pair. However, if one drives a Hungarian four-in-hand on a good road it can trot for hours, and can be difficult to hold back. With English harness, of course, horses are bitted with curbs and possibly also with a bridoon, so they will hardly try to pull the reins out of the driver's hands; Hungarian blood horses, on the other hand, are bitted only with snaffles.

Since a four-in-hand is a necessity in the Hungarian terrain, it is often unavoidable putting horses together which are of different temperaments and varying characters. They are, however, always bitted with snaffles even though one or two horses may be particularly high-spirited or bad in the mouth, may throw their heads about and try to pull the reins out of the driver's hands. Under such circumstances it is extremely difficult to hold four individual reins, and have to gather them up to the right length, at the same time holding the horses together. For this reason, Hungarian reins are buckled together with a so-called 'frog' (a hand-piece buckled between the reins). It also explains why the English style of 'four-in-hand' driving could never catch on in Hungary.

The basic 'Hungarian Style' position is to hold the reins with the left hand in the centre of this hand-piece. To make a right- or left-hand turn, the hand holds on to either the right-hand or the left-hand side of the hand-piece – depending upon the turn, pulling one side back and thus releasing the other side, but the releasing should be greater than the pulling. The principle is in fact similar to Achenbach's method, namely to drive a turn by 'giving' the outside rein.

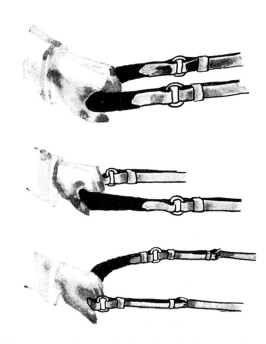

Hungarian method of driving. Reading from top. Basic position; left-hand turn; right-hand turn

134

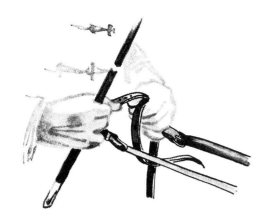

Hungarian style – basic position

When driving a four-in-hand the lead-reins are buckled to this hand-piece. To drive a left-hand turn, the hand-piece is taken in the right hand, the left hand loops the left-hand lead-rein, and at the same time, shortens the right-hand wheel-rein. For a right-hand turn, the hand-piece remains in the left hand and the loops are made with the right hand.

From the standard position all points are made. It would take too long to explain all of them in detail in this chapter. I only wanted to mention the main characteristics. A great advantage of the 'frog' is that the reins can be adjusted from the box seat. However, the adjustment is more complicated than with the Achenbach reins.

In contrast to the English turnout, personal taste has no limitations either in respect of harness or in the dress of the coachman – providing the Hungarian characteristics are maintained.

The influence of personal taste shows particularly in Hungarian gala costume. Whereas in other European countries, for instance for official state receptions, the dress is laid down for the respective occasion and alterations are not possible, the Hungarian gala costume is not bound by any rules, but is left to individual taste. At the same time, descending from a democratic-aristocratic instinct, it does not allow a display of rank. The most important factor is that colour, cut and style of the individual livery must show the characteristics of

Hungarian tradition – this requires a knowledge of styles covering four centuries which must not be mixed up. (The same applies to the selection of the coachman's uniform.)

Likewise, there is no limitation to personal taste in harness. Every owner is interested in the design and decoration of his riding and driving equipment. Typical are the 'Sallangs' and the 'Pillangos'. Sallangs are plaited decorations of many shapes, originally designed as a protection against flies and midges, but later made in such marvellous patterns that they became the typical decoration for all Hungarian harness. The Pillangos (butterflies) are made from coloured cloth and further decorate the harness. For four-, five- or seven-in-hands, open bells with a striker (not closed bells) are attached to the outside trace buckle, or one larger bell is tied round the neck of the right-hand leader.

As regards colour combinations, the coachman's uniform matches the harness decorations and the costume colours of the owner. The coachman's raincoat is the so-called 'Szürss' which has a richly-embroidered back part in the

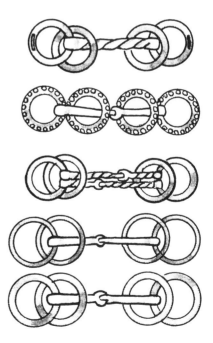

Hungarian snaffle bits

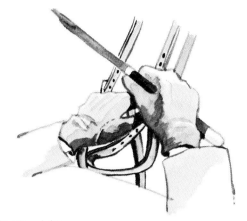

Turning right

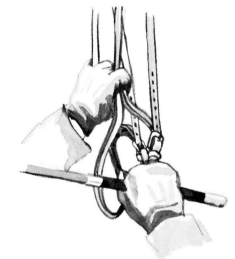

Left turn with counter resistance

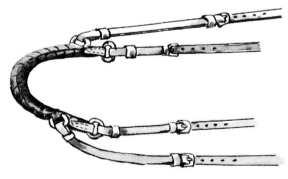

Four-in-Hand reins with hand part. Reading from top. Left lead-rein; left wheel rein; right lead-rein; right wheel-rein

colours of the owner. When used, this back part hangs down over the rear of the box seat as a type of decoration. In the winter, Hungarian furs and fur hats in the same colours are worn, with cord trimmings and embellishments.

Hungarian teams are always bitted with four-ring snaffles. The rings are smooth if the harness fittings are smooth, and notched if the harness fittings are notched.

The Hungarian whip is a straight stick; an English bow-topped whip or a German cane whip are not considered correct.

The light vehicle for fast driving on bad roads is a Hungarian invention and the 'Kocsi' is derived from the Hungarian village, Kocs, where this type of carriage was made. The name 'Kocsi' occurs in every European language: German 'Kutsche', English 'Coach', French 'Coche', Spanish 'Coche', Swedish 'Kush', Italian 'Cocci', Polish 'Kocz', etc. The word had already appeared in the Hungarian language by the fifteenth century, whereas in other European countries it had not appeared until the sixteenth century.

All Hungarian carriages are made much lighter than those built in England, Germany or, particularly, in France.

For driving in town, horses of the same colour and height are preferred and they should match in conformation. In the country very often contrasting colours are used, like greys and chestnuts or greys and blacks. They are put to crosswise, with the strongest horse – as in Germany – in the right-hand wheel. In Britain the biggest horse is the left-hand wheeler, as the British drive on the left-hand side of the road.

Manes and tails are trimmed, but left full, and the manes are brushed to the outside. Hogged manes are not Hungarian style as they contradict the intention of protecting the horses from flies. This also explains why tails are never docked, but left as long as possible and feathered at the end to a point.

The pace of a Hungarian turnout is the trot, not the canter, but it is always driven at speed.

32

Country Turnout

This chapter will be of interest to farmers and breeders who not only use their teams daily, but wish to compete with them at horse shows in 'Working' competitions. In these classes the turnout, i.e. vehicle and harness, is of lesser importance, although there are sometimes special prizes for the most correct turnout. Hence the following explanations which will show how such horses should be turned out. The aim is to eliminate everything that serves no particular purpose.

Anybody who studies the country turnout in detail will already see from the above whether or not his team fits into this category. Refer also to Chapter 23.

As far as training is concerned, there is no difference between town and country turnout, but it is recommended you refer back to Chapter 21.

What requirements should be fulfilled by a country turnout? There are no firm rules; your aims must be based on the fact that the turnout should be able to go anywhere, taking into consideration that which is customary for the area, and what the competitor has available. Therefore, he need not buy anything new for a show. He should turn out his team as well and as accurately as possible within his limits. He should check his equipment for bad faults and remedy these. He should concentrate on seeing that everything matches and that the general picture looks good.

Cleanliness and tidiness are the first and foremost demands. The horses must be spotless; manes, tails, and shoes in first-class condition; every part of the harness must be clean and safe to use. All metal parts must be either well

varnished or polished, whether buckles, carriage parts or livery buttons. The carriage must be clean and well-greased. The brake, if there is one, should function; the cushions should be brushed and the driver himself be clean and tidy – this obviously means that he must be clean-shaven. Naturally, in bad weather, dirty wheels and mud splashes are unavoidable, but it will be

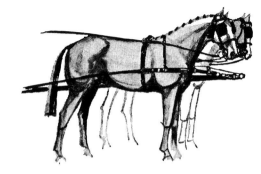

Correct country turnout for a pair with breast

Incorrect turnout for country – too smart with full patent leather collars and crests on winkers

obvious whether or not the vehicle was clean originally. In 'Working' competitions the horses play the most important and decisive part. Their conformation, action and training – and, for a pair or four-in-hand, the matching – must be of first consideration. If competing turnouts are equally good, the horses are the deciding factor. However, if serious mistakes have been made in the turnout, this shows in the marks for 'turning out of horses and carriage'.

The harness must fit the horses, and must be fitted correctly. What this implies has been explained in detail in previous chapters.

Well-fitting full-collar harness is always preferable to breast-collar harness. It can be used with any carriage, and the full collar makes the draught easier for the horse because it lies on a part of the body where there are no joints or movable bones. The breast collar never lies in such a favourable position and it hinders the horse in its movement. Breast collars may be used with light vehicles (not with six-seaters) and light, small horses. For horses of coaching type and for heavy vehicles, breast collars are not considered correct. Full-collar harness must always have curb bits. If the unbroken mouthpiece is not wanted, curb bits with broken mouthpieces are obtainable which, when buckled plain cheek, have the same effect as a snaffle. With country turnouts leather pole straps are correct.

Movable bars are always preferable for country turnouts. With full collars, fixed roller bolts are permissible but they would be wrong with breast collars as their rigidity would result in sore chests. Most country vehicles have bars attached to a movable main bar (swingle bar). I do not completely disapprove of this, because they distribute the load of the vehicle evenly over the two horses on heavy tracks, and, with 'sleeping' drivers, prevent a keen horse '-ploughing' the road with the front wheels. When used at a show on firm ground, however, 'swingle bars' should be fixed with straps so that they only move very little.

With single harness, the kicking strap is essential, and with heavy carriages without brakes a breeching is a must. With four-wheeled vehicles, iron tugs (Tilbury Tugs) are used with which the shafts can be firmly buckled to the wide single-harness pad. With two-wheeled vehicles, oval-shaped leather tugs (London Tugs) are used to take the shafts of a well balanced vehicle.

For a country turnout any vehicle may be used which fits the size of the horses and is suitable for tracks with heavy going and deep ruts. This last demand, therefore, excludes vehicles with rubber tyres because they grind through heavy going and make it harder work for the horses. Besides, the rubber suffers on such bad tracks and for this reason is unsuitable.

The most practical vehicles are those which run as easily as possible, namely with high wheels and short bodies. For long carriages a 'perch' is desirable. The box seat should not be too low because it is difficult to drive from a low seat. The higher the driver sits above the horses, the better he can survey the road and control his team. With low vehicles it is difficult to look over the horses. Besides, the reins are nearly horizontal, can touch the horses' backs, and can get caught under their tails.

The advantage of high wheels is the accompanying higher driving seat; the disadvantage, that they make mounting more difficult. However, this is more than compensated for, as they considerably ease the load for the horses.

The same applies to carriages with a perch. They run much more easily because the flexibility of the carriage springs is isolated from the draught. Although the perch prevents very sharp turns, a good driver can overcome this by turning with a rein-back.

When judging a vehicle, of first and foremost importance is its suitability for country driving; then the quality, and finally its looks. The German 'Jagdwagen' is almost always suitable. Even more so is the Hungarian Esterhazy Wagon, which is also built with a hood that can be moved to cover either the front or the rear seats. Also very suitable is the wagonette, or brake. Before the war, light, high-wheeled vehicles made of hickory wood were imported

Carriages suitable for driving in the country. Reading from left to right. *1st column*: Varnished dogcart (two or four horses), Jucker wagon (two, four or five horses), Stanhope Phaeton (two horses); *2nd column*: Esterhazy wagon (two, four or five horses), Pursch wagon (two horses), Vis-à-vis (two horses); *3rd column*: Country Vis-à-vis (two or four horses), Jagdwagon (two horses), Governess cart (single pony); *4th column*: Landrats wagon (two horses), Landaulet (single or pair), Country dogcart (single horse)

from America. These were copied in Germany and used in the country. Because of their lightness and suitability of design, they are highly recommended, and one can overlook the disadvantage of the low seat and the difficult mounting. A landau, because of its length, is heavy, and is therefore not recommended for country roads.

Many other things must also be taken into consideration; for instance, whether a four-seater is adequate, or whether it would be better to choose a six-seater which means it becomes longer, bigger and therefore heavier.

The 'Achenbach Wagon', built by Zimmermann of Potsdam, has a brake which is easy to operate; comfortable wide steps; doors that prevent things from falling out, open easily and, in winter, keep out draughts. It can seat four to six people, is of natural wood, with whipcord or moquette trim.

If the 'Achenbach Wagon' is used with a four-in-hand, or with very big horses, it is advisable to have a special cushion made to raise the driver's seat. For trimming, a sand-coloured whipcord or melton cloth is preferable to moquette.

Whipcord trim or melton cloth complement natural wood. Any mixing is in bad taste; for example – natural wood and coloured panels on one vehicle; natural wood and very dark or very light trim; or painted vehicles and whipcord trim. Practical and inexpensive are: panels and floor of poplar wood; supports and joists of beech wood; wheels, axle, splinter bar, bars and pole of ash; mudguard and dashboard of poplar or ash; rear and front full elliptic springs.

"Achenbach" shooting wagon

The above advice, which applies to pair-horse vehicles, naturally applies also to those for a single or a four-in-hand. High wheels, which ease the draught, are even more essential for vehicles used with a single horse than for those used with a pair. Four-wheeled vehicles particularly, when used with a single horse, must be light and run easily. Two-wheeled vehicles must be so well-balanced that the shafts can be held horizontally with ease. Correctly put to, the shafts should be horizontal and not point downwards. A slightly upwards pointing position is not too bad; with a gig loaded with only one person, it is difficult to avoid.

To produce a four-in-hand in country style, ensure that the box seat is high enough and that the vehicle does not appear too small behind the horses. High hunting carts and wagonettes are suitable, and for Jucker type, also the Esterhazy Wagon. A coachman may also use an Omnibus.

The dress of the driver must conform to the vehicle and harness. With a Phaeton, the Gentleman driver may wear a black coat and black hat, although with a country turnout, an ordinary tweed suit and soft hat looks more correct. Lady drivers should wear neat, tailored clothes and small hats. Brown leather gloves should always be worn when driving.

A turnout must always be accompanied by a coachman or groom (clean-shaven). If he wears livery it must be correct.

If a country riding-and-driving club exhibits turnouts made up from horses belonging to its members, say a four-in-hand, there is no objection to driver and grooms wearing the club uniform – for instance, hunting cap, dark jacket, and white breeches with boots. Of course, everything else must conform.

The most suitable dress for the grooms is always stable livery, i.e. jacket and trousers, or breeches and leggings, either in a dark-coloured material, or else a pepper-and-salt coloured tweed, with ordinary bone buttons – never with silver or brass buttons – and with a collar and tie. The hat should be a bowler, or a cap of the same colour as the suit.

The driver is seated on the right-hand side

with the groom beside him. On carriages with back seats (rumble seats) and those which have front and rear seats, the groom sits in the centre of the rear seat. He should sit upright but not stiff, with his hands on his thighs and not with his arms crossed. At the halt, the groom stands in front of the horses.

In the handling of the reins, the Achenbach system applies.

With breast-collar harness the Hungarian Jucker whip should be used, and with full-collar harness the English bow-topped whip.

At a show, the Jury is also required to judge a turnout's uniformity of style. With a country turnout, the best is always the most suitable for the purpose for which it is used. This viewpoint has been explained before; it does not concern luxury turnouts, but those used daily. Apart from the suitability, it is of course important that correct fitting and condition create a good general impression. The horses must be well trained and fulfil any demands which justifiably may be expected. For a four-in-hand, the horses should match and work together evenly and nicely, with correct head positioning. The trot should be 'ground-covering' and the extended trot should show an energetic forward trend.

As driving is likely to centre more and more in the country, it would be advisable, when purchasing, to look for a correct country turnout.

33

General Aspects on the Putting To of a Nobleman's Turnout

(Original text of Achenbach)

The most usual varieties of turnouts are:

1 English, 2 American, 3 Hungarian, 4 Russian.

Each has different attributes (trimmings) depending upon place and time; (comparison: state dress, town suit, sporting outfit).

In order to achieve an attractive overall picture, it is recommended to assemble a nobleman's turnout by following the established precedents.

Mixing the different styles can never produce a good overall picture – the differences between them being: State; Semi-State; Town; Park; and country turnout.

For State and Semi-State turnouts, both the American and the Jucker style are unsuitable because carriages, horses and harness are too light, and therefore would look out of place on ceremonial occasions.

For full State turnout, plain-coloured, (i.e. grey, black, or bay) coach-horses of the heaviest type with proper long tails should be used (Coronation carriages and State carriages are exemplary in London and Vienna).

State and semi-state turnout

For these, either a pair, a four-, six- or an eight-in-hand is driven from the saddle (postillion) when the carriage has no box seat. With a box-seat, a pair, or a four-in-hand; a six- or eight-in-hand is driven from the box but with a postillion rider on the left-hand leader. A Semi-State turnout may use a six-in-hand with a postillion rider on the left-hand leader, and one on the wheeler (who drives the middle horses with long reins) or else with a postillion rider on each of the left-hand horses.

Postillion riders' saddles should be without knee rolls, should have black girths, and stirrup leathers under the saddle flaps. The right-hand horses have driving saddles (not pads) with bearing-rein hooks but no terrets, and the hames of the ridden horses and their respective lead horses have no hame terrets either. If each left-hand horse is ridden, only long traces are used.

However, if one or more of the horses are driven from the box seat, or the centre horses of a six-in-hand are driven by a postillion rider, then the pair in front of the wheelers is attached to swingle bars (with polished metal fittings) which consist of one main bar and two bars. Only with a mail turnout with rope traces is the lead bar in one piece.

The horses of the out-riders in front wear driving bridles, crupper straps, and matching breast-plates; the horse of the 'Pikor' (the first of the out-riders) should have an ornate riding bridle.

The postillion riders carry riding crops pointing left upwards. The out-riders' hunting whips are carried on the right-hand side pointing down, with the end of the unfurled whip in the right hand.

Town or park turnouts

1 Victoria, Vis-à-Vis, Barouche, Landau are driven by a coachman from the box seat, or by a postillion rider. For C–sprung vehicles, long-tailed horses are used, and a footman (house servant), not a groom, accompanies the turnout. Jucker Teams: Victoria or Coupé, either Hungarian or English livery with very light full-collar harness.

2 Owner-driven: Mail Phaeton, Demi-Mail Phaeton; Stanhope Phaeton; Spider Phaeton; Lady's Phaeton; Duc, Drag; *char-à-bancs*; Tandem; Gig; Buggy (American four-wheeler) etc. Jucker Teams: a pair, four- or five-in-hand, to an Esterhazy or Cziraki Wagon etc.

The Gentleman driver does not wear a double-breasted morning coat or white gloves.

Country teams

All country vehicles: brakes, wagonettes, runabouts, tandems, dogcarts, road cart, hunting cart, omnibus.

Assembling a nobleman's turnout

When producing a nobleman's turnout, the horses are usually the most expensive and difficult items to obtain. Carriages, harness and liveries cost the same whether they are of the right type and correct, or in bad taste. If they are well made and looked after properly they last for a long time. Therefore only buy 'style' and good quality.

On a good, stylish nobleman's turnout nothing should be fake – for instance, no false hub caps; no faked C–springs; no front boot with blind buckles (which can neither be opened nor closed) on carriages without a box seat; no imitation leather boot-tops made of plastic; or, in place of well-polished livery boots, those made of patent leather; no white linen or cloth breeches (instead of buckskin), with fake buttons. Neither should bits, pole fittings, chains, bar fittings be chromium-plated to cover up bad cleaning; they should all be polished steel.

Only for State harness should pole-hooks, pole-ends and fittings be silver- or gold-plated;

for all other town or park carriages, owner or coachman driven, they are made of polished (burnished) steel. For simple closed town or country carriages, such as landaus or coupés, black-painted pole fittings are preferred. This applies for every country turnout whether English, German, Hungarian, American or Russian.

The lines of carriage and harness should match, both either being rounded or square. Carriage fittings, harness and livery fittings should be either all brass-coloured or all silver-coloured. A combination of gold-plating and nickel, for example, would be undesirable.

For town and park carriages which require 'town' (promenade) dress: black brass – or – silver-mounted harness. Collar, pad, cushion and inside of the winkers should be black.

For country turnouts both German and English, brown full-collar harness is permissible (but not practical), particularly with natural wood vehicles.

Noblemen's turnouts

(a) The Coachman: good position on the box seat. Grooms' arms not crossed. For English turnout: handling of whip and reins English fashion; correct, fluent driving; livery to suit the turnout; coachman and groom to be clean-shaven.

(b) The turnout: vehicles and harness need not be new, but with good care and maintenance they must make a thoroughly grand impression. This also applies to the livery.

The horses should have good action, match in action and conformation, and work evenly as if they all had the same keenness. Any unevenness of work should not be covered up by traces that are too tight; on the contrary, even at the halt, the collars should lie flat against the shoulders, and due to correct adjustment of the reins at the coupling, the horses should all be evenly in draught. They must also suit the carriage in size and type. For instance, two Juckers (blood horses) should not be put to a landau, nor two heavy coach-horses to a light, owner-driven carriage. Docked horses are wrong for a Troika, and typical Russian horses do not suit the English turnout. Hunters may be used (docked or with long tails) for a coach, a tandem and a phaeton, but never *heavy* coach-horses. Manes should be brushed over to the right-hand side.

(c) Harness: breast collars are used only for full ceremonial state turnouts, for Jucker or American turnouts, for the leader of a tandem, and for ponies. Otherwise full-collar harness of suitable strength should be used.

For single harness: saddle with kicking strap, or for heavy vehicles, with breeching. Winkers are essential and should not be shaped. Driving snaffles only to be used with breast-collar harness. Trace buckles must be attached to trace tugs, not to the end of the traces. On bridles with curb bits, the cheek pieces must go through the noseband in order to allow adjustment if the bit is placed either higher or lower.

Cruppers without buckles are always preferable because they prevent bare patches, and the tail hairs do not get caught in them.

The hame terrets must always be movable and lie against the collar, particularly for pairs, four-in-hands etc., and tandems. With a single, this is not so important. The hame-strap buckle must be on the inside. For owner-driven carriages English-style, use polished pole chains with oval links. One end of the pole chain has a ring and the other a simple snap hook. The length of the chain is 90–95 cm. With all other teams (this also applies to country turnouts in England) a leather pole strap is used, the exception being a Road Coach which has black-painted pole chains, no snap hook, but a hook with a rubber ring.

With any English turnout, use a bow-topped whip; with Juckers in breast collars, a Jucker whip. A driving crop is used only with an American turnout.

Additional advice for the presentation of noblemen's turnouts:

Owner-driven singles

(a) Ladies' Park Carriages (Duc) etc. (this also applies in America). Horses: small or medium-sized, elegant, with naturally good head carriage, high action, perfectly trained. No hogged manes.

Harness: as for the Victoria. Bow-topped whip. Groom wears either white or light brown gloves.

(b) Two-wheeled Ladies' and Gentlemen's carriages: cabriolet, buggy, gig, dogcart, road cart (American), governess cart etc. Horses: depending upon the size of the carriage. (For cabriolets, elegant 'steppers' of reasonable light type, with bearing-rein and Buxton bit). No hogged manes.

Harness: for the cabriolet, coupé harness should be used but not of *brown* leather. For a cabriolet, and for carriages with fixed shafts which therefore have parallelogram springs, Tilbury tugs are used. Bow-topped whip.

Other carriages: gig harness with loosely-buckled belly-band (leather tugs), preferably black. For road carts, black American harness is essential. Driving crop is only used with a long-tailed trotter.

Driver, coachman and groom with owner-driven carriages wear light brown gloves.

(c) Four-wheeled owner-driven carriages: Spider Phaeton, show wagon, runabout. For these, English harness is used unless pulled by long-tailed trotters – then American breast collars are correct. If a footman is carried with a trotter turnout, he will always wear stable livery, with plain buttons (not metal) and a bowler hat.

Coachman-driven singles

Horses: Cob-type, suitable for the size of the carriage, with high action and naturally high head carriage. Trimmed manes but not hogged. Tails may be docked but the tail hair should not be cut too short.

Harness: black, chromium- or nickel-plated, full-collar harness with saddle; Buxton bit with bearing-rein or Liverpool bit with or without bearing-rein; breast-plate (false martingale) fixed to the noseband is undesirable, fixing it to the bit is wrong. Trace buckles are attached to the tugs, not to the traces.

(d) Victoria (Mylord).

Horses: depending upon the size of the carriage, with high action. Mane and tail as above.

Harness: light, black full-collar harness. Light saddle in preference to pad. Buxton bit with bearing-rein or Liverpool bit with or without bearing-rein.

Owner-driven pairs

Suitable carriages are: Mail Phaeton; Demi-Mail Phaeton; Stanhope Phaeton; Spider Phaeton; Ladies' Phaeton; Duc; Curricle; four-wheeled dogcart; Hungarian Jucker Wagon.

(a) English style: horses should have plenty of even, front action. Same colour and trimmed manes preferred.

Harness: black full-collar harness (Mail Phaeton: coach wheeler harness or similar). For other carriages lighter harness, particularly for Spider and Ladies' Phaeton. Curb bits with or without bearing-rein. Steel pole chains.

(b) Hungarian style: Hungarian carriages like Esterhazy, Cziraki, etc.

Horses: Jucker, same colour not necessary, but speed and action essential.

Harness: black breast-collar harness with or without Pillangos or Shalanks. No bearing-rein. Always movable bars. Private livery or national costume. Flat reins, snaffle bits. Round traces preferred. Trace buckles at the side part of the breast collar, not at the end of the traces. Leather pole straps. Shortened or well-cared-for long tails. (For town team also English turnout.)

(c) American Style: this is very different to the Russian style. With the Russian style everything is old-fashioned, highly picturesque and, for our speedy times, mostly impractical. With the Americans, everything aims for lightness, simplicity, speed. The turnout is sober, plain and unpicturesque. With its

fresh, well-fed and high-stepping horses, the Russian turnout *looks* fast; the American turnout *is* fast.

The second American type of driving is to put hackneys or other fast half-breeds to light American vehicles with English harness. The horses are always put to in their appropriate harness. This applies to double harness with the pole yoke. The third type is the great 'mixture', the Americanized English style. The fourth type is for 'heavy harness horses'. The turnout does not differ from the English style except for the exaggerated top hat shapes.

Because of the great American passion for equestrian sports, horse shows sprouted like mushrooms. Naturally everybody wanted to know the correct appointments to achieve the best overall picture. In Britain there were no books or written regulations on this subject. Therefore the Americans attempted to satisfy their thirst for knowledge by writing down everything they could find out. In doing this, they very often overshot their goal, misunderstood the English-style turnout which had developed from centuries of experience, and incorporated some nonsense in otherwise excellent books. Of course it is not of basic importance whether a strap is buckled one way or the other, but experts and judges should be clear about everything so that they can give advice if they are asked by a competitor. However, in addition to the horses, a perfect turnout requires correct harnessing, bitting and driving, which always have room for further knowledge.

(d) Russian Style: to us, the Russian Style is more of artistic and comparative interest than of practical importance. I mention it here only because of its originality. In single harness, the trotter goes in a collar between the shafts which, at the points, have a side support through the duga. Manes and tails are left untrimmed and full. Very often the trotter has on his left-hand side a 'Galopin' – usually in a breast collar, which is tied to the shafts by a strap. He has only one rein which pulls his head to the outside. If the trotter has a 'Galopin' on both sides (each attached to a bar), the turnout is called a Troika. The driver holds four individual reins made of webbing, with the two right-hand reins in his right hand, and the two left-hand reins in his left. If a whip, which is only a very short stick, is carried, it hangs over the right wrist above the horses' quarters. Metal buttons connect the webbing hand-parts of the reins with the leather front part. These heavy buttons (if possible, hidden) are sometimes used to urge on the horses. The harness has no winkers, no crupper straps, no curb bits, and only the front half of the noseband. Plain double-ring snaffles would not be quite correct. The plated snaffles hide other secrets; for instance, a rope that goes round the jaw and which, accurately fitted, squeezes this only so far as the snaffle permits. It is typical that genuine harness has very few buckles, nearly all straps taper down to narrow laces, and the horses are more tied to the carriage than buckled. The side horses canter with low head carriage, positioned to the outside, but not tied down with side-reins, inside leg leading. Troika harness is basically very plain and then heavily plated; the duga is flat and heavy, mostly metal-plated at the end, and very often attractively painted in many colours on a silver background. Driving a pair with a pole between them is not typically Russian. In our opinion the Russian carriages and sleighs are too small. With a Troika, the driver wears a feather beret, for the single turnout a small felt hat. The unsophisticated style of driving two or three horses is carried out with four individual reins held with arms outstretched and hands far apart.

Coachman-driven pairs

Vehicles: Coupé; Coupé d'Orsay; Victoria (Mylord); Vis-à-Vis; Landau; Berline; Barouche.

Horses: with long fronts, good and even action, if possible of the same colour, medium-length tails, trimmed manes.

Harness: heavy, black, full-collar harness, pole straps. Quarter strap and small numnah under the plain leather pad are permissible. A Buxton bit is preferred with bearing-rein. No elbow or other coaching bits, but Liverpool with cross-bar permissible. With Coupé d'Orsay, eight-spring Victoria, Berline, and Barouche: silk browbands, large rosettes, numnah, quarter strap or breeching.

With these semi-ceremonial carriages the coachman and footman should wear frock-coats, white gloves and knee breeches; in the winter, long overcoats. In summer, stockings and buckled shoes can be worn; gaiters may be substituted in winter.

Tandem

Vehicles: tandem cart, high dogcart, high gig, suitable for the size of the two horses. (Wheel height and weight depend entirely on the height of the horses.) The cart has to be sufficiently high for the shafts, which are fairly straight, to be nearly horizontal when put to. A movable bar, preferably attached to the axle by chains.

Horses: Wheeler – strong, deep short-limbed. Leader – elegant, lively, with plenty of action, if possible under 1.60 m. [16 h.h.]. Shortened tail. The leader should be lighter, but not smaller, than the wheeler.

Harness: black leather. Full-collar harness with leather tugs. Leader may have breast-collar harness but never use half a set of double harness. Lead pad 9 cm. wide, wheel pad 14–15 cm. Lead traces hooked to the trace buckle-eye of the wheeler. Length of lead traces for horses 1.68 m. high [16.2 h.h.] should be 3.10–3.20 m. including snap hook (double bar recommended). The pad terrets of the wheeler have a half-moon-shaped bar in the centre so that the lower part leaves sufficient room for the wheel-rein to be pulled through correctly. If the cart has no brake, a breeching is required, otherwise a kicking strap is used. Curb bit, or, if the leader is in breast collar, a snaffle may be used. Hame terrets must be movable, otherwise the lead-reins may get caught under the hames. With sensitive horses this could be dangerous as the wheel-rein can easily get caught either in front of, or behind, the rein terret. Length of wheel-traces to the bar (attached by chains to the axle) which hangs below the travers (cross-bar), 1.90 m. with cock-eye. Points to centre-hole 22 cm. (3 holes), girth well tightened, belly-band loose to allow play for the shafts. Rein terrets for lead-reins at the throatlash.

Reins: lead-reins 7.20 m., wheel-reins 4.20 m., of plain natural leather; no buckled hand-parts; four individual reins.

Coach horn and umbrella basket not necessary.

Owner-driven teams of four, or more, horses in hand.

Vehicles: Drag (private coach); Road Coach; char-à-banc; Wagonette; Brake, and original Jucker Wagons (not Paris Phaetons, without hood, or four-wheeled dogcarts).

Horses: for English carriages, Park teams with high action, or road teams of hunter type but with long tails. Wheelers: strong, deep, short-limbed. Leaders: same type but lighter, of more quality, not smaller. For Park Drags, good quality horses with a lot of action. Matched colours preferred. Manes brushed over to the right.

For Hungarian Carriages; Jucker horses of blood type, fast, matching in colour, not essential, but should match in conformation.

Harness: for English carriages, English four-in-hand harness, not two sets of double harness, because the wheel pads would have no centre terrets and the traces are too weak. The leaders should not be tied together with a strap or chain. However, the lead-traces may be wound round each other but not crossed. The side bars must be free, i.e. not connected by a link or a chain. All screw heads must be visible, including those of the lead-traces. To avoid squeaking, and wear on the crab, the fittings of the bars should be slightly greased before putting to. Pole chains are safest if they are completely doubled. I recommend having chains of 90–95 cm. for a pole height of 1.10 m. from pole end to the ground, in order to nurse the wheelers. A brake-shoe is only required for journeys with steep uphill gradients. Footboard lamps are of no practical value as they do not shine on to the road but on the wheelers; in fact they only impede the driver.

The brake lever should move easily and smoothly, and should be free in the ratchet in order to work safely. It is therefore difficult to understand why every time a carriage goes back to the coachbuilder, the lever invariably is tightened against the teeth of the ratchet. Repeatedly, 'pull' brakes have been altered to 'push' brakes (which are not safe), only because the pull brake is difficult to operate due to the strong pressure against the ratchet. During the day, coach lamps should always be in the carriage. With char-à-bancs they do not protrude as far as on a coach, and therefore are less likely to be used as foot-rests by passengers. Well-fitting candles of best quality should be in the lamps, and should also be carried as spares. The wooden shutters of the coach should be closed.

The groom, or maybe a stable boy, sits on the back seat. If the seats above the body are unoccupied, the back rests (lazy backs) are put down. With a Drag (the private coach) the back seat (only for coachman and groom) rests on iron supports, and the step-ladder hangs between them. On a Road Coach, where all seats were bookable, the back seat is supported at the sides and at the back by wooden supports and is made to carry four people; the step-ladder hangs between the rear wheels. Lining the bars on the top is more practical since the lining can be touched up by a conscientious coachman. The same lining, about 10 mm. wide, should be on the hub, the wheel fellies, springs, and on the undercarriage and footboard. All these parts, including pole and bar, are always the same colour; the back panels follow the colour of the body; cushions and trim should be cloth. The length of the pole should be approximately 2.80 m. from splinter bar to pole end. The lead-reins should be 7.20 m. long, the wheel-reins 4.20 m., the outside lead-trace, including cock-eye, 1.80 m., but the inside lead-trace 50 mm. shorter; the outside wheel-trace when attached to the roller bolts should measure 2 m., inside wheel-trace 1.75 m., and both must not be less than 43 mm. wide. With bars, the wheel-traces should be 15 m. shorter. Rein terrets should be on the outside of the throatlashes of the wheelers. A bow-topped whip must be used.

Coachman and groom wear light brown gloves. Coachman sits at the rear on the right, and at the halt stands by the right-hand wheeler. Groom stands in front of the leaders, passing along the left-hand side of the horses when moving off.

Jucker Team

Horses: light, very fast blood horses, any colour.

Harness: Hungarian black leather. Trace buckles not at the back, snaffle bits, flat reins. Round traces preferred. Jucker whip, movable bars, leather pole straps, private livery or national costume. For Town teams, English harness is permissible (full collars and livery). Four-in-hand rein terrets on the outside, but the three-ring system may also be used.

Coachman-driven country turnouts

Vehicles: Landau, Vis-à-vis, Victoria, Brake, Wagonette, Hunting Cart, Omnibus.

Horses: four safe, well-trained horses. Jucker style may also use a five-in-hand.

Harness: black leather preferred, but essential for Jucker style.

H.R.H. The Duke of Edinburgh and his team of bays negotiating a water obstacle

Mr. Vance Coulthard driving the Caperne Wray Farms team of chestnuts through the water obstacle at the European Championships, 1979

Mr. Ewald Welde, of Austria, with his pair through a water obstacle

Gyorgy Bardos, the 1979 and 1981 European Champion and 1980 World Champion in the Obstacle Driving Competition

34

Essential Maintenance

Previous chapters have already outlined the basic requirements of harness and carriages, their general condition, and how to ease the daily work for the horses.

However, it appears appropriate to go further into the maintenance of carriages, and demonstrate the necessity for frequent greasing of turntable and wheels.

It is essential to keep the turntable of all carriages clean and lightly greased. Only very few coachmen know how this is done on carriages with a perch. With light vehicles, particularly if the horses are put to a little tighter, the lack of grease does not show up as much. However, with heavy carriages which have a perch and have to be driven with the pole chains reasonably slack, it is essential to carry an oil can in your spares. A small oil can, like those used for bicycles, will suffice. On dusty or dirty roads the turntable of a carriage with a perch dries up and the fore-carriage starts to judder from side to side. Immediately this is noticed, pull up and turn the fore-carriage, clean the dry parts of the perch as well as the areas of the turntable away from the pin by turning the fore-carriage, and oil them lightly.

It usually takes some time for coachmen to agree that the transom plates of vehicles with perches must be greased prior to each journey and sometimes even during a journey. Usually he thinks that the owner is just nagging. On many carriages with perches, although of the same design, the transom plates dry up in different places. This is because the axle-tree and perch touch too much at the outside, and not enough or not at all, in the centre. Once a stubborn coachman has experienced a pole that is

out of control, particularly on a wet tarmac road, he is cured for ever.

Every driver, whether Gentleman driver or coachman, must know how to lubricate Collinge as well as Mail axles. He should keep a watchful eye on his axles; unfortunately, this is not done often enough, although it is of the utmost importance. When buying a secondhand carriage, always get at least the front wheels taken off and check whether the axle-arms are in good condition and not worn. Any good coachman knows he must *oil* Collinge axles. Mail axles (found only with the coach, the Mail Phaeton, and the tandem cart) have to be lubricated with *grease*, not oil. It is important that the 'Guv'nor' knows the procedure thoroughly. To ensure that the nuts and bolts do not get mixed up, I recommend cutting a mark at the rear of the collar above the bolts, and cutting the same mark on the relevant screws (chalk marks are unreliable). The large moon plate should also be marked so that the correct bolts are put back into their respective holes.

After the screws have been removed, pull off the wheel and clean the moon plate, collar, leather washers, disc, axle area and the part of the axle bed which lies between the spring and the collar with turpentine or petrol. At the same time check whether the screws of the spring clips are tight. Then fill the cleaned oil groove with grease and push the wheel slowly, so that the lubricant does not squeeze out, back on to the axle-arm and the three holes of the plate, positioning carefully on to the respective bolts; wipe off the thread of the bolts and paste them with an iron varnish so that the nuts get a good hold. The screws are then tightened evenly until the wheel is firm. The greased wheels must have a little play so that they can run freely and absorb unevenness of roads. It also ensures a better distribution of the lubricant along the axle-arm. The play on the axles should be approximately the thickness of a straw (2–3 mm.). To achieve this, turn each nut one-eighth of a turn on the bolt, pull the wheel forward and then push it back. Very important are good leather washers. I also recommend carrying a few spare screws on a coach, because the heavily-loaded front wheels have to suffer more than those of a Mail Phaeton, or the large wheels of a tandem.

On Collinge axles, the wheels only need enough play to allow them to run smoothly. They should not move backwards and forwards on the axle-arm. When lubricating the wheels, it is important that hub cap, split pin, screws and washers are kept on a clean piece of paper and do not come into contact with sand or dust. One grain of sand is enough to ruin the polished axle-arm.

When removing the wheels, the jack must be placed at each wheel – *never* in the centre of the axle which is the weak point where the axles are welded together. Having cleaned both nuts, collar, axle-arm, box, and oil groove, pour bone- or castor-oil into the oil groove and a little on to the axle-arm. To re-assemble the wheel, firstly put on the leather washer, then slide the wheel on to the oiled axle-arm. Next the collar goes into place, and then the first nut, which is screwed on tightly. The wheel should now be firm. If this is not the case, the leather washer is too thin and should be replaced immediately. If the wheel *is* firm, loosen the nut until the wheel turns easily but without play on the axle-arm (which is necessary with a Mail axle). Then, screw on the second, smaller nut which has the thread in the opposite direction. Tighten it, and push in the split pin. Always keep a few split pins in reserve. Finally, pour a little light grease or thick oil into the hub cap and screw it tightly into the box which is sealed by a leather washer.

The axle-arm of a Collinge axle is cylindrical, with an oil groove running longitudinally. Towards the outside, and opposite the axle-shoulder, the axle-arm has a flat piece which prevents the collet from turning. In front of this, the arm has two threads running different ways (one right and one left) which hold the nuts. Outside the nuts there is a small pin (split pin) which passes through the reduced end of the axle-arm. Finally, the hub cap, which screws into the box and consequently into the hub (not on the axle) and therefore turns with the wheel. Close to the inside end of the box is a recess which acts as a container for the lubricant. The leather washer immediately in front of the axle-shoulder must always be in good condition, otherwise the wheel will still wobble even if the nuts are tight.

The Mail axle finishes where the Collinge axle tapers down to hold the collet. It is therefore much shorter and less likely to be hit and thus bent. It is also not weakened either by tapering it down or by the threads. Mail axles obtained their name from the old 'Royal Mail'. Nearly all Road Coaches and all genuine Mail Phaetons and Mail Carts have Mail axles; so, too, do a large number of Private Drags. The Mail axle has either an oil groove at the top or more often a slightly-sloped area. The outside of the axle-arm collar has a narrow ring like a piece of welded-on wire. This ring cuts slightly into the leather washer – thus preventing the oil from escaping. The large moon plate is put on each axle-half before they are welded together in the centre. A large leather washer which also has three holes for the bolts is placed immediately behind the axle-arm collar, and one in front of it. The bolt heads, as well as the respective nuts, are always square, *never* octagonal. The rear end of the box goes over the axle-arm collar and fits flush over it. It has however, like the collar, a sharp edge to it which cuts into the leather washer and seals the box.

There are arguments both for and against the Collinge and the Mail axles. The advantages of the Collinge axle are that it runs easily, is well sealed, and only requires oiling every three months. The disadvantages are that, because of the longer axle-arm, it is easier to hit corners and trees and thus bend the axle. Should this occur, the wheel will not run true, the hub cap can get lost, and dust and sand can penetrate into the box between collet and axle-arm.

When buying a secondhand carriage check and measure the track of both front and rear wheels at the axle.

Because of the higher number of revolutions, the smaller front wheels are likely to dry out much quicker. Therefore, start by checking these. If they still are sufficiently lubricated, there is no need to check the rear wheels.

The turntable and wheels of farm and trade wagons and carts require the same attention, only more often because they are in constant use. Badly-maintained and -greased carriages are hard on the horses and, in the long run, good maintenance and prompt repairs are far more economical.

35

Driving in Agriculture and with Trade Vehicles (Swingle trees/Swingle bars)

In agricultural driving, Achenbach's main demand should still be a foregone conclusion, i.e. that harness and way of driving must be guided by the aim to make the horses' daily work as easy as possible. Horses worked with this in mind will thank their owners by being able to serve them for a longer time.

Any farmer or haulier should therefore consider what he can do to achieve this.

In the previous chapter, but particularly in Chapter 6, important points have been raised which should give food for thought.

Of course, this does not mean that horses in the plough should be driven Achenbach fashion. Driving with cross-reins can only be done where it is possible.

However, when driving a trade turnout, or a working pair of horses into town, the points mentioned in previous chapters about harness and driving still apply.

'Horse preservers' and swingle bars (See illustrations I. and II. and III. to VI. on opposite page.)

If heavy loads have to be pulled, try and ease the work by using 'horse preservers'. These are strong steel spiral springs which are either attached between trace and bar, or bars and main bar. They make pulling heavy loads much easier. There are also swingle bars which are constructed in such a way that the bars are attached to two movable iron arms, connected by a strong iron spiral spring behind the main bar.

Swingle bars

In previous chapters, I have argued *against* the use of swingle bars, but now they should be explained in detail since they are regularly used in farming and for trade turnouts where their usefulness cannot be denied.

Swingle bars, however, should be used only for pairs that work evenly and slowly. With horses of uneven temperaments (particularly blood horses) they are not recommended, because the keener and more lively horse will become upset when the draught resistance changes continually, and the lazy horse becomes lazier.

Talking to the handler of a pair about the effect of the swingle bars he may argue that 'only the horse which moves first pulls the bar forward, and the cart remains at a standstill, so it is only when the other horse starts that the vehicle moves'. If you follow that with, 'Why do you hold back the keen horse and only urge on the lazy one?', he is at a loss to explain.

The effect of the swingle bars depends on how their three pivot points are positioned to each other. If the three pivot points are in a straight line, the three levers are of the same length and both horses have to pull the same load. In III the centre of the three holes is intended for hooking up the bar.

If the middle one of the three pivot points lies back (see dotted line IV), the leverage gets shorter when one horse moves off, and it has to pull harder.

152

If the middle pivot point is forward, V, the leverage of the horse that hangs back will get shorter; the horse therefore has to pull harder. See illustration, C, opposite.

The swingle bars of a show four-in-hand in VI below has the same effect as IV; the horse that moves off first has the heavier load to pull.

The most favourable construction of the swingle bars for agricultural and trade turnouts is as shown in III. If the centre holes are used, both horses have the same load of work. This has nothing to do with one horse being keener than the other. This swingle bar has the advantage that the horse which should be eased in work can be given longer leverage by hooking the swingle bar either in the right- or left-hand hole. It would be wrong to hold the right-hand horse back just by a loop rein which is attached to the left-hand corner of the swingle bar. In fact, the use of the loop rein is not advocated at all.

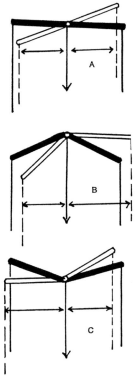

The effect of leverage

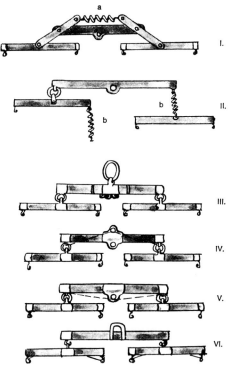

'Horse preservers' (also known as 'eveners') are illustrated in I. and II. above with swingle bars III. to VI. below.

The aim which must be achieved is to distribute the work evenly on both horses. The swingle bars have to be so adjusted that the bigger and stronger horse relieves the weaker horse.

As well as the swingle bars in III, those depicted in IV are also very practical. With both, the leverage can be adjusted. See also the illustration above where the different effects of the leverage are demonstrated.

The disadvantage of having the swingle bars over the splinter bar is that it is not possible to drive as tight a turn. With the swingle bar, the position of bars, main bar and pole towards each other alters continually, because the tractive power only attacks at one point, i.e. the connecting point of swingle bar and turntable. Therefore, the turn is carried out on a wider curve.

This is necessary for heavy carts, the more so if the going is heavy, because in a tight turn, front and rear wheels have to break new tracks.

The advantage of the swingle bar (or loose bar) is that the tensile resistance relative to ground friction is reduced, since the draught is always straight. Because of this advantage, swingle bars are used widely in agricultural and trade turnouts. They ease the work of the horses on bad roads with deep ruts, as well as in heavy going.

Draught direction of the traces

If we consider how the draught is transmitted to the carriage – namely, starting from the splinter bar, via the turntable, to the front axle and front wheels, then via the perch, or the king pin, to the rear carriage, the rear axle and the rear wheels – it must become apparent that the heavier the going, the larger is the angle of draught. We know that the draught angle should be 10–20°. On a flat, smooth road it is not necessary for the draught to be 'lifting'. However, this alters as soon as the ground friction increases. Let us take an example: in heavy going, the load becomes so heavy that it exceeds the sum of the draught resistances, which exceeds the tractive power. Therefore the tractive power must start as low as possible, i.e. the swingle bars must be attached below the pole, so that the draught can start with a leverage. As a result, if we want to make work easier for the horses, we must not overlook the influence of the direction of the traces. It is obvious that the angle of draught alters, depending upon the height of the fore-carriage (front wheels) and the size of the horses, and accordingly the swingle bars have to be attached either above or below the pole. If a lead pair is required, the farmer or driver must ensure that the direction of the leaders' draught does not pull the pole down, as this would pull the collars on to the wheelers' necks.

Shoeing

It must also be mentioned that, for heavy work, correct shoeing is of great importance. It makes work considerably easier. Observe how the horses have to go into their collars when they start to move a heavy load. They require, particularly at the toe, 'slip protection'. The toe hold is almost more important than studs.

The reins

Agricultural vehicles, and vehicles with heavy

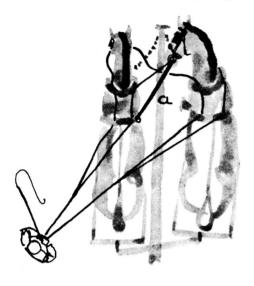

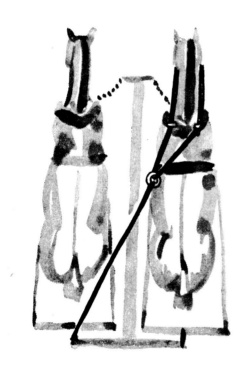

Agricultural turnouts, incorrectly driven (from the ground) but the lower illustration is preferable

154

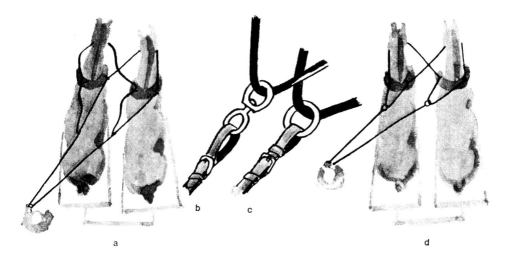

The use of the ring

loads, are not usually driven from the box seat. The horses are manoeuvred by the driver walking alongside.

In order to have the horses always under control, the easiest method for a working pair is to have a simple pair rein which regulates itself.

It does not matter whether the driver sits on the box, or walks alongside on the right- or left-hand side. The reins can always be lengthened or shortened. The ring fitted on to the reins going to the bits allows the driving rein to slide into the correct position wherever the driver may be, and the horses are always on the bit. This type of self-regulating rein is suitable for horses of similar temperament. It is easily made and guarantees correct driving at all times.

However, it is not possible to adjust it to suit horses with different temperaments; this must be balanced at the swingle bars.

The top rein (bearing-rein)

Bearing-reins for working horses are used to stop them eating during work. However, they must always be long enough to allow the horse to stretch its neck when pulling heavy loads.

Connecting rein

The disadvantages of the connecting rein are that it makes horses unsuitable for riding and pleasure driving because they get one-sided.

Collar or 'hamen'

The word 'hamen' is mentioned here because the large, heavy, working collar is frequently called a 'hamen'.

Working harness

To fit working harness, the same principles apply as for driving harness. Naturally, due to the heavy loads, it must in all parts be much stronger. This will apply to a working harness with full collars, and a working harness with breast collars. With the collar harness the noseband is missing which is essential for correct positioning of the winkers. With the breast-collar harness the neck strap is correctly placed in front of the withers, and pulled through the pole-chain ring. However, the girth should be less tight.

Working harness with full collar

Working harness with breast collar

Working harness with breast collar

Horses in two-wheeled carts

It is often said that the draught arms of the collar should be low, and that the collar should widen considerably towards the top to achieve as near as possible a draught angle of 90°. This is incorrect and contains two serious errors. Altering the draught angle can be achieved only by lowering the 'point of attack' at the cart, and *not* by placing it higher on the collar. Therefore, 'from experience', the draught arms of the collar are low, and close to the point of the shoulder, which contradicts the above theory. The collars are not wide at the top to achieve rectangular draught, because it is impossible to achieve it this way – the direction of the traces, the position of the shoulder, and the surface covered by the collar, determine the angle, never the front line of the collar!

How is it possible, therefore, that with the low draught arms and the horizontal chains of tipcarts, the collar does not slide upwards on the shoulders and press on the windpipe of the horse? Firstly, the shoulders of heavy horses are less sloping; secondly, the heavy weight of the collar itself holds it down. The weight is balanced out with an upward tendency during the draught. Only then is the vertical front line of the collar of importance, because the weight of the collar has its strongest effect in the downward direction.

I will try to explain this process, which is worth clarifying. The horse is harnessed to a two-wheeled tip-cart; compared to it is a feed-box with sloping lid (shoulder) on which is placed a box with a deep-hinged lid. It would slide down were it not held by the 'traces' – positioned as on the tip-cart. Imagine the box with open and closed lid. The acute angle which is formed between the 'traces' and the slope (shoulder), remains the same, whether the traces are fastened as Z or Z1. To move Z up to Z2 would be wrong, as it would actually worsen the 'point of attack' at the shoulder. The chain ends must not go down because it would be impossible to make use of the favourable length of the spokes. It therefore only remains to weigh down the collar and box to stop the collar, or here the box, from riding up. This is what practical collar-makers have done: they have not tried to widen the acute angle by placing the draught arms higher, but have increased the weight of the collar. This is the purpose of the heavy collar. If one takes the trouble to look at this closely, one must see and feel that the only suitable angle is that formed by trace and shoulder or collar surface. Where and how the front line of the collar runs is of no interest whatsoever.

Many mistakes with two-wheeled carts occur through a bad distribution of the load. The cart should be loaded in such a way that the shafts just rest in the tugs of the back-band and belly-band, i.e. neither front- nor back-heavy. Unfortunately, very often the front is overloaded. As a result the horses' action becomes tied. If the lazy driver then goes and sits in the front of the cart, it produces even more 'front weight'.

Loading of four-wheeled wagons

The weight of many carriages is sometimes so high that even the unladen cart requires tractive power; how much more, then, does a loaded or badly-loaded wagon require? The most suitable design for a wagon is as follows.

The wagon should be as short as possible with the largest loading space over the strong rear axle. It should not be too high above the axles,

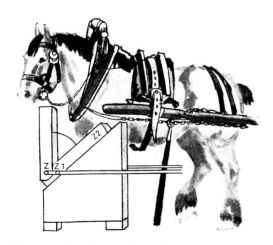

Heavy working harness for a tip-cart

and should have high, easily-manoeuverable wheels. The swingle bars should be as close as possible to the front axle, and be attachable either above, or below, the pole, which should have a constant height at the front. The wagon, whose basic weight should not exceed 700–750 kg., should be sturdily and toughly built, with a wide track width. Ideal are vehicles with rubber tyres and ball-bearings; but these are expensive.

When buying a new vehicle the decisive factor should be: how can I save tractive power?

The load should be distributed as follows: one-third on the front axle, and two-thirds on the rear axle.

The weight of the horses in relation to the weight of the laden cart should be 1:3, that is, the horses can pull three times their own body weight on flat, good roads. If we take, say, two shire-horses of 750 kg. each (a total of 1,500 kg.), this means that they can pull a wagon of 4,500 kg.

On bad roads, or in hilly country, the proportion alters to 1:2. On very bad roads, in fields, on sand, or in the mountains, it drops to 1:1.

These figures refer to continuous work with occasional heavy draughts and short rest periods.

The weight of a pair of horses may be assumed as follows:

Light horses (large Panje – type of Russian horse) about 14.2 h.h. at 450 kg. each = 900 kg.

Light horses at 600 kg. each (East Prussians, Hannoverians, Cobs) = 1200 kg.

Medium horses at 750 kg. each (heavy Hannoverians, Irish draught horses etc) = 1500 kg.

Heavy horses of 900 kg. each (Shires, Percherons etc.) = 1800 kg.

Every owner of draught horses should take the trouble to find out the unladen weight of his carts and wagons and have this inscribed on the pole, or elsewhere.

In Germany, the Animal Protection Law penalises anybody who overloads his vehicles.

It is very difficult to intervene, as no government insists on proof of qualifications of cart-horse drivers, grooms and coachmen. Sometime in the future, perhaps, a form of licence will be introduced, and drivers will have to pass a test at a state institution.

Any method of driving and harnessing should give first consideration to the care of the horse. What this entails is once again summarized here:

1 Treat your horse well, talk to it, do not beat it or push it or press it unnecessarily.
2 Start the above rule in the stable when harnessing, and continue to do so during work.
3 Drive only with 'giving' aids, not with rough jerks in the mouth.
4 Do not demand anything which is beyond your horse's capabilities. If a special effort is required, achieve it by kindness and not by roughness.
5 Ensure correct shoeing (slip protection and studs).
6 After extra exertion, give your horses a breather. When halting on a steep incline, put on the brake or place a brake-shoe under the rear wheels.

7 Ensure that wheels and turntable are always properly lubricated.
8 If your horse is sweating, cover it with a rug if you halt in a windy spot. Never let it stand unprotected in the sun or in the cold.
9 In the summer keep the flies away.
10 In hot weather, water your horse whenever possible.
11 Use the bearing-rein so that the horse cannot eat during work but can still stretch its neck.
12 Do not use curb bits, but thick snaffle-bits.
13 Use a breeching. It makes it easier to hold back the cart, particularly in hilly country.
14 Load your cart correctly, and never couple together loaded vehicles, because the longer the load, the heavier the draught.
15 Try to distribute the work evenly by adjusting the reins and altering the leverage of the swingle bars.
16 Consider your horses to be your best workmates and they will repay your kindness.

36

Care and Maintenance
of Carriages

A carriage which has been maintained properly from the start saves trouble and money, for the life of a carriage does not depend only on quality. One is too easily prepared to blame defects found during use on to the manufacturers, even if such defects are due to improper maintenance and negligence.

Housing of carriages

The carriage-house should be dry, free of dust, and airy; adequate ventilation is essential. In a wet or damp place the varnish goes dull, polished parts oxidize, wooden parts warp, upholstery and leather go mouldy. The room should be light, but not too light; sunlight should be kept out with curtains or blinds as it will fade colour and varnishing. Frosted glass windows are recommended. The coach-house should not be in the immediate vicinity of the stables; dung heaps or sewers are very detrimental because the ammonia fumes cause dullness and cracking of the paintwork. If the coach-house is heated in the winter, care must be taken that the heater is not in the same room, and that any heating pipes are not close to the carriages. Blocking off the source of heat with a guard is not sufficient; temperature in the room will still vary and even the driest wood will shrink, causing both wood and varnish to crack, and dulling the varnish and paintwork. Unused vehicles which have been kept in a locked room for some time should occasionally be brought out for an airing and treated as described in the following. The carriage-house itself should frequently be thoroughly aired.

Cleaning

Start by cleaning carpets and upholstery. Material is always brushed against the grain. Silk is cleaned with a soft brush or a feather duster. Patent and kid leather is rubbed down with a soft cloth, very dirty leather is cleaned with luke-warm water and a little soap added. Occasionally on the leather use a little olive oil; it keeps it soft and pliable and stops it from perishing. Stains on material and silk are removed with cleaning spirit or other modern stain removers. Cushions and carpets should frequently be beaten to prevent moths settling in them. Leather hoods are dusted with a feather duster and then rubbed down with a soft cloth. Here again, occasional treatment with olive oil is recommended, but only very lightly. After a drive in very cold weather do not close the hood immediately. The same applies to wet sail-cloth hoods, or hoods of waterproof material. Sail-cloth hoods rolled up or covered, when they are wet, become musty, and water-proofed materials lose their water resistance. After beating cushions and upholstery, do not forget to brush the piping, or braid, because they are traps for moth eggs. The same applies to the pockets in the doors and on the box.

Washing the carriage

Careful washing is of utmost importance in the care and maintenance of carriages. After each journey the vehicle must be thoroughly washed. Washing, however, does not mean flooding. Pressure hosing should always be avoided because it floods the carriage, the water comes in too large quantities and with too much pressure, damages the paintwork at the joints, between the carvings and fillings, gets in the doors and into corners where it cannot be dried off. Too much water is damaging for carriages and a main cause for their perishing. The wooden parts rot and the metal parts rust. Therefore, use water in moderation.

Washing should be done with clean water, without additives, and with a sponge – one sponge to be used for the body and another for the undercarriage. Dry off with a chamois leather. Stubborn dirt should be removed by repeated rinsing with a hose or watering-can, not by rubbing. Rubbing only spreads the dirt; it will act like sand-paper and leave ugly marks on the varnished surfaces. Never use a brush. Carriages covered with mud must be cleaned immediately after use, because if the mud dries, it leaves marks which are difficult to remove or cannot be removed at all. Never wash carriages in the sun; the heat causes the varnish to blister. It is possible to remove stains on the varnish by 'water polishing', with cottonwool or a soft cloth. Then polish with dry cottonwool until no water is left, and the surface is shining again. Remember, varnish not only improves the look of a carriage, but is also a protection. Therefore, never wait until the varnish has become dull, or whole patches have rubbed off, before touching up or re-varnishing.

Metal parts of the carriage

Brass or nickel parts are cleaned with a liquid polish, but take care that this polish (which usually contains acid) does not touch the varnish. Even the tiniest drop will leave a permanent mark. Before cleaning polished parts inside the carriage, cover the trimmings with cardboard or paper cut to fit round the shape of the metal part to be cleaned. Silver parts are rubbed with a suede or chamois leather. For windows use a damp chamois leather and then polish with a soft cloth or tissue paper.

General

Polished parts, window frames etc. should occasionally be rubbed down with linseed oil, and then re-polished. This gives them a certain greasiness from which the water runs off. Thus polished parts gain a measure of weather resistance.

Varnished parts which have become dull can be restored temporarily with polish, but remember that polish does not replace varnish. Every carriage must be repaired and re-varnished from time to time by a conscientious expert. It is therefore recommended to send the carriage to a coach-builder for re-varnishing, because small repairs are usually necessary before re-varnishing. Repairs undoubtedly increase the life of a carriage and, if carried out in time, save a lot of money.

37

Cleaning and Maintenance of Harness

The life and condition of harness depends upon proper care and maintenance.

First, clean all harness parts immediately after use. This saves a lot of work and trouble since it is much easier to remove fresh dirt than when it has dried. In particular, sponge immediately all parts which came into contact with the horse's body. Use luke-warm water with a small addition of soda. On no account use hot water as this is bad for leather. Remove dirt with a soft brush.

It is wrong to soak harness in water in order to soften dried dirt. It makes the leather spongy, and when it has dried, very hard. It is also wrong to use only leather polish, as it blocks the pores of the leather, which stops 'breathing' and gets hard, dry, and perished. Only leather treated with oil retains its suppleness. However, the use of oil must not be overdone, and never use more than the leather can absorb. In the winter, or in cold weather, the oil sets, and therefore does not penetrate into the leather; oiling, therefore, should only be done in the warmth. Only use animal fats, the most suitable being fish oil, lard,

or other good animal fats which a harness-maker will advise. A good natural shine is achieved by applying a boot polish or good floor polish. Only apply it thinly to the harness once it has been taken apart, is dry, and has previously been cleaned. Then polish and re-assemble the set.

All metal parts should be polished with a brass cleaning liquid. If the parts are clean and shiny it is sufficient to wash them in soapy water and then polish with a dry, soft cloth. Steel parts, like bits and pole chains should be immediately placed in a bucket of water. This will not make them rust. Add either soda or a soft soap to the water, but never use a 'sand cloth' on the polished steel parts afterwards, or they will become dull. After they have been dried, use a burnishing chain or a burnishing cushion.

A good treatment for metal parts is to place them in a bag filled with bran.

Never use saddle-soap to clean the reins; saddle-soap makes the reins slippery when they get wet, and difficult to hold with leather gloves.

38

Trimming and Clipping Horses

Badly and unevenly trimmed horses ruin the picture of any turnout. Therefore, every owner and breeder should know how to trim a horse. It is a bad habit to hog the mane of a carriage horse because the neck strap of the breast collar, or the collar itself, will rub on the stubble and leave sore places. If a mane is pulled well, a harness horse very rarely gets sore with a properly fitted collar. Horses which are not ridden should have the forelock removed completely because browband and winker-stays fit better.

Hogged manes are often a sign of a lazy groom. Well groomed horses should have evenly-pulled manes brushed over to the right. This applies to riding horses as well as to driving horses. If a mane does not lie easily, clip out a third or half of the right-hand side of the mane. It will then brush over easily. The hogged part, however, must be re-clipped every three weeks. It only takes a few minutes but saves a lot of work. A hogged mane is also unpleasant for the horses because they cannot shake off flies. Well-groomed manes are essential for a pleasure team as well as for a team of working horses.

For the grooming of manes and tails, a mane comb, a dandy brush and a water brush are required. If a mane is dirty and neglected it must be washed with soap and thoroughly rinsed. It is then brushed over to the right with dandy brush and mane comb. When the mane has dried, smooth it down again with brush and comb. Now start pulling the mane to achieve a good shape, and thin it so that it finally lies flat along the neck about 10 cm. down. To get a mane to lie nicely, it must be pulled correctly. Thinning

scissors should never be used because the remaining short hairs will stand up.

Start at the head behind the ears, take a few strands of hair between thumb and index finger of the left hand, and with the index, middle finger and thumb of the right hand, hold the hair in front of the left hand and pull enough hair upwards. This will leave sufficient hair in the left hand to be pulled out comfortably. The right hand, which slides back to the left hand, will then pull out the hair by putting the right index finger over the hair, whilst thumb and middle finger press against it from underneath. It is advisable to wear gloves when pulling manes or blisters may occur.

The above method will produce the best result. Pulling the mane with a mane comb is not as neat and accurate.

Proceed in this manner along the mane down to the withers, always smoothing the mane down with brush and comb. If there are still some odd long hairs showing, pull these out with thumb and index finger.

Manes which are cut with scissors look terrible and indicate bad grooming.

To ensure a flat-lying mane for a horse show, prepare a solution of starch, brush it over the hair, pull a stable rubber or small blanket over the mane from left to right and leave it there for a little while. When the mane is dry, it is as stiff as a board. All that is now required is to beat the starch out with your hand and the 'hair-do' is perfect.

Pulling tails at the dock, whether long or short, is done in much the same manner. Never

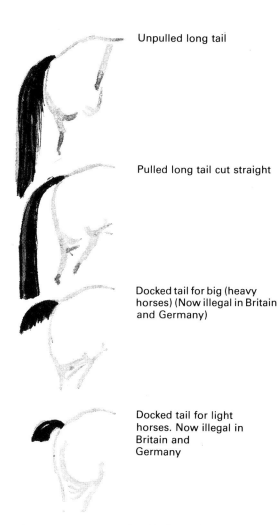

Unpulled long tail

Pulled long tail cut straight

Docked tail for big (heavy horses) (Now illegal in Britain and Germany)

Docked tail for light horses. Now illegal in Britain and Germany

Plaiting manes for a horse show indicates that special trouble has been taken for the occasion. However, do not leave manes plaited for any length of time, or plait them too tightly, because the hair will fall out.

To pull the tail at the dock to a length of about 20–30 cm. is to show the muscles of the hind quarters to better advantage.

Do not use a mane comb for the tail. It takes out too many long hairs. The result is a 'pheasant tail' that gets shorter and shorter.

'Pheasant tails' belong to Hungarian turnout; they may be permissible for a country turnout but a long tail, cut straight across at the bottom, is much nicer.

Turning out a horse correctly also includes removing excessive fetlock hair. If a clipping machine is used, this must be worked in the direction of the hair, not against it, otherwise the fetlock hair will look dull. It is much better to use bent fetlock scissors.

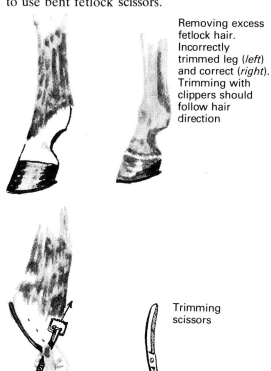

Removing excess fetlock hair. Incorrectly trimmed leg (*left*) and correct (*right*). Trimming with clippers should follow hair direction

Trimming scissors

take too many strands of hair or the horse may become restless, apart from the danger that too much could get pulled out in one place. The slower one proceeds, the more even the tail becomes on both sides. Never use scissors or razors. Only pull the 'under hair', not the top hair. Do not pull out so much that the dock looks bald and thin like a rat's tail.

If the dock is trimmed with scissors or a razor, it looks dull compared to the shiny top hair.

Naturally, the type of tail must suit the horse. The same applies to the mane. The mane of a heavy horse stallion which hangs down both sides of the neck should be about 20 cm. long. The more elegant the horse, the thinner the neck and the lighter the mane should be.

163

With heavy horses the heels usually are not trimmed; excessively long feathers are only thinned out.

Long hair under the belly, the head, along the throat, and on other parts of the body (of course not the 'whiskers') are singed off with a candle or a singeing iron.

Ear hair is trimmed by squeezing the ear together and running along the ear with a pair of scissors, cutting off the hairs that stick out.

Thinning scissors are in my opinion only useful to prepare heavy horse foals. Cut continually down with thinning scissors, never in one place.

Achenbach says the following about clipping horses: 'Horses in the same stable and with the same amount of work often grow their winter coats at different times. Even then the coat could be short and smooth with one horse, and long and woolly with another. Therefore horses should be trimmed at their appropriate times if each is to look well groomed. Before the war, I had five dark chestnut horses, one of which was always ready for clipping in October, i.e. he sweated unnecessarily in work and always broke out again in the stables. After the first clipping, he still matched the others in colour, but after the second, he was near enough dun. The fifth horse only had to be clipped at the beginning or middle of December. I thus had one dun, three chestnuts, and one dark chestnut which remained very dark even after having been clipped. However, although they no longer matched, the horses remained lively and did not have to be rubbed dry for a long time, nor did they break out in the stable. If one is short of staff it is always a great help if the horses dry quickly and do not break out again because, particularly if one has been out with the coach, there are masses of things to do like cleaning the coach and its many steel parts, and wiping over the brass-mounted harness. During the summer, I always had the two horses who did not break out in the stables, returned to their boxes where they rolled immediately; the other two I kept outside and had their feet washed. They dried quicker in the open air than they would have done in the stables.

Years ago, in late autumn, I watched a friend's young, unclipped horses return after a coaching trip. At 11 p.m. they were still soaking wet despite their warm, but nevertheless airy, night rugs. After these young and unfit horses had been clipped for a few days they were lively, fresh, and full of stamina. But now, at times, the owner could hardly control them.

In my opinion it is best not to clip the legs. Horses which are ridden should also not be clipped under the saddle because the long, soft hair reduces any pressure of saddle and girth. Horses' legs cannot be rugged up, and if the horses are in stalls and not in loose boxes, every time the stable door opens, the cold air blows round their legs. Also, horses which have to wait outside, or perhaps slip and fall on the road can cut their knees and hocks; and one can only hope that no dirt gets into the wounds. In cases like these, the winter coat is the best protection.

I have never used a clipping machine to trim out heels but have always done it with fetlock scissors over a comb, just as hairdressers do. This prevents mud fever and also gives a better transition between the clipped-out heels and the rest of the leg. Only the hair around the coronet is best done with clippers – lift the foot, pull it forward and cut upwards along the coronet.

Clipping along the coronet also helps the hoof oil to penetrate into the horn of the hoof. Cut over an ordinary comb, not a metal one. The hair inside the heel remains about 1 cm. long. Feet treated in this manner look tidy and, if cared for properly, are protected from mud fever.

Apart from trimming out the heel, to give the leg a good shape without clipping it only trim the back of the fetlock joint with scissors over the comb.

When trimming out the ear, it is sufficient to pull forward the hair inside the ear and trim it with the fetlock scissors. I have always treated freshly-clipped horses as follows: two people brushed them down with a dandy brush, and then rubbed them over with a woollen rag. I then rode them immediately to get the blood circulating, but not long enough to get them sweating, and put them back in the stable covered with an extra blanket. None of the horses ever caught a cold. Riding them got them warmer than when they were in the clipping box where the door had to be kept open so as to get a better light. My reason for riding the horses after clipping, preferably in an indoor arena, was because I have frequently seen horses shivering for hours after they had been clipped, even though they were well covered with rugs. Also because I know myself that sometimes when sitting indoors, even with a blanket over my knees, I cannot get warm; but after running around outside – even in freezing cold – I get warm and remain so for the rest of the day.

Always pick a still day for clipping; and, preferably, clip three times a year – at the beginning of October, mid-November, and again if neces-sary at the end of February – rather than take off the winter coat on a cold November day. Horses that were clipped at the beginning of October I would clip again when they began to look untidy. A horse which I had for many years was always clipped for the third time at the end of January, sometimes even later. The others were only clipped twice. Therefore all the horses looked clean and tidy all winter, although they were then very different in colour.

For working horses I recommend that the legs and the whole of the back remain unclipped. This gives the horses excellent protection against rain and snow. They carry a natural rug which keeps their kidneys and backs warm, but have sufficient clipped areas to stop them sweating too much. The condensation on the back is thus more even, more natural, and better than when

Different styles of clipping

165

under waterproof rugs which on a still day collects only damp air, while on a windy one it blows icy across the (clipped) loins.

When using clipping machines, most grooms make the mistake of not cleaning the clipping blades often enough. They should be cleaned with a little brush. One drop of oil every five minutes is better than a lot of oil every ten minutes. This stops the clipping machine from getting hot and also reduces the wear of the machine. All other parts need oiling only once a day. The clipped parts of the horse must be rugged up as soon as possible. Most people forget this because they themselves get warm while doing the clipping, whereas the horse stands and shivers.

Clipping machines suffer most when they are used for clipping fetlocks and legs, because the hair there is rarely free of sand or dirt. Therefore, save money in the right spot: horses and machine are better off for not clipping the legs.'

39

Shoeing

The importance of correct shoeing is already mentioned in Chapter 24.

Therefore, full attention to proper shoeing is a necessity. Never drive off without checking beforehand that all shoes are in good condition. From experience it has been found that most foot complaints are due to bad shoeing and incorrect or neglected treatment of the foot. When shoeing, the following should be observed: the groom who usually attends the horse should assist the farrier. He should ensure that the horse is treated quietly and kindly, is not frightened but gains confidence. This is particularly important with difficult and high-spirited horses. They can easily be ruined by rough treatment from a farrier, but will probably stand quietly and willingly with a person they know.

When lifting a leg, never forget firstly to run your hand down the leg and loosen the foot by slight pressure on shoulder or hip with the other hand. Never lift the foot higher than is necessary, and never pull it to the side.

Shoes should not be *torn* off but *taken* off: the clenches are raised from the hoof with chisel and hammer, and then cut off with pliers; the pliers will then loosen the shoe first at the outside, and then at the inside of the heel, and then the nails are pulled out individually. There is no set period after which shoes should be renewed; it depends entirely on the wear of the shoe and the condition and growth of the hoof. Under normal conditions shoes should be removed about every five weeks, but it is advisable to get either the veterinary surgeon or the farrier to determine exactly when the horse should be shod.

Apart from correct shoeing, frequent cleaning of the feet with a hoof pick and water is of utmost importance in order to keep the feet sound. It is the first duty of any groom always to clean the feet before leading the horse into the stable.

In the following paragraphs I recommend anti-slip shoes and studs for use on oily roads; also measures for use in the winter. The wide variety of ground conditions must be taken into consideration and shoeing carried out accordingly. It must be determined whether special shoes for winter are required, or for use on slippery roads.

In winter, studs should be used which penetrate into snow and ice, and pads which prevent snow from collecting in the hoof. Sloping the surface of the shoe also helps to prevent this. It is important to grease the sole of the hoof with fat, oil or tar.

The most widely used hoof pads are those made of plaited straw or hemp, also rubber, felt or cork pad. Or you can simply use an infill of hoof putty.

As a precaution against slipping on asphalt, tarmac, or cobble-stone roads, choose a rough-surfaced shoe with pads. There are pads and anti-slip shoes of various types.

Pads:
1 Rubber pad
2 Plaited-straw pad
3 Plaited-hemp pad
4 Cork pad
5 Felt pad. The hoof putty mentioned in a previous paragraph can be obtained in sheets. It is heated and then pressed into the hoof where it hardens and gives excellent protection.

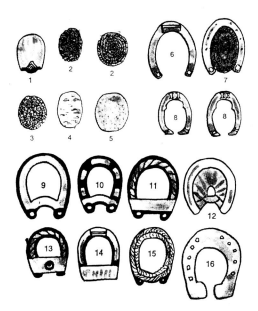

studs, which were developed later, have grains of this hard metal welded on to the surface of the studs with a softer binding material, and the steel/rubber studs are a combination of a steel casing with rubber filling. There is also the Hartring stud which consists of a metal ring interspersed with hard metal pieces in a steel casing. All these studs have the advantage, particularly in the summer, of being low. In the winter it will not be possible, especially in the mountains, to do without a certain 'grip height'. It is not intended here to recommend one type of stud more than another, but as a comparison, it is wise to have the horses shod at the same time with different types of studs. One will then easily find the most suitable.

On long journeys, when horses get tired,

Different types of hoof pads and special shoes

Anti-slip Shoes:

6 Shoe with screw studs and pin
7 Shoe with screw studs and straw pad
8 Sloped front and hind shoes with caulkings
9 Shoe with rubber inlay
10 Shoe with rubber inlay in certain places
11 Shoe with rope inlay and rubber cross-support
12 Shoe with rubber buffer
13 Shoe with rope inlay and felt pad which can be screwed on
14 Box shoe with wire brush which can be screwed on
15 Shoe with double-rope inlay
16 Rubber shoe

In addition to pads and anti-slip shoes, modern studs can be obtained which have the advantage that they can be re-used. They are therefore cheaper in the long run. All these studs have one common factor, namely that they use a combination of materials. Mordax studs, which were developed in Switzerland and have been proven for a number of years, include in the steel body of the studs a considerably harder metal pin. Widak

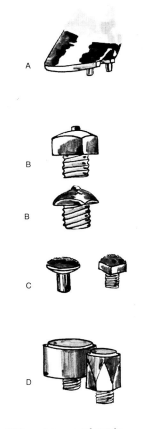

Different types of studs

168

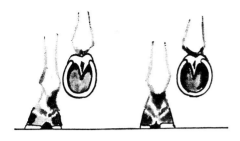

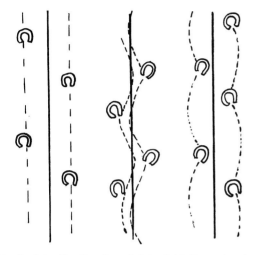

Hoof prints. Reading from left to right. Normal; splay-footed; pigeon-toed

'brushing' can easily occur. It is important to find out what causes this.

As most horses stand with their hind feet slightly turned out, brushing occurs more often behind than in front. If a horse has obviously brushed for the first time, a brushing mark will show which is either free of dirt or bloody. Remember to point this area out to the farrier because he will have to make the new shoe accordingly. He may have to put more weight at the toe or at the sides, or even make a special shoe. This would be fashioned so that at one particular place the hoof protrudes slightly over the shoe, and the hoof is well rounded at the edge. Horses which brush always turn the foot from the inside to the outside. Therefore the shoe should have a side clip which prevents the shoe moving to the inside. In addition to the slightly turned-out hind feet, there is the slant of the thigh from the stifle to the hock. Therefore, even with vertically-standing cannon bones, the weight of the body presses the fetlocks to the inside when the foot is put down. This can be seen very clearly if you stand behind one of the horse's legs and have the other lifted up. A correctly-fitted and properly-rasped brushing shoe will often not be sufficient to prevent brushing. To allow the brush wound to heal, it is necessary to consider the position of the foot on the ground and treat it accordingly. This at times is not done, partly because of the owner's lack of knowledge, and partly because the farrier believes that the foot should not be cut down incorrectly. Of course no joint should be *forced* into a certain position, but by heightening the inside arm of the shoe and slightly cutting down the outside wall of the hoof, the weight will press the fetlock less to the inside. The horse will then walk like a human does in slightly-worn heels, which take the ankles further apart.

169

40

Developing the Action

Experience has proved that both young and old horses get excited when shown in hand. Knowledgeable horse dealers will take advantage of this by getting their stable-hands to deliberately incite a horse to 'step out' in front of a potential buyer. The horse will put up its tail and show a lot of action. Many buyers fall for this trick. Even the oldest horse will behave like this when fresh from the stable. It has nothing to do with the natural action of the horse. Never buy a horse on that basis; wait until it has calmed down and the tail hangs down normally when the horse walks – only then is it possible to get a proper impression. Nevertheless, action can be improved by appropriate training.

B.H.S. Hollenter, when he was first Stallmeister at the Royal Prussian Military Riding Academy in Hanover, wrote an excellent book called *Training of the Riding and Driving Horse in the Pilars* (Hanover Halusche Book Store, 1896). In the discussion on equipment Hollenter mentions a pair of 'Rattlers':

'A rattler consists of six wooden balls, each with a diameter of 4.5 cm. They all have a hole, and are connected by a round, stitched strap with a buckle and a point. These rattlers are either buckled above or below the fetlock joint. The weight and the rattling which occurs as soon as the horse moves will encourage the horse to step out more lively and actively. Horses which, as a result of previous lameness, have weak muscles, take a shorter stride with the weak leg and therefore show less elevated steps. In this instance, the rattler is only used on the weak leg.' Hollenter comments also on 'Pellet bags':

'These are made from soft leather lined with buckskin. They are 36 cm. long and 6.5 cm. wide. The front has an incision in the centre with 6 to 8 loops either side. After the bag has been filled with pellets, a cord is threaded through the holes, and the opening laced up. One end of the bag has a buckle and the other a point. It is used for the same reason as the rattler; but the heavier weight of up to a kilogram of pellets achieves a more energetic use of the lifting muscles. The bags are also effective for riding horses which are too hurried in their action; they immediately slow down. In these cases the bags are used on all four legs. However, patience is required as the lifting muscles must regain strength.'

In Britain very experienced people use a contraption whereby ropes are fastened round the pasterns and guided through a ring on the girth, thus lifting up the legs. Rubber bands, called expanders, act similarly, but work with such contraptions requires a great deal of experience and it is not recommended to experiment with

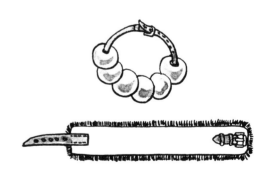

Anklets: Rattlers, and weighted variety

Cavaletti – work on
the double lunge

them. Besides, it does not achieve the desired result of action *and* a ground-covering stride. Rattlers and pellet bags round the pastern, however, have produced remarkable successes, as I know from my own experience.

Lungeing in very deep straw, or sand, and trotting over poles spaced apart (cavalettis) are also excellent exercises. Start with one heavy pole and then gradually increase the number to eight or ten. Generally a distance between the poles of 1 m. is sufficient, but watch whether the horse hits several poles. If he does, place the poles a more suitable distance apart, depending upon the stride of the horse, say 1.3 m. to 1.4 m. Lungeing a horse over poles teaches it cadence and rhythm and also makes it more relaxed.

41

Driver's Test and Solving a Driving Problem

During my first commission in Berlin in 1923 with Achenbach I had to drive the following driving test daily, firstly with a pair, then with a four, and later also with a six-in-hand. The Master, sitting beside me on the box, always knew how to find quiet roads where he faced me with this test, or variations of it, having first made me practise it on the driving apparatus at his home. It was not easy to please him, particularly as the six-in-hand, which was placed at my disposal, was rather difficult. During this period he wrote his book *Putting to and Driving* in which he mentions the following test. It was then included in the old German Horse Show Regulations as Driving Problem No. 1. It is an excellent exercise which tests the skill of the driver in a very confined space. See illustration.

The Test

A lane 7.50 m. wide with an L-shaped bend marked by signs (hurdles, cones or poles) has to be driven through observing the traffic regulations, i.e. the left-hand turn as wide as possible and the right-hand turn as small as possible.

The left-hand bend is to be driven at a slow trot, and the right-hand bend (on the return journey) at a walk. After the first L-bend (left turn), about-turn at a certain spot, usually a left-hand turn. (On the corner at the centre of the road is a large cone, a 'Traffic Policeman'.)

After the sharp right-hand turn, halt at an appointed spot, close to the 'kerb'. From this point, drive across to the left, and halt at a designated spot on the left-hand side. Here, right about-turn and again halt on the right-hand side. Finish.

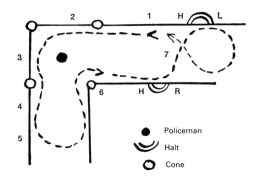

Diagram of a driving test

The whole exercise is to be driven fluently. Safety and correct driving are valued higher than speed. Losing time through indecisiveness, however, is a bad fault.

Main faults that occur: driving with incorrectly-adjusted reins and bridles, disturbing the horses with rough aids, using the whip incorrectly, unnecessary use of the voice. Before the left-hand turns: turn round and do not forget to signal with the whip; in the right-hand turns look round for the kerb (cone). It may also be required to turn round with a rein-back. In this case, if the going is heavy, or if the same team is to be driven through the same test by other drivers, starting correctly, followed by a description by the candidate as to how he would proceed, is sufficient.

If the test is driven with a four-in-hand it might also be requested that the driver use the four-in-hand whip at the end of the test. This should be done at the halt. The driver might be asked to hit an object on a pole placed level with the pads of the leaders.

The test can be driven with a pair, a four-in-hand, a six-in-hand or a tandem. The measurements (length, not width, of the road) may be altered to make the test more difficult or easier.

The following section explains how Achenbach advised that the test should be driven with a four-in-hand or a tandem.

See the illustration below.

The team to start from H.L. and should make a correct left-hand turn round the policeman (cone) X. To achieve this, make the opposition point at the time of moving off by placing the right-hand wheel-rein on the left index finger. If this brings the horses too close to the right, it is better to move the left hand to the right, rather than let go of the opposition point, as this may be required on reaching the 'policeman'.

As soon as the heads of the leaders reach 2, make a loop of approximately 15 cm. If the wheelers turn insufficiently, as is shown here, there is no point in making another loop, as it would not stop the horses from going over the border. Once the loop at 2 has been made to bring round the leaders, there is no need to worry about them for a moment. Concentrate on guiding round the wheelers. If they fail to turn enough, as shown at 3, there are several aids which can be given, but it depends on the circumstances whether they should be given individually or together. Firstly, as soon as the danger of hitting the cone is over, move the left hand to the right and release the opposition point on the index finger. If the corner is very tight, take up the left-hand wheel-rein with the right hand and apply a little pressure in order to hold back the wheelers. Experienced drivers place the left wheel-rein over the thumb to avoid leaning forward and having to reduce the speed, and to avoid turning the pole with the pole strap. This leaves the right hand free, and it is possible to push on the right-hand wheeler, i.e. the outside horse, if there is no other way to successfully manoeuvre the corner.

Apart from getting the wheelers away from 3, let the loop slide to enable the leaders to carry on in the direction of the road (dotted line). However, the last bit of the loop should be released only when the rear wheels are completely parallel with the road. If the loop is released too early, the leaders will learn to hang on to the outside rein and lean into the turn (as shown at 4 with the dotted line).

In order to make the left about-turn at 5 using the whole width of the road, do not make a right-hand loop at 4, not even a little loop. This would only turn the heads and the forelegs of the leaders. Make the opposition point at 4, i.e. right wheel-rein on the index finger, if necessary moving the left hand to the left. As a result the wheelers and the carriage move close to the

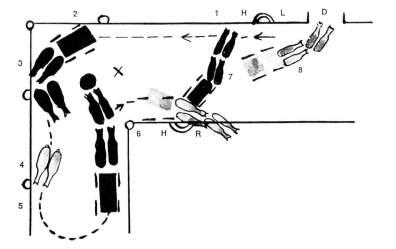

Execution of a driving test

right-hand side. Look quickly round, signal clearly with the whip, then make the first left loop, immediately followed by the second loop; at the same time let go of the opposition point on the index finger, which makes a large second loop.

In order to drive the right-hand corner between the policeman (cone) and point 6 and halt H.R., do not loop the left-hand rein to avoid hitting 6. This would only result in the leaders going towards the policeman or straight on to the left-hand side of the road. To take corner 6 well, and arrive as close as possible to H.R. (halt point marked by several small cones in front of a hurdle), first make sure that the right-hand wheeler is paying attention. (By using the least space, the turn is best made.) Then move the left hand sharply right into the turn, take a large right loop and place it under the left index finger.

As soon as the danger of hitting 6 with the rear wheel is over, move the left hand out of the turn, i.e. to the left, let the loop out quickly and place four fingertips of the right hand on the right-hand wheel-rein, back of the hand facing up, over which at the same time the right-hand lead-rein slides. This manoeuvre will place the carriage correctly after the turn.

If the loop in the right-hand turn was not released early and quickly, the position of the team would be as shown at H.R. with the dotted line.

In order to cross from H.R. to H.L., look quickly round, signal clearly with the whip and, if the road is clear, place both left-hand reins over the base of the left thumb and move off. As soon as the leaders reach the left-hand kerb, make a small right-hand loop. The two left-hand reins remain over the thumb until the carriage has arrived at H.L. Then release the right-hand loop slowly until the whole turnout is straight and close to the left-hand kerb. Only then

release the opposition point of the two left-hand reins from the thumb.

To make the right about-turn from the halt, release the brake quietly. (Remember to have your reins short.) The about-turn should be made in half steps, and the wheelers must remain standing until the second loop is made. If the wheelers do not move quickly round immediately afterwards, but go half-right forward, there is a danger of damage to the coronets in the second part of the turn and also that the swingle bars may hit the chest of the right-hand wheeler.

If the wheelers turn, as shown at 7, instead of following sharply to the left, push on the right-hand horse. Whether this has to be done before or after the right-hand loop has been made depends on how the horses are going. The dotted line at 8 shows how one never reaches point H.L. but where one arrives if a left-hand loop is made at H.R., namely exit D.

To arrive close at the right-hand kerb after a right about-turn, the left-hand loop must be made in good time; opposition point on the left index finger which brings both wheelers to the right-hand kerb, then release opposition point and loop skilfully so that the carriage stops again parallel to the kerb with leaders and wheelers absolutely straight.

To demonstrate the use of the four-in-hand whip, a steward could place a pole about 1.20 m. high in line with the pads of the leaders (about 1 m. away), with a box on top. Unfurl the whip, hit the box, catch the whip and furl it up again.

The driving test can be made easier or more difficult, but the solution is not easily accomplished without proper instructions as given in this chapter. With short distances, the judges can observe everything from point X, otherwise they have to move within the area. One judge should sit alongside the competitor on the box seat.

42

Horse Show and Dressage Competitions

Preparing for a show

If the owner/driver of a team feels that his horses are sufficiently well trained to compete with success at a horse show, it is advisable for him to discuss his plans with his coachman or head man in good time, and make a detailed list of all the equipment needed.

In F.E.I. driving competitions, the first phase is 'Presentation', and there are also competitions for harness horses where a special prize is given for the most correct turnout. When competing in such competitions, preparations must be thorough. For instance, the carriage may need touching up, the harness may need a little more polish and the horses may have to be clipped again. Nothing should be left to the last minute, particularly shoeing. Ensure that grooming kit and cleaning materials for harness and carriage are taken. The following are essentials:

Grooming kit

    Curry comb
    Dandy brush
    Body brush
    Water brush
    Hoof pick
    Stable rubber
    Hoof oil
    Sponge

Cleaning materials for harness

    Brass polish
    Shoe polish
    Saddle-soap
    Sponge
    Quantity of rags

    Soft polishing brush
    Soft flannel cloth

Cleaning utensils for carriage

    Sponge
    Chamois leather
    Soft, clean duster
    Grease rags
    Small greasing can
    Burnishing cushion or burnishing chain if the carriage has sfeel fittings

Other items

    Clothes brush
    Velvet pad for top hat
    Boot brush and shoe polish

The night before the competition everything should be polished. If it has rained, ensure that the water has been wiped off all steel fittings and the harness, and if more rain is expected, rub all steel parts lightly with a greasy rag, turn over the cushions or cover the whole carriage with a waterproof cover.

On the day of the competition, thoroughly check the whole turnout. Make sure the bridles are properly fitted, the bits are lying correctly, all points are in their keepers. Check that the horses are put to correctly and that the grooms look clean and tidy.

Never say 'it will do' but get as near to perfection as possible, and go into the competition confident that you have laid as much foundation to success as you possibly can.

Never leave things to the last minute; preparations must be made well in advance, and these include working your horses for the competition and practising yourself.

DRESSAGE TEST No. 2 (advanced)   Time: 10 minutes

		Movements	To be judged	Marks 0—10
1	A X	Enter at collected trot Halt – salute	Driving in on straight line standing on the bit	....
2	XCMB FAK	Collected trot	Impulsion regularity, collection	....
3	KXM MCH HXF FAX	Extended trot Collected trot Extended trot Collected trot	Extension, regularity, transitions	....
4	XG G	Walk on the bit Halt – immobility 10 seconds – Rein-back 3 metres	Regularity, immobility, transitions, straightness	....
5	GCHXF	Walk on the bit	Regularity, impulsion	....
6	FAK EHC C	Collected trot Circle – 20 metres diameter	Position, accuracy of figure	....
7	CM MF FAD	Collected trot 10 metres deviation from side with reins in one hand Working trot, reins at discretion	Regularity, position, accuracy of figure	....
8	D	Circle right 20 m. diameter followed by circle left 20 m. diameter	Regularity, position, accuracy of figure	....
9	DXG G	Extended trot Collected trot	Extension, regularity transitions	....
10	C – A	Serpentine of five loops commencing on the left rein	Position, accuracy of figure	....
11	DXG G	Extended trot Halt – Salute	Extension, regularity, transitions, immobility, straightness	....

Leave arena at working trot

176

Dressage competitions for driving horses

In the years just before the war, dressage competitions for harness horses had become more and more popular. They followed the demand for increased dressage training for carriage horses, and aimed to give the keen driver the opportunity to demonstrate his expertise in the art of driving as well as training his horses. The tests laid down in the F.E.I. Rules give judges the opportunity to comment on the individual movements of a test; this gives keen drivers the opportunity to improve their own knowledge and further the education of their horses. In the following, a dressage test for pairs or four-in-hands is given. The test can be practised at home in a field of 40 x 100 m., and practising the movements required in the test will further the drivers' own knowledge – particularly if he has studied in detail the requirements of training as described in Chapter 46 as well as Article 923 of the F.E.I. Rules. It is also good practice to have a friend or coachman drive the test, and watch him. Bearing in mind the principles of Chapter 46, watching your own team driven by someone else tremendously improves your eye for expert driving. Until you can drive the test from memory, take a friend or groom with you on the box seat to read out the test to you.

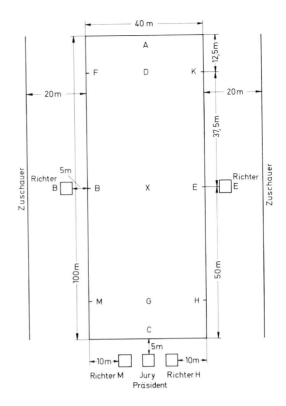

177

43

Trotting

To be thorough, I mention here trotting equipment, and explain how horses are raced to a Sulky. In principle, trotting races have no connection with the art of driving. Good trotters driven sensibly to a light carriage, either Hungarian style or in country harness, look very nice, and the owner of several trotters can probably use them for pleasure driving. In fact, trotters in general have very good temperaments.

The trotting harness will include the overcheck which is used to give the horse more support during a race, and head, neck and foreleg muscles have more freedom in a forward movement.

Most of the special trotting harness serves the purpose of balancing the horse. The braces hold the 'leggings' in position, which again protect the knee. Elbow protectors are used to ensure that the girth does not rub, leather boots protect the tendons, and rubber overreach boots protect heels and coronets. Pellet rings round the fetlocks (additional weight at the toe of the shoe) are intended to produce a long trotting stride. However, the application of these items in training, as well as in the race, require thorough knowledge and understanding by the trainer.

If you want trotters for pleasure driving, buy big, young animals which have either never raced, or proved too slow for racing. It is unwise to buy old trotters after they have finished their racing career.

Trotting Sulky and harness

44

Summary of the Main Principles of the Achenbach Method

In conclusion, I summarize the principles and doctrines of Achenbach covered in previous chapters. This summary illustrates more clearly his doctrine on the driving of harness horses.

Fixed splinter bars

All carriages must have fixed splinter bars. Without them, warm-blooded horses can neither be driven straight, nor safely, through turns and corners, but additional swingle trees are desirable.

The English reins (Achenbach reins)

Inseparable from carriages with the fixed splinter bar are correctly-made cross-reins, the design and measurements of which are known. The hand-part with the buckle is attached to the right-hand horse. The billets at the bit should have only one hole, and the coupling reins should have 11 holes each, distributed over a distance of 40 cm. This enables adjustment of the reins from the box seat whenever necessary. When breaking horses to harness, cross-reins are very useful because they can be altered on the move and do not require the horses to stand while adjustments are being made.

Measuring the reins

Hamelmann wrote over 50 years ago that the reins should be fixed at the right-hand horse and taken up correctly when mounting: 'Before mounting, the driver must measure his reins accurately, because if they are too long or are uneven the horses could move off during mounting. As a result the driver would lose control and, apart from the disorder, nasty accidents could happen. The driver, therefore, has to take the correctly-measured reins into his left hand and mount the carriage from the left.' This principle must *always* be observed. It will avoid many problems with young, untrained horses, whether as a pair or a four-in-hand, as a tandem or a six-in-hand.

Adjusting the reins

Practise this at the driving apparatus unless you wish to remain a 'beginner' for ever. Realize that, in principle, driving with your 'head' is as important as hands and fingers, but once the head decides what is required, arms, hands and fingers must be sufficiently well trained to carry out the necessary with ease and confidence.

Giving rein

'Ham-fistedness' is very often in the mind. For instance, if a pair of horses pull, think how to reduce the pain in the mouth. First, settle the horses down to a walk, then, without word of command, only by giving rein, trot on gradually at a quiet pace, which will reduce the pressure on the horses' bars. 'Giving rein', which must be practised, is a main principle in the art of driving, and demonstrates a 'kind' hand.

The steady hand

Hand and fingers need not be particularly

flexible. More important is that elbow, shoulder-joints and shoulder-blades are relaxed. Wrist and fingers only have to acquire the strength to hold the reins firmly, so that they do not slide through the fingers, thus get too long, and have to be shortened every few minutes. This will cause permanent disruption and unsettle high-spirited and sensitive horses. With quiet horses, this is not so bad, as one may get away with paying little attention. However, one thing is certain – a steady and attentive hand, correctly guided by the 'head', can even with a weak, elderly person achieve as much or more than a strong, young driver with less experience.

Seeing, not feeling

A well-trained driver will soon discover that he cannot *feel* whether one horse pulls or two. He must *see* this. If it is only one horse, couple it one or two holes shorter at the coupling: bitting the horse more severely would be a bad mistake. If the shorter 'coupling' and a little 'travelling speed' do not bring the desired result, only then may the curb chain be shortened and the horse bitted a *little* more severely.

Look for your own faults

If you wish to progress, always watch and observe carefully; try and find the fault with yourself, never assume unwillingness of the horse. If a horse makes a mistake, first ask yourself what did I do? What was the reason?

Halt aids and braking

Halt aids, in conjunction with the use of the brake, should only be given downhill on wet tarmac and to prevent accidents; otherwise, halt aids should be given gradually and in good time, because even the most obedient horse will jib as a result of rough halt aids.

Winkers

Only very reliable horses, which have been trained unwinkered in other work, may be driven without winkers. Even then it has the disadvantage that the right-hand horse keeps looking to the left for the whip, particularly if it has already been struck with it. This brings its shoulder away from the pole and the chances are that it brushes its off foreleg.

Reins first, then whip

With horses of different temperaments it is wrong to shout, click, hiss, or whiz the whip through the air. This would only affect keen horses. The lazy horse does not take the slightest notice. Should you use the whip at all? A rider would say 'yes', but a driver must think more carefully. First, see whether adjustments of the reins can solve the problem, and only when all possibilities have been exhausted may the whip be used.

Correct head position

Never pull the inside rein in a turn because the inside horse will, as a result of the pull, try to influence the direction of the pole with the pole strap; on the contrary, give with the outside rein so that the change of direction is achieved by the outside horse from the splinter bar. Also, never pull the outside rein to increase a curve whether driving a four- or a six-in-hand; make large loops, they prevent the leaders from leaning into the turn. Let the inside wheeler out or even urge him forward. He will push out the leaders via the inside traces (shoulder-in). This applies for a four-in-hand as well as for a six-in-hand. However, nothing should be exaggerated. Mastering the art of driving a four- or 'more'-in-hand depends basically on correct head positions of the horses. If these are wrongly positioned to the outside, the horses, however many there may be, can lean into a turn. The 'perfect' driver may occasionally maintain pressure on the outside rein, but only enough to maintain the correct head position of all horses.

Hand in the turn

Particularly when driving a team, the left hand must be moved into the right-hand turn and must remain there until any danger of hitting the kerb with the right-hand rear wheel is

Four-in-hand to a Mail Phaeton, driven by Miss Michele Macfarlane of San Diego, California

A Barouche with a pair of Windsor Greys. Photographed in the Royal Mews, Buckingham Palace

A State Landau with a pair of Cleveland Bays

The Glass Coach and a State Landau in winter dress

The Irish State Coach, drawn by six Windsor Greys

Mrs. Cynthia Haydon driving Mrs. McDougald's team of Bay Hackneys for the lap of honour, after winning the Championship at the Royal Windsor Horse Show, 1979

H.R.H. The Duke of Edinburgh takes the salute of Mr. Alwyn Holder with his team of Welsh cobs

over. It must then move straight back to the centre of the body or, if one wants to get very close to the right-hand kerb, in front of the left hip. The occasional pressure allowed on the outside rein must always be combined with pressure of the inside rein, if the intention is to give a fairly strong aid to halt. If no halt is intended, only an enlargement of the turn, the right hand goes forward, not to pull back, but to be able to give rein with the left hand. This is the safest way of getting the inside horse to move the whole turnout to the outside (enlarging the curve). If it does this too emphatically, the aid was too clumsy. If the correct head position was lost, it can be corrected once the mistake has been recognized.

Lead-reins outside, not inside

It is imperative that the lead-reins must pass along the outside of the wheelers' heads. If passed through on the inside, even the largest loop will not shorten the outside lead-rein. The leaders would remain too much in draught, and in a narrow turn, particularly if the vehicle has a perch, the pole could snap quite easily.

Why no looping when driving a pair?

In a left-hand turn, horses in double harness are pulled away from the driver by the pole straps; hence it is necessary to give with the outside rein. It would be silly to squeeze the horses, which are pulled forward by pole and pole strap, with 'over-reach' or loop and expect them to do something which is impossible. Therefore, in right-hand turns, where the horses are coming towards the driver, he must *maintain* the pressure, and for a left-hand turn *reduce* the pressure – in the case of a left about-turn, by a considerable amount. Looping would therefore be contradictory.

Looping with a four-in-hand

With a four-in-hand the matter is different. Firstly, in a turn, the leaders should be out of draught (on very rare occasions they may be slightly in draught). Secondly, they are not forcibly moved away from the driver by pole and

pole strap. Thirdly, when the driver places the left loop under the thumb, initially only a 'pressure' (opposition) point is created. As a result the leaders start to turn – *start* only – the loop is now increased until the driver thinks it is sufficient. Remember here that this does not work quite the same way as on the driving apparatus, where the driver stands still and pulls the weights towards himself. On the box seat of a carriage, he is continually in a forward motion, i.e. he does not get closer to the leaders. He has to loop the rein to achieve direction and head position, and to maintain contact, which would be lost if the leaders had not been brought back but only slowed down.

Watching a turn carefully will show that looping does not only shorten the inside lead-rein in the turn, but also the outside lead-rein. This is because the lead-reins go along the outside of the wheelers' heads and therefore in every turn the leaders go away from the head of the outside wheeler.

Why loops with centre horses despite the centre pole?

If the centre reins of a six-in-hand are looped, one might imagine that this is contradictory to the demand never to loop with a pair (as they, too, go alongside a centre pole). The comment that the horses are pulled away from the driver by the pole straps does not apply to centre horses, and in fact, because it is attached to the hook of the pole with a seven-link chain, can even move backwards.

To sum up, driving is an art calling for a precision to which thought, understanding and much practice is given. The driver must distribute the work expertly and skilfully between the individual horses, and with more horses in hand, between the various pairs. However, he will only be able to do this if he has learnt to see, and to understand, what is important in the wide variety of situations that can occur. Enthusiasm for seeing, acknowledging and meditating, and thoroughness in the study of the basic principles of driving, are conditions which the driver owes to his horses.

45

The Animal Protection Law

As this law varies from country to country it has not been translated. However, F.E.I. Rules apply in all member countries of that body and, therefore, attention is drawn to these Rules, in particular Article 150 General Regulations, and Article 911 Rules for Driving Events. In addition, drivers must acquaint themselves with Animal Protection Laws in their respective countries apart from bearing in mind the basic principle to treat their horses kindly and well. This does not mean pampering them. They will repay men's kindness and care with long and faithful service.

46

Demands on Harness Horses in Dressage

Here again, rather than translate the requirements of the German National Rules, the relevant Articles of the F.E.I. Rules for Driving are quoted, namely Article 920 – paragraphs 7 to 11.

'7 At the halt, the horses should stand attentive, motionless and straight, with the weight evenly distributed over all four legs, and be ready to move off at the slightest indication of the competitor.

8 Walk. A free, regular and unconstrained walk of moderate extension is required. The horses should walk energetically but calmly, with even and determined steps.

9 The following trots are recognized: working, collected and extended.

(a) Working trot – This is a pace between the extended and the collected trot and is more rounded than the extended trot. The horses go forward freely and straight, engaging the hind legs with good hock action, on a taut but light rein, the position being balanced and unconstrained. The steps should be as even as possible, hind feet precisely following the tracks of the forefeet.

The degree of energy and impulsion displayed at the working trot denotes clearly the degree of suppleness and balance of the horses.

(b) Collected trot – The neck is raised, thus enabling the shoulders to move with greater ease in all directions, the hocks being well engaged and maintaining energetic impulsion, despite the slower movement. The horses' steps are shorter, but they are lighter and more mobile.

(c) Extended trot – The horses cover as much ground as possible. They lengthen their stride, remaining on the bit with light contact. As a result of great impulsion from the quarters, the horses use their shoulders, covering more ground at each step without their action becoming higher.

10 The rein-back is a kind of walk backwards, the legs being raised and set down simultaneously by diagonal pairs, the hind legs remaining well in line and the legs being well raised.

11 The changes of pace and speed should always be made quickly, be smooth, and not abrupt. The cadence of a pace should be maintained up to the moment when the pace is changed or the horses halt. The horses remain light in hand, calm, and maintained in a correct position.'

Dressage competitions demand a high degree of training, suppleness, obedience and safety. In all paces and movements the horses must be on the bit, correctly positioned. Cadence and impulsion must be retained throughout the test. The horses should go neither in front of the bit nor behind it, and should follow all aids willingly. In a pair, or a four-in-hand, they must give a picture of harmony, and should match in conformation and action. Even in the collected paces they must maintain impulsion and the urge to go forward. They should not resist the bit, toss their heads, pull, or bore. They should be attentive at all times. Their necks should be raised and the poll should be the highest point. They should be champing at the bit and maintaining light contact with the driver's hand. In all paces, freedom and regularity must be maintained. In the collected paces the horses should maintain energetic impulsion despite the slower movement, and in the extended paces they should cover as much ground as possible by lengthening the stride, rather than going faster, but should remain on the bit.

47

Participation in International Driving Competitions

Continental and World Championships – C.A.I.s and C.A.I.O.s.

Since 1970, when international driving rules were first published, driving competitions have been held based on these new rules. The first three articles of the rules are:

Article 900

These rules are not intended to standardize driving competitions, but international competitions must be strictly fair to all competitors. It is therefore necessary to lay down a number of strict and comprehensive rules, which must be carefully observed. At the same time, within these rules organizing committees have the right to use their discretion to make their events interesting for the competitors and attractive for the spectators.

Article 901 – Organising Committees

1 These rules provide for three types of competitions:
   Competition A: Section I Presentation
                    Section II Dressage
   Competition B: Marathon
   Competition C: Obstacle Driving
   A combination of any of these will be known as a Combined Driving Competition.

2 The organizing committee of an international event may decide which of these competitions are suitable for their particular event, and may include any one, two, or all three. It is emphasized that the Marathon (Competition B) should always be regarded as the most important. Competition A may take place before or after Competition B, but Competition C must always be the last.

3 (a) At C.A.I.s, C.A.I.O.s and Championship Events, the organizing committee may arrange international competitions outside the championship or official team competitions, but these must comply with these rules and may be for Dressage and Obstacle Driving only; different courses may be used.

3 (b) The Organising Committee may arrange a Free Dressage Test provided it is not a part of the Combined Event. The method of scoring must be laid down in the schedule but in principle the judges should give one set of marks for the contents and another for the general impression. The program selected by the competitor may not exceed 7 minutes. The bell is sounded for the first time after 6 minutes and for the second time after 7 minutes to indicate to the competitor that he has to bring his performance to an end immediately. Music may be used.

4 Continental and World Championships must consist of all three competitions.

5 The F.E.I. is fully aware of the practical difficulties facing organizing committees under modern road and traffic conditions, and the inevitable variety in vehicles and harness. It therefore accepts that they will have to use their discretion in many matters not specified in these rules. It is however important that all championships, and any event described as 'International', should follow these rules.

6 To ensure uniformity, organizing committees

must send a draft schedule for their event to the Secretary General of the F.E.I. not less than sixteen weeks before the event, setting out the general conditions of each competition and any particular conditions, not provided for in these rules, which they wish to introduce.

7 These rules and conditions are provided for competitors driving teams of four horses, but they are equally applicable for pairs, tandems, or horses in single harness, and classes for ponies in the same combinations. All these may take part in the same event, but each type will be classified separately.

8 When an Event is open to competitors other than for teams of 4 horses, the Organising Committee must specify the rules regarding vehicles, harness, the number of people carried and any other details that differ from these rules or which are not covered by these rules.

These events must be similar in principle to those described in these rules.

Article 902 – Competitions

1 The object of Competition A, Section I – Presentation – is to judge the turnout, cleanliness, and general condition and impression of the horses, harness and vehicle. The teams are judged at the halt.

2 The object of Competition A, Section II – Dressage – is to judge the freedom, regularity of paces, harmony, lightness, ease of movement, impulsion, and the correct positioning of the horses on the move. The competitor will also be judged on his style of driving, accuracy, and general command of his team.

3 The object of Competition B – Marathon – is to test the standard of fitness and stamina of the horses, and the judgement of pace and horsemastership of the competitor.

4 The object of Competition C – Obstacle Driving – is to test the fitness, obedience, and suppleness of the horses after the Marathon, and the skill and competence of the competitor.

5 Competition A (Sections I and II) and Competition C will take place within an arena (but not necessarily the same arena). Competition B will take place over roads and tracks typical of the country, including natural and artificial obstacles.

Index